Programming with VisualAge for Java Version 2.0

The VisualAge Series

Akerley, Li, and Parlavecchia
Programming with VisualAge for Java, Version 2

Bitterer, Brassard, Nadal, and Wong
VisualAge and Transaction Processing in a Client/Server Environment

Bitterer, Hamada, Oosthuizen, Porciello, and Rambek
AS/400 Application Development with VisualAge for Smalltalk

Bitterer and Carrel-Billiard
World Wide Web Programming: VisualAge for C++ and Smalltalk

Carrel-Billiard and Akerley
Programming with VisualAge for Java

Carrel-Billiard, Jakab, Mauny, and Vetter
Object-Oriented Application Development with VisualAge for C++ for OS/2

Carrel-Billiard, Friess, and Mauny
Programming with VisualAge for C++ for Windows

Fang, Chu, and Weyerhäuser
VisualAge for Smalltalk and SOMobjects: Developing Distributed Object Applications

Fang, Guyet, Haven, Vilmi, and Eckmann
VisualAge for Smalltalk Distributed: Developing Distributed Object Applications

Nilsson and Jakab
VisualAge for C++: Visual Programmer's Handbook

Programming with
VisualAge for Java
Version 2.0

John Akerley
Nina Li
Antonello Parlavecchia

INTERNATIONAL TECHNICAL SUPPORT ORGANIZATION
SAN JOSE, CALIFORNIA 95120

PRENTICE HALL PTR
UPPER SADDLE RIVER, NEW JERSEY 07458

This edition applies to Version 2.0 of the VisualAge for Java product set, and to all subsequent releases and modifications until otherwise indicated in new editions.

Comments about ITSO Technical Bulletins may be addressed to:
IBM Corporation ITSO, 471/80-E2, 650 Harry Road, San Jose, California 95120-6099

For information about redbooks:

http://www.redbooks.ibm.com

Send comments to:

redbook@us.ibm.com

Published by Prentice Hall PTR
Prentice-Hall, Inc.
Upper Saddle River, NJ 07458

Acquisitions Editor: *Michael E. Meehan*
Editorial Assistant: *Bart Blanken*
Manufacturing Manager: *Pat Brown*
Cover Design: *Andreas Bitterer*
Copy Editor: *Maggie Cutler*
Production Supervision: *Mary Sudul*

The publisher offers discounts on this book when ordered in bulk quantities. For more information, contact:
Corporate Sales Department, Prentice Hall PTR, One Lake Street, Upper Saddle River, NJ 07458
Phone: 800-382-3419; FAX: 201-236-7141; E-mail (Internet): corpsales@prenhall.com

Printed in the United States of America

10   9   8   7   6   5   4

ISBN   0-13-021298-9

Prentice-Hall International (UK) Limited, *London*
Prentice-Hall of Australia Pty. Limited, *Sydney*
Prentice-Hall Canada Inc., *Toronto*
Prentice-Hall Hispanoamericana, S.A., *Mexico*
Prentice-Hall of India Private Limited, *New Delhi*
Prentice-Hall of Japan, Inc., *Tokyo*
Editora Prentice-Hall do Brasil, Ltda., Rio de Janeiro

To the members of my family, who are only a little surprised by what I do

John

To my parents for their continuous undivided support

Nina

To my parents

Antonello

Foreword

When we set about to create a VisualAge programming environment for Java, we first needed to understand the kinds of applications that businesses wanted to build, applications that could leverage the capability that Java brought to the Web. We discovered that businesses wanted to create real applications that leveraged their existing environments and data. VisualAge for Java accepts this business goal and is making it a reality today for our customers, large and small.

VisualAge for Java is object-based and tied closely to the dynamic nature of Java to support incremental compilation and debug, plus automatic version control down to the method level. In this book you will learn all about VisualAge for Java; work through real programming examples that explain the VisualAge for Java Integrated Development Environment, JavaBeans, and user interface programming; and explore visual programming with the VisualAge Visual Composition Editor. The ability to develop applets and JavaBeans through visual programming and code generation make VisualAge for Java a powerful rapid application development environment.

The CD-ROM that accompanies the book contains Version 2.0 of VisualAge for Java Entry. This version is a full function edition of the product that is limited only by the total number of classes you can create. Along with this book I am sure VisualAge for Java Entry will launch you into the exciting world of Java and the Internet. Install it on your own system and give it a try.

Welcome to the world of VisualAge!

Paul Buck
Solution Manager - IBM VisualAge for Java
IBM Corporation
October, 1998

Preface

Java is definitely here to stay. The number of developers working with Java continues to increase dramatically, while Sun and other Java development organizations continue to release new developments, such as the Java Foundation Classes and Enterprise JavaBeans.

In 1998, the focus of Java development changed somewhat — from applets to encompass servlets and enterprise computing. As a typical Java developer, you no longer whip up a simple applet in an afternoon. Today you need a serious development environment to create large and complex applications. You need an environment with code management, powerful searching and browsing, GUI building, and JavaBean creation and manipulation capabilities. You need an environment that helps you think in terms of objects. With the new and improved features of Version 2, VisualAge for Java is *the* development tool for serious Java development.

Programming with VisualAge for Java Version 2 shows you how to use VisualAge for Java to develop Java applets, applications, and servlets. You will learn the right way of coding with VisualAge for Java and how to use the tool productively.

Who Should Read This Book?

This book teaches you how to program in the VisualAge for Java environment. You should already have some knowledge of object-oriented programming and the Java language. You should also know a little about the Internet and TCP/IP to understand the concepts introduced.

For Chapter 7, "Making Your Data Persistent", you should have some knowledge of relational databases and SQL.

How to Use This Book

The book is organized as a tutorial where many chapters build on the examples in the previous chapters. Specifically:

❑ Chapter 6, "Finishing the ATM Application", depends on the ATM model you build in Chapter 3, Beginning the ATM Project.

❑ Chapter 7, "Making Your Data Persistent", Chapter 8, "Creating Servlets", Chapter 9, "Internationalization" and Chapter 11, "Advanced Topics" depend somewhat on the code you develop for the Bookmark List in Chapter 4, "Building User Interfaces".

The book is not a complete set of documentation for VisualAge for Java. Use the online documentation included with the product for specific reference material or to see another way of approaching some of the topics.

CD-ROM

The CD-ROM that accompanies this book contains the IBM VisualAge for Java Entry Edition as well as other required software. Refer to the README.TXT file in the root directory of the CD-ROM for the latest information about installing VisualAge for Java and the sample code on your machine.

For updates to the sample code or the book, see:

```
ftp://www.redbooks.ibm.com/redbooks/SG245264/
```

The Java and Internet world is forever changing. The software on the CD-ROM may be several months old by the time you buy this book. You are encouraged to download the current evaluation copies of the software or, even better, to buy the software at the latest level.

How This Document Is Organized

Chapter 1, Introduction to the Environment
In this chapter you are introduced to the VisualAge family and to the new features of VisualAge for Java. You build your first applets and applications, learn to use the Scrapbook, and customize the VisualAge for Java environment.

Chapter 2, Organizing Your Code
This chapter explains how you work with code in VisualAge for Java and introduces you to the windows and views of the development environment and the code import and export features of VisualAge for Java.

Chapter 3, Beginning the ATM Project
In this chapter you implement the business logic for the Automated Teller Machine (ATM) application, one of the examples you will use throughout the book. You step through the design and

implementation of the ATM application. Along the way you learn how to use VisualAge for Java to build JavaBeans from the BeanInfo page of the Class Browser.

Chapter 4, Building User Interfaces

In this chapter you use the Java Foundation Classes (JFC) to build a Bookmark List to save your favorite URLs. The VisualAge for Java Visual Composition Editor features for building user interfaces with the JFC are explained.

Chapter 5, Managing and Fixing Your Code

This chapter explains the code management features of VisualAge for Java, including the workspace and repository concepts. You also learn how to use the Inspectors and debugger to trace and fix your code.

Chapter 6, Finishing the ATM Application

This chapter guides you through the process of implementing a complex application by using card layouts, multiple panels, inner classes, and variables.

Chapter 7, Making Your Data Persistent

This chapter shows you how to add persistence to your Bookmark List applet through serialization or a relational database.

Chapter 8, Creating Servlets

In this chapter you learn how to use VisualAge for Java to create and debug servlets. You implement the Bookmark List as a servlet.

Chapter 9, Internationalization

This chapter explains VisualAge for Java support for creating applets and applications that can run in a variety of locales.

Chapter 10, Deploying Your Java Programs

In this chapter you walk through the steps required to deploy applets, servlets, and applications.

Chapter 11, Advanced Topics

In this chapter you learn about several advanced VisualAge for Java features, including the interface to external SCM tools, Remote Method Invocation, AgentRunner: Lotus Domino Connection, and the Tool Integration Framework.

Conventions Used in This Book

Bold font is used for headings and things you can select, such as buttons and menu items.

Italic font is used for the names of fields in the interface as well as the first use of terms.

Monospace font is used for code samples, project, package, object, attribute, variable, and type names, or anything that you enter.

 Tips are placed throughout the book. Read these to find out how to be more productive in VisualAge for Java. "Tips" on page xxix lists all the Tips found in the book.

New in V2! Wherever you see this icon, a new feature of VisualAge for Java Version 2 is introduced.

Improved in V2! Wherever you see this icon, a feature of VisualAge for Java Version 2 has been improved from the previous version.

Examples in This Book

The examples in this book were created with VisualAge for Java Professional Version 2 on Windows NT. If you are using VisualAge for Java Enterprise, or VisualAge for Java Professional on another platform, you may experience differences in creating the examples. If so, please let the authors know at redbook@us.ibm.com and the differences will be posted to the ftp site: www.redbooks.ibm.com/SG245264/. The examples were created using the original released version of the product. You should download the available fixpacks for the product from www.software.ibm.com/vadd. If you install fixpacks, some of the behavior outlined in the examples may change.

You can find the examples at:

```
ftp://www.redbooks.ibm.com/redbooks/SG245264/
```

World Wide Web Addresses in This Book

The URLs given in this book were correct at the time the book was created. Given the dynamic nature of the Web, these addresses may no longer exist when you read this book. Use the search services of the IBM web site or other search services to locate the correct sites if they still exist.

ITSO on the Internet

Internet users can find information about redbooks on the ITSO World Wide Web home page. Point your Web browser to:

http://www.redbooks.ibm.com/

IBM internal users can also access redbooks from the internal IBM Redbooks home page:

http://w3.itso.ibm.com/

The FTP server, *www.redbooks.ibm.com*, stores the samples from the accompanying CD-ROM. To retrieve the sample files, check the contents of the */redbooks/SG245264* directory.

If any errors are discovered in the book, the errata will also be in the ftp directory.

VisualAge for Java Service and Support

VisualAge for Java Service and Support is staffed by knowledgeable developers who handle everything from how-tos to complex technical problems. The most common way of contacting VisualAge for Java Service and Support is through this Web site: http://www.software.ibm.com/ad/vajava. The site has links to newsgroups, fixes, announcements, and other information. Check the site periodically for information.

VisualAge for Java Service and Support monitors several VisualAge for Java newsgroups:

ibm.software.vajava.beans
ibm.software.vajava.enterprise
ibm.software.vajava.ide
ibm.software.vajava.install
ibm.software.vajava.language
ibm.software.vajava.non-technical

If a new version of VisualAge for Java is being beta-tested, there may also be an ibm.software.vajava.beta forum.

You can find these newsgroups at news.software.ibm.com.

IBM employees can also participate in internal VisualAge for Java forums.

About the Authors

This book was produced by a team of specialists from around the world working at the IBM International Technical Support Organization, San Jose Center.

John Akerley

John Akerley is a consultant at the IBM International Technical Support Organization, San Jose Center, California. Mr. Akerley previously worked on the VisualAge for Java certification team at the IBM Toronto Lab where he helped create certification programs, taught, wrote, and consulted on VisualAge for Java.

Nina Li

Nina Li is completing her Master's degree in Computer Science at the Université de Montréal. She joined IBM Canada in 1996 as a member of the national technical support team for OS/2-related products. Nina is currently a member of IBM's Global Services, providing national support for all VisualAge family products.

Antonio Parlavecchia

Antonello Parlavecchia is a Consultant IT Specialist at Telecom Italia Mobile (TIM). Before joining TIM, he worked as an IT Specialist for the IBM Java Technology Center in Bari, Italy. Antonello's areas of expertise include object-oriented technologies, component object architectures such as JavaBeans, COM/ActiveX, and application development in object-oriented languages such as C++ and Java.

Acknowledgments

Thanks to the following people for their invaluable contributions to this project:

Ueli Wahli, International Technical Support Organization, San Jose Center, who started this project.

David Williams of the VisualAge Services team at the IBM Raleigh Lab, Christina Li of the VisualAge support team at the IBM Toronto Lab, and John Connell of the Carle Clinic Association, for their extensive technical reviews.

Craig Edwards of IBM Australia, who had the original idea for the BaseLine tool.

As always thanks to Jasna Krmpotic for her insights on technical writing, and, in this case, indexing.

The authors also wish to thank Maggie Cutler for her editing of the book and the technical professionals and staff at the International Technical Support Organization, San Jose Center, who make writing these books possible and, more importantly, pleasurable.

Comments Welcome

Your comments are important to us!

We want our redbooks to be as helpful as possible. Please send us your comments about this or other redbooks in one of the following ways:

❏ Fax the evaluation form found in "ITSO Redbook Evaluation" on page 393 to the fax number shown on the form.

❏ Use the electronic evaluation form found on the Redbooks Web sites:

For Internet users: http://www.redbooks.ibm.com
For IBM Intranet users: http://w3.itso.ibm.com

❏ Send us a note at the following address: redbook@us.ibm.com

Contents

Figures

Tables

Tips

1 Introduction to the Environment

VisualAge for Java is an integrated, visual development environment that supports the complete cycle of Java program development. With the VisualAge for Java programming environment, you can build 100% pure Java applications, applets, and JavaBean components. Using the true rapid application development (RAD) provided by VisualAge for Java, you can shorten the development life cycle of your applications and improve their time to market.

In this chapter you will find a short description of the VisualAge for Java product family and an overview of VisualAge for Java Version 2. You will learn the basic terms that you need to understand to create your first program. Before you finish reading this chapter, you will have your first Java program up and running!

VisualAge for Java Product Family

VisualAge for Java Version 2 is available in three versions:

- VisualAge for Java Professional
- VisualAge for Java Entry
- VisualAge for Java Enterprise

This book covers the VisualAge for Java Version 2 Professional and Entry editions without describing the features of VisualAge for Java Enterprise.

IBM also has several other offerings related to VisualAge for Java, including:

- VisualAge Developers Domain Subscription for Java, which provides a single access point on the World Wide Web for everything you need to build business-critical Java applications, including Java-related samples, education, support, and the ability to network with a community of Java professionals. VisualAge Developers Domain is also the place for registered owners of VisualAge for Java products to obtain updates and fixes. For example, as VisualAge for Java updates the Java development Kit (JDK) and Java Foundation Classes (JFC) it uses, you can download the updates from the VisualAge Developers Domain.

  You can learn more about VisualAge Developers Domain at www.software.ibm.com/vadd.

- WebSphere Application Server, which serves as the foundation for building advanced Web sites with true functionality. It includes two key components to help you transition easily from simple Web applications to powerful e-business applications:

  - A secure and scalable runtime environment that supports Hypertext Transfer protocol (HTTP), Internet Inter-ORB protocol (IIOP), and Enterprise JavaBeans.

  - An integrated tools environment, IBM WebSphere Studio, where you can easily create dynamic content and Java-based applications.

  For more information see http://www.software.ibm.com/webservers.

VisualAge for Java Professional

VisualAge for Java Professional features an *Integrated development environment* (IDE), which enables you to create classes, or change methods, and then incrementally compile without the need to exit the testing phase of development. The IDE includes:

- Incremental compiler

  Changes to your code are compiled "on the fly" as you work with individual methods and class declarations. Errors in your code are immediately flagged so that they can be fixed while you are concentrating on that part of the code.

❑ Repository-based environment

All of the code in the development environment is stored in a *repository*. This repository enables incremental compilation and provides for very powerful search capabilities. The code that you are working with is stored in a *workspace*. Version management is built into the repository, and versions or *editions* of code are automatically stored when you change any *program element* (method, class, package, or project) in your workspace.

VisualAge for Java Professional is a single-user, repository-based environment. If you work as part of a development team, you may want to consider using VisualAge for Java Enterprise.

❑ Project-based development

VisualAge for Java provides *projects*. The basic Java environments provide only the concept of a package to organize your work. In VisualAge for Java you organize your packages in projects.

❑ Source code editor

A full-featured syntax editor, which helps you write error-free source code.

❑ Advanced coding tools such as automatic formatting, automatic code completion, and fix-on-save

❑ An integrated debugger

❑ A Visual Composition Editor, which enables you to develop your application visually

❑ A JavaBean creation tool to create 100% pure Java beans that you can use with the Visual Composition Editor

New powerful features that come with Version 2.0 of VisualAge for Java Professional include:

❑ Java Virtual Machine and JDK Release 1.1.6

❑ Visual Composition Editor support for the JFC Release 1.0.2 (Swing)

❑ Inner class support

❑ National language support

❑ Tool integration API

❑ Database access beans

❑ Notes Domino access

❑ Interface to external software configuration management tools

VisualAge for Java Version 2 comes with extensive online, searchable documentation and many examples. Click the **Help** menu item at any time to access the documentation.

Anywhere in this book where new or improved features are discussed, you will see, to the left of the text, the icons shown in Figure 1.

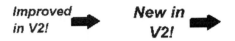

Figure 1. Improved and New Icons

VisualAge for Java Entry

The VisualAge for Java Entry edition provides the same functions as VisualAge for Java Professional, with a limit of 500 Java types (classes and interfaces). You can get it for free from the Web (www.software.ibm.com/ad/vajava).

When using the VisualAge for Java Entry edition, you can see how many classes you can still create by selecting the **Help→About** menu bar item.

VisualAge for Java Enterprise

VisualAge for Java Enterprise is an extremely powerful team development environment. It extends VisualAge for Java Professional with more features, including:

❑ Data Access Builder for accessing enterprise data managed by database servers, such as IBM's DB2, through the JDBC specification for accessing relational databases from Java programs

❑ CICS Access Builder for building Java programs that interface with CICS transactions

❑ RMI Access Builder for building pure, distributed Java applications that use the Java remote method invocation (RMI) specification

❑ C++ Access Builder for building distributed Java applications that connect to C++ application servers

New features of VisualAge for Java Enterprise Version 2 include:

❑ Team programming support

❑ Servlet building support including form and HTML support

- More access builders: TXSeries and SAP R/3
- IIOP support for CORBA 2.0 ORBs, specifically for IBM Component Broker
- AS/400 access tools
- A high-performance Java compiler, for platform-native code generation
- The Bean Extender, for building more specialized beans from other beans
- Remote debugging, for debugging Java applications from a remote console

Updates to VisualAge for Java

Updates to the different versions of VisualAge for Java are provided at the VisualAge Developers Domain Web site: www.software.ibm.com/vadd.

Building Your First Applet

Now that you have an idea of the capabilities of VisualAge for Java, you can build your first applet.

Before starting, you should familiarize yourself with the terms in Table 1. If you are not familiar with any of the terms in Table 1 or you are new to the Java language itself, try to read some of the resources listed in "Related Publications" on page 365.

Table 1. Object-Oriented Terms

Term	Definition
Class	A template for creating objects. A class defines the behavior and properties that are common to all objects of that class.
Interface	A specification of behavior that a class must provide if it implements the interface.
Object	An instance of a class. An object shares the behavior of all objects of the same class, but each object can have a different state.
Applet	A special kind of class introduced in Java. Its instances usually run in a Web browser such as Netscape Navigator.
Attribute or field	A data variable held by a class.

Term	Definition
Access modifier	In Java the access modifiers are public, private, protected, and default or package.
Method or message	Objects communicate with each other by sending messages. When an object receives a message, a corresponding method, defined in the class definition, is invoked to perform the required task.
Package	A collection of Java classes that typically serve a common purpose. This is Java's way of organizing classes into logical entities that are easier to maintain and understand than a huge set of classes at the same level.

Let's Get Started!

Before you go any further, you must have VisualAge for Java installed on your computer. For the latest changes, make sure you also read the installation instructions (README.TXT) included with the CD-ROM that accompanies this book. Use the instructions on the CD-ROM and with the installation images of the product if you need any assistance installing VisualAge for Java or the other products on the CD-ROM.

Your first Java class is a simple applet that displays the text of your choice in the applet's window. You launch VisualAge for Java by double-clicking the **IBM VisualAge for Java** icon in the IBM VisualAge for Java folder or selecting **Start→Programs→IBM VisualAge for Java for Windows→IBM VisualAge for Java**.

If this is the first time you have started VisualAge for Java, a dialog box will inform you that some features are being installed. Next, the Welcome to VisualAge dialog (Figure 2) is displayed. The Welcome to VisualAge dialog box is shown when you start the VisualAge for Java IDE, unless you deselect the checkbox at the bottom of the window. Click **Close** to close the dialog box.

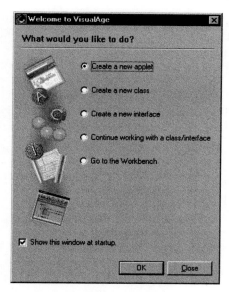

Figure 2. The Welcome to VisualAge Dialog Box

Somewhat confusingly, a different dialog, the Quick Start, is available from the **Workbench→File** menu (see Figure 3).

The Workbench window opens the first time you start VisualAge for Java. The Workbench is where you usually create and manipulate your classes. From the Workbench you can also launch the Quick Start window. Open the Quick Start now, by selecting **File→Quick Start** from the menu bar.

New in V2!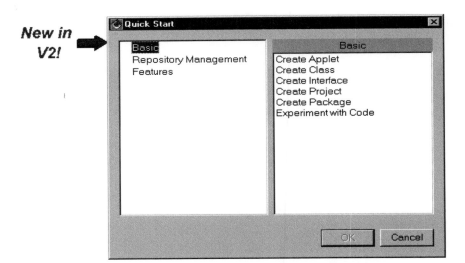

Figure 3. The Quick Start Dialog Box

Using the Quick Start dialog, you can select from three options:

❑ Basic: Create a new applet, class, interface, project, or package or experiment with code

❑ Repository Management: Compact the repository (see "Compacting the Repository" on page 165)

❑ Features: Add new features to your environment (see "Loading Available Editions" on page 162)

You are going to create an applet so select **Basic→Create Applet** and click **OK**.

SmartGuides

VisualAge for Java uses SmartGuides (which are similar to Wizards in other products) to help you create Java applets and applications. Clicking the **OK** button on the Quick Start window opens the Create Applet SmartGuide (Figure 4), which guides you through the process of creating your new applet class.

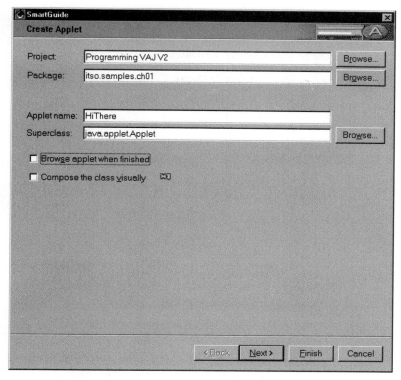

Figure 4. The Create Applet SmartGuide

To create your applet, fill in the text fields (Project, Package, and Applet name) as shown in Figure 4 and deselect the **Browse applet when finished** and **Compose the class visually** checkboxes. The *Superclass* field already has java.applet.Applet entered because you selected **Create Applet**. Click the **Finish** button to complete your work with the SmartGuide window. VisualAge for Java now creates the code needed for your new applet. The dialog closes and lets you work with the Workbench window (Figure 5).

Believe it or not, you have just created your first applet with VisualAge for Java! Now you can use the WorkBench to examine and run your applet.

The Workbench

The Workbench is the main control center of the VisualAge for Java IDE. From the Workbench, you can access projects, packages, and classes and modify and test your code with just a few mouse clicks.

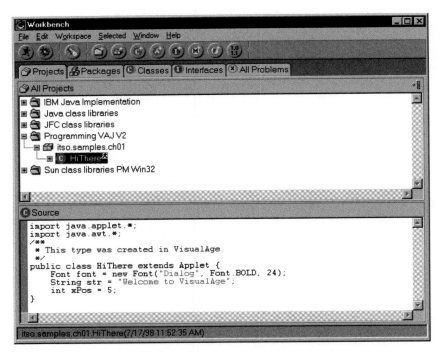

Figure 5. The Workbench

To test your newly created applet, click the plus sign next to your project and your package to expand them and then select the **HiThere** applet. Select **Selected→Run→In Applet Viewer** from the menu bar of the Workbench to run the applet. You can also run your applet by clicking the **Run** button (the left-most button with the picture of the running person).

The Applet Viewer opens and runs your applet (Figure 6). The Applet Viewer is a utility that lets you test your applets without having to use a Web browser. You may have to resize the window to see the complete message.

Figure 6. Your First Applet Running in the Applet Viewer

Congratulations, you have built and tested your first applet with VisualAge for Java!

Modifying Your Applet

To modify the applet to show different text, select your class in the Workbench. The class definition of the applet is displayed in the Source pane of the Workbench window and looks like this:

```
import java.applet.*;
import java.awt.*;
/**
 * This type was created in VisualAge.
 */
public class HiThere extends Applet {
    Font font = new Font("Dialog", Font.BOLD, 24);
    String str = "Welcome to VisualAge";
    int xPos = 5;
}
```

To change the text "Welcome to VisualAge" to any string you like, just type over the text. Save your changes by selecting **Edit→Save** from the menu bar. VisualAge for Java compiles the code immediately, and you can test the result by again selecting **Selected→Run→In Applet Viewer** from the menu bar.

You do not even have to close the Applet Viewer to see the changes! Change and save the text, then select **Applet→Reload** from the menu bar of the running Applet Viewer.

This simple example shows how VisualAge for Java can help you create Java programs. You did not have to edit, save or compile any file. You simply changed the code generated automatically by VisualAge for Java, saved it, and ran it. This reduced development time is a reality thanks to the incremental compiler, which compiles changes to your code on the fly when you save it.

Creating an Animated Applet

Integrated development environment

Now that you are becoming more familiar with the VisualAge for Java IDE, it is time to create your second applet. With VisualAge for Java, it is easy to create applets that scroll text from one side of the applet to another.

This time you create a new class without using the Quick Start. Instead, expand the Programming with VAJ V2 project by clicking on the + (plus sign) and then select the **itso.samples.ch01** package. Next, click on the **Create Applet** icon (the one with the capital A on it) on the tool bar of the Workbench. The SmartGuide appears again, requesting you to fill in information about your second applet. Because you selected the package, the Project and Package fields are already filled in (if not use the same names as in your first applet). Enter HiThereAgain in the *Applet Name* field and make sure the **Browse applet when finished** checkbox is not selected. Click the **Next**> button to access the second page of the SmartGuide (Figure 7).

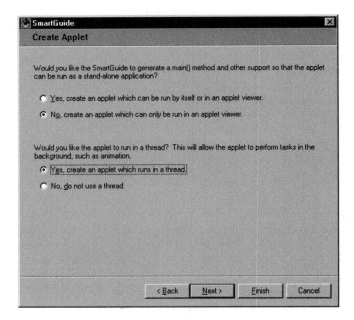

Figure 7. Creating an Animated Applet

Select the **Yes, create an applet which runs in a thread** radio button, and click the **Finish** button. Run the applet by selecting it in the Workbench and then selecting **Selected→Run→In Applet Viewer** from the menu bar.

The Selected Menu
The Selected menu is contextual, that is, it differs according to the item selected.
You can also access the Selected menu by holding down the right mouse button once you have selected an item.

Your application should show a marquee text scrolling from left to right. You have just built an animated applet.

Changing the Properties of the Applet

New in V2! An HTML applet tag is required to run an applet within a browser, and within that tag there are some required fields. VisualAge for Java automatically creates the applet tag for you. If you want to change any of the properties or add new ones, you open the Properties window for the class. Select the **HiThere** class in the Workbench and then select **Selected→Properties**. The window shown in Figure 8 on page 14 appears.

The first time you ran your HiThere applet (Figure 6 on page 11), the applet size was not perfect. On the Applet page of the Properties window, change the *Width* to 300 and the *Height* to 100 and run your applet again. In the other pages of this window you can set the class path for the applet (where the Applet Viewer looks for external classes) and see other properties of the class. If this class were a Java application (which you are about to build), you could set the command line parameters here.

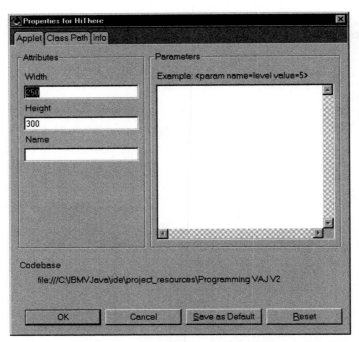

Figure 8. Class Properties Window for the HiThere Class

Building Your First Application

In this section you create a Java *application* that prints a string to the VisualAge for Java Console. The Console is a window that displays messages sent by your application to the standard output of the operating system and where you enter input for your applications. To create a class that can be run as an application, without the Applet Viewer or a Web browser, you have to implement a method called main in your class.

Now start creating your application. In the Workbench, select the package you created (itso.samples.ch01), then select **Selected→Add→Class** from the menu bar. Enter HiAgain in the *Class Name* field (see Figure 9).

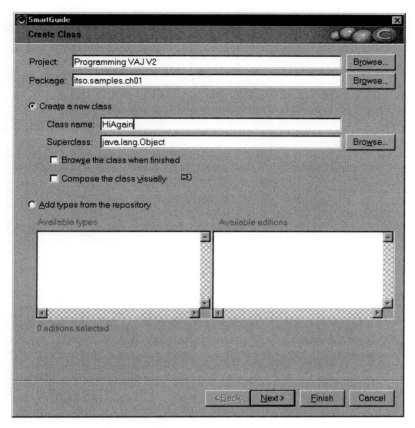

Figure 9. Creating the HiAgain Application

When you created your applet the superclass was java.applet.Applet. Now because you are creating a class that does not need a user interface and does not reuse the behavior of other objects, the superclass is java.lang.Object.

Deselect the **Browse the class when finished** and **Compose the class visually** checkboxes.

Click the **Next>** button to access the second page of the SmartGuide (Figure 10), where you specify attributes of your new class.

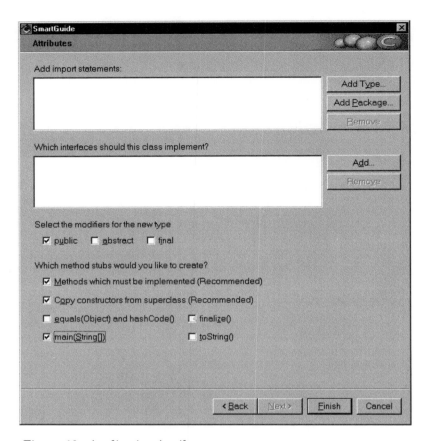

Figure 10. Application Attributes

Select the **main(String [])** checkbox under *Which method stubs would you like to create* and click the **Finish** button. VisualAge for Java creates a class declaration and constructor for HiAgain and a stub, or skeleton code, for the main method.

VisualAge for Java can automatically generate method skeletons for:

❑ The common methods listed on the SmartGuide

❑ Constructors declared in the superclass

❑ Methods that must be implemented because of abstract inheritance or interfaces that the class implements

In the Source pane of the Workbench you can see the definition of your newly created class. In the Browse pane, expand the class by clicking the plus sign to the left of it, and you can see the main method. Select this method, and the

Source pane shows you the method implementation. Only a stub of the method has been generated, but you can change that by adding the following code to the method body:

System.out.println("This is my first application!");

The System.out.println() statement prints a string to the standard output, which in turn is displayed in the VisualAge for Java Console window.

Your main method should now look like this:

```
/**
 * Starts the application.
 * @param args an array of command-line arguments
 */
public static void main(java.lang.String[] args) {
    System.out.println("This is my first application!");
}
```

Save the changes you made, using the menu bar (**Edit→Save**) or the Control-S key combination, and you are ready to see the results of your work. Select **Selected→Run→Run Main** from the menu bar. The **Console** window (Figure 11) opens to display the result. Notice that you do not have to select the class itself; the Run function knows which class you are working with and runs that class.

Figure 11. The VisualAge for Java Console

You have successfully created a Java application. The Console window displaying the text that your application generated is used as a standard output window for messages and for entering input through the standard input.

Improved in V2!

For each Java program that writes to or reads from the Console that you are running, the Console shows a line in the All Programs pane. To view the output or enter input for that program, select it in the All Programs pane.

Running a Program As an Applet and Application

With VisualAge for Java, you can easily build an applet that can be run as an application, but your applet has to implement the main method to handle opening a window without an Applet Viewer or a Web browser.

To create this kind of applet, click the **Applet** icon in the tool bar, and the SmartGuide creates the necessary implementation for you. After providing names for the project, package, and class, select the Write source code for the applet radio button and click the **Next** button to access the Applet Properties SmartGuide. Select the **Yes, create an Applet which can be run by itself or in an Applet viewer** radio button, and click the **Finish** button. Notice that the **Selected→Run** menu has both **Run main** and **In Applet Viewer** options available if you select the class in the Workbench.

The VisualAge for Java Scrapbook

The Scrapbook enables you to evaluate Java expressions. Just type in any expression, highlight it, and execute it. The Scrapbook can have several pages. You can consider each page of the Scrapbook to be a separate JVM that compiles or runs separate code fragments.

The Scrapbook As Editor

You can also use the Scrapbook to open files in the file system for reading or editing. You need not use a text editor that is external to VisualAge. If you do not save pages to files, when you close the Scrapbook, VisualAge prompts you to save any pages that you modified.

Using the Scrapbook

To enter and run Java code in the Scrapbook:

1. From the Workbench menu bar select **Window→Scrapbook** (Figure 12) to display the Scrapbook window (Figure 13).

2. Type some Java code (for example, the code shown in Figure 13) into the Scrapbook and highlight the text by using the mouse or the shift and cursor keys.

3. From the menu bar select **Edit→Run** or click the **Run** button on the tool bar.

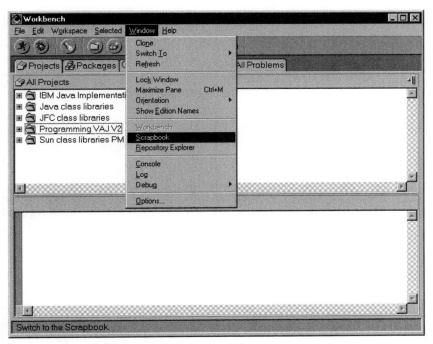

Figure 12. Launching the Scrapbook in VisualAge for Java

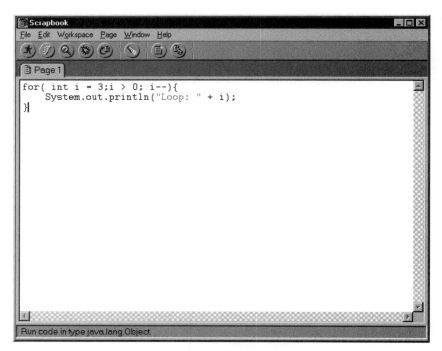

Figure 13. Evaluating Java Code in the Scrapbook

By highlighting the Java statements and selecting **Edit→Run**, you instruct the compiler to compile the statements and execute them immediately. A Console window opens, and the output of the `System.out.println("Loop: " + i);` statement is displayed (Figure 14).

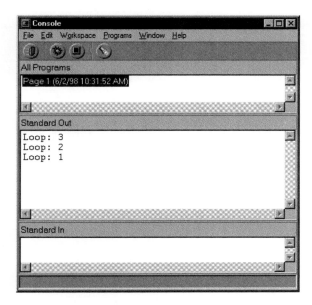

Figure 14. Console Output of the for Loop Executed in the Scrapbook

If you want to save the code you have created in the Scrapbook, select **File→Save** from the menu bar, and you can save the Java source code into a text file.

Figure 15 shows some examples of using operators in the Scrapbook.

```
Scrapbook                                              _ □ ✕
File  Edit  Workspace  Page  Window  Help

  loop.scp   Page 2

int x = 10;
int y = ~x;
System.out.println(y);

x = 3;
y = x & 1;
System.out.println(y);

x = 16;
y = x >> 1;
System.out.println(y);

int test=-3;
do{
        System.out.println("In while loop");
        test = 0;
}while( test > 0);
System.out.println("Out of do loop");|

Run code in type java.lang.Object.
```

Figure 15. Using Operators in the Scrapbook

Scrapbook Context
When you execute code in the Scrapbook, the code runs in the context of a static method in the Object class. Select **Page→Run In** to change the context in which the code runs.

Changing the context is not always that useful because you still cannot access instance variables or methods of the type. However, you can create an instance of the type and then perform operations on it. The benefit of the **Page→Run In** selection is that you do not have to use absolute package names and you are running with private access permission on the class. Because the context is defined by the Run In function, you cannot use import statements in the Scrapbook.

Correcting Errors in the Scrapbook

If you make a coding mistake, for example, you forget the closing parenthesis at the end of the System.out.println("Loop number" + i) statement, VisualAge for Java places a highlighted message where it detects the mistake (Figure 16).

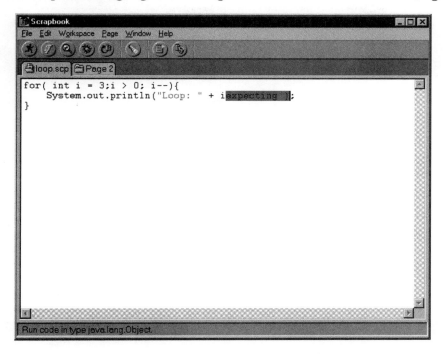

Figure 16. An Error Message in the Scrapbook Window

In this case, four simple steps will correct the error:

1. Read the error message to determine what is wrong.
2. Press the Delete key to delete the compiler information.
3. Correct your code.
4. Run your example again.

VisualAge for Java also provides *Automatic Code Completion*, also known as *Code Assist* or *Code Clue*. Code Assist can help you locate the correct type, method, or field while you are coding. You can invoke it from method source, Scrapbook, Inspector windows, the event-to-code editor and the conditional breakpoint editor. To see Code Assist in action, go to the Scrapbook window. Type System.out, hold down the Control key, and press the spacebar. A dialog appears showing all possible methods you could call in the System.out context (see Figure 17 on page 24).

When you save methods, VisualAge for Java provides you with a list of suggested corrections for errors in your code. You can select the correction, save the code as is, or cancel the save.

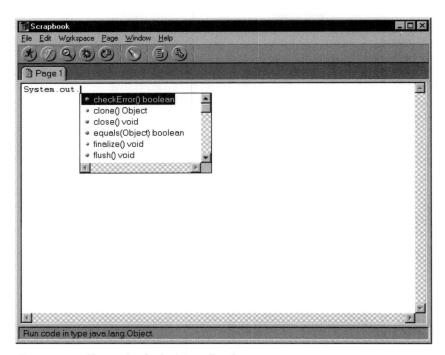

Figure 17. Using the Code Assist Facility

If Your Scrapbook Page Remains Busy
Whenever a code fragment is evaluated in a Scrapbook page, that page is made inactive (busy) for the duration of the evaluation. Two visual cues indicate that a page is busy: The document icon in the tab contains a small clock icon, or the status line for the busy page contains the following text: "This page is busy running the selected code."
The page remains busy until the selected code fragment is finished running. Your page may remain busy because the code actually takes a long time to evaluate, or you are debugging a thread started from that page.
To terminate the evaluation of the code and return the page to its original state, select **Page→Restart Page** from the menu bar. Note that all threads, and therefore all windows, started from that page will be stopped and closed.

Customizing VisualAge for Java

You may have noticed by now that your windows may not look exactly like those in this book. We changed our environments to make the screen captures as readable as possible. It is possible to customize VisualAge for Java in several ways:

❑ Workbench Options

❑ Tool Integration Framework

❑ Palette modification

In this section you will learn about the Workbench Options. The Tool Integration Framework is described in "Tool Integration Framework" on page 377, and palette modification is discussed in "Beans Palette Modification" on page 115.

Workbench Options

The Workbench Options (accessed by selecting **Window→Options** from the Workbench menu bar), enable you to customize the VisualAge for Java environment in many ways (see Figure 18 on page 26).

New in
V2! ➡

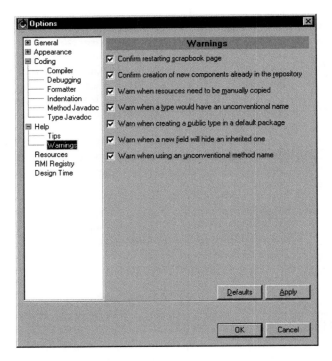

Figure 18. Workbench Options

For a complete description of the options see the VisualAge for Java product documentation. Some of the options you may use throughout this book are:

❏ General

• Cache

The new Cache feature improves the performance of the VisualAge for Java IDE considerably. You can set the number of classes cached in memory and on your hard drive.

❏ Appearance

• Source

To make your source code easy to debug, you can choose the font type, size, and foreground and background color of the source code. You can customize different colors for the default code, its comments, keywords, literals, and errors.

• Printer

This option lets you chose the default printer for VisualAge for Java.

❏ Coding

- Debugging -The debugger options are discussed in "The Debugger" on page 177.

- Formatter - Many developers are stringent about the formatting of their code. With VisualAge for Java Version 2 you can set the way your code is formatted:

  - Compound statements begin a new line

  - Opening braces begin a new line

- Method Javadoc

  This option provides a text template for comments added when you create a method with the Add Method SmartGuide. The comment is inserted into Javadoc-style comments.

- Type Javadoc

  This option provides a text template for comments added when you create a class or interface with the Add Class or Add Interface SmartGuide. The comment is inserted into Javadoc-style comments.

❑ RMI Registry - With VisualAge for Java Professional you can develop distributed Java applications that use RMI. You can:

- Start the RMI registry on VisualAge startup

- Use the default or another RMI port

- Restart or stop the RMI registry

❑ Design Time

- Generate meta data method - In VisualAge for Java Version 2 you can save the visual builder information directly into source code (using the getBuilderData method). If you subsequently import the Java code into another VisualAge for Java environment, the builder information is not lost.

2 Organizing Your Code

With VisualAge for Java you use projects and packages to organize your work. Projects are a feature of VisualAge for Java that provide a high-level means of grouping the development efforts of a project. Packages are the standard Java scheme of organizing classes and interfaces that are intended to work together.

In this chapter you will learn to work with projects and packages in VisualAge for Java.

Projects in VisualAge for Java

You have already created a project, Programming VAJ V2, to organize all of the work you do while reading this book. Projects provide a way of organizing your Java code at the highest level. Whenever you create a new package, you must place it in a new or existing project. Projects do not have any equivalent in the Java language.

The first time you start VisualAge for Java and go to the Workbench, you see several projects in your workspace, all of which contain several packages. Table 2 lists these projects and their contents.

Table 2. Default VisualAge for Java Projects and Their Contents

Project	Contents
IBM Java Implementation	com.ibm.uvm.* packages, which enable and support the VisualAge for Java VM and environment
Java Class Libraries	java.* packages, which contain the Java Class Libraries
JFC Class Libraries	The Java Foundation (Swing) Class library
Sun Class Libraries PM Win32	sun.* packages, which are extensions to standard java.* packages

The code in the projects in Table 2 cannot be modified or deleted. It is required by VisualAge for Java to function correctly.

Additional projects are available in VisualAge for Java and are described in Chapter 5, "Managing and Fixing Your Code" on page 153.

The Workbench

To understand how VisualAge for Java organizes projects and packages, you have to know a little more about the Workbench.

The Workbench provides different views of your current development environment or workspace. The layout of the Workbench window depends on the tab selection above the pane. To switch between the Projects, Packages, Classes, Interfaces, and All Problems pages, just click on the corresponding tab. The menu bar of these pages also changes as you switch from tab to tab.

From any Workbench page you can access the menu of the currently selected item (project, package, class, interface, or method) in two different ways. You can:

❑ Access the pop-up menu by right-clicking the selected item

❑ Use the menu bar

The pop-up menu of the Source pane and the Edit menu in the menu bar have the same contents. The Browse pane's pop-up menu is the same as the Selected menu in the menu bar.

The Workbench also provides a toolbar for quick access to functions. Figure 19 shows the toolbar and Table 3 describes the icons.

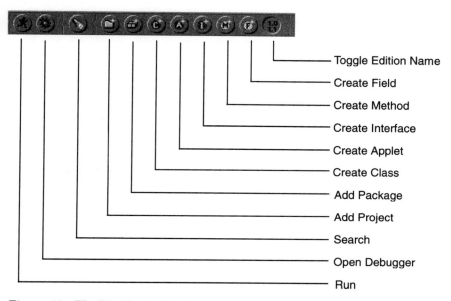

Figure 19. The Workbench Toolbar

Table 3. Toolbar Icon Descriptions

Icon	Description
Run	Run the selected class or a class from the selected project or package.
Open Debugger	Start the debugger.
Search	Search for a reference or declaration of a field, method, or class.
Add Project	Add a project to the current workspace.
Add Package	Add a package to the current selected project.
Create Class	Invoke the Create a new Class Smart-Guide.

Icon	Description
Create Applet	Invoke the Create a new Applet Smart-Guide.
Create Interface	Invoke the Create a new Interface Smart-Guide.
Create Method	Invoke the Create a new Method Smart-Guide on an existing class.
Create Field	Invoke the Create a new Field Smart-Guide on an existing class.
Toggle Edition Names	Show or hide the edition names of program elements.

The Workbench Projects Page

The Projects page of the Workbench (Figure 20) contains two panes: a Browse pane and a Source or Comment pane.

Title Bar
Menu Bar

Tool Bar

Tab Selection

Browse Pane

Source Pane

Status Bar

Bookmarks

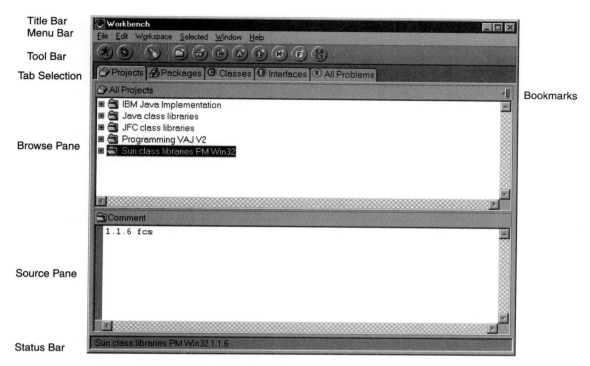

Figure 20. Workbench Projects Page

The orientation of the panes is by default set to horizontal. If you want to change the orientation, you can select **Window→Orientation** and choose **Vertical** instead of **Horizontal**.

If you select a program element in the Browse pane, which contains code, such as a class, interface, or method, the other pane is labeled Source and contains source code. If you select a package or project, the other pane is labeled Comment and contains any comments you have added to the project or package.

A tree view of the projects, packages, classes, and interfaces that are currently loaded in your workspace is shown in the Browse pane when you select the Projects, Packages, Classes, or Interfaces views. The Projects view is the default view shown when you open the Workbench for the first time. To collapse or expand any item in the list, click the plus or minus sign to the left of the item (or use the plus sign and minus sign keys). To show the source code for an item in the Source pane, select the item, using your mouse.

You can create new projects by selecting **Selected→Add→Project** in any browser window.

Using the VisualAge for Java Windows
VisualAge for Java provides many useful features for viewing different parts of your projects. Three of these features are:
- The Projects page enables you to set bookmarks. In the upper-right corner of the Browse pane, click on the plus sign to set a bookmark. When you want to return to a particular piece of code, click the number that appeared when you created the bookmark.
- You can clone any window in VisualAge for Java. Selecting **Window→Clone** opens another window in the same context. A clone of a window can be very useful when you need two similar views, but be careful about updating the same class in two views. It is possible to overwrite changes you have made in one view with changes made in another window.
- Double-clicking on the title bar of any pane maximizes that pane within the window. Double-click again to restore the normal view. You can also select **Window→Maximize Pane/Restore Pane**.

The Workbench Packages View

The Packages page of the Workbench (Figure 21) contains three Browse panes — All Packages, Types, and Methods — and one Source pane.

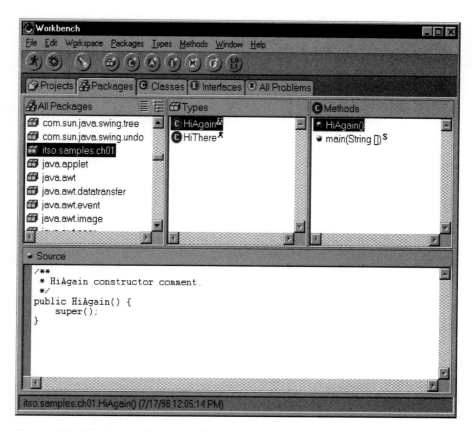

Figure 21. Workbench Packages Page

You can use **Packages→Layout** to customize your view, and you can choose
between **Tree Layout** or **List Layout**. You can access the same functionality
through the layout icons at the top right of the All Packages pane.

The **Orientation** option is also available for this view under **Window**.

Creating Packages

With the JDK, directories are used to organize packages on your file system,
whereas in VisualAge for Java packages and classes are kept in the
workspace.

The workspace contains all of the program elements with which you are
currently working. Rather than creating directory structures, VisualAge for
Java organizes its packages and classes internally. If you export classes, the
directory structure is created on your file system. This approach makes

managing packages and classes simple. Although classes of your projects are kept in the workspace, any resources of those projects are kept separately in your local file system in this directory:

```
\ibmvjava\ide\project_resources\project_name
```

In Java you can declare a class to be part of a package by using the *package* keyword at the top of your Java source file:

```
package account;

public class BankAccount{
    private string accountId;
    private double balance;
}
```

In VisualAge for Java you select the package that will contain each new type that you create. If you specify a package name that does not exist, that package will be created for you. After creating new classes in a selected package, the package name is not shown in the code; it is implied in the list of classes in the package.

You can also create or import code that has been defined with the default package, the package used when no package is explicitly defined. Because you cannot access members of a default package from other packages, the use of a default package is not recommended.

You can also create new packages by selecting **Selected→Add→Package** in any browser window. To create the Automated Teller Machine (ATM) application used throughout this book, you need two packages:

```
itso.atm.model
itso.atm.view
```

Create these two packages now by selecting the Programming VAJ V2 project and then **Selected→Add Package**. Fill in the *Create a new package named with* field with the name of the first package and click **Finish**, then repeat the process for the second package.

Using Types from Other Packages

With VisualAge for Java or the JDK environment, you have two ways of using a class from another package:

❑ Refer to the class by using the fully qualified name

❑ Use the import keyword

You can either import all types defined within a package or be more selective. Note that importing a package does not import the subpackages of that package, you have to import them separately. You can use the star notation (java.awt.*) to import all types within a package, but you have to separately import any subpackages, such as java.awt.event.

If you already know which packages you will need within your class when you are creating it, use the Attributes dialog box (which opens when you click **Next** in the Create Class or Interface SmartGuide). The Attributes dialog box enables you to specify the packages to be imported. Use the **Add Class** and **Add Package** buttons to browse and select classes and packages to import into your class (Figure 22).

You can also add the import statements manually by editing the class declaration.

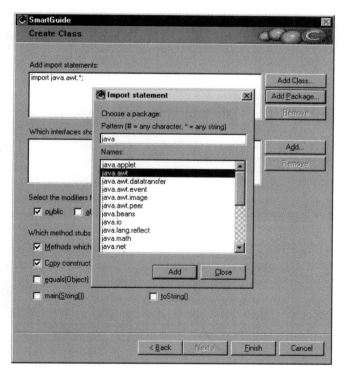

Figure 22. Create Class SmartGuide: Import Statement Dialog Box

The Workbench Classes Page

The Classes page of the Workbench (Figure 23) contains three panes: Class Hierarchy, Methods, and Source.

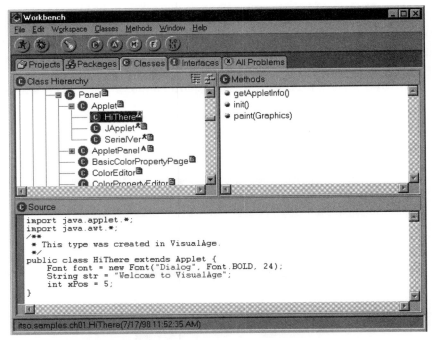

Figure 23. Workbench Classes Page

You can change the layout of your classes, using **Classes→Layout** from the menu or the layout icons at the top right of the **Class Hierarchy** pane. You can also select the orientation of the Browse pane, using **Window→Orientation.**

The Classes view is useful because it shows the class hierarchy of types, and you can quickly follow the inheritance tree of classes. In the Classes view you can quickly find a class you are interested in by selecting **Classes→Go To Class** and then typing in the class name until the complete name shows up in the list.

Navigation Aids

The Go To Class function is just one of the many navigation aids in the WorkBench. Here are some other aids:

- Each window has a different **Go To** option.
- Each window has an **Open To**, which opens the selected item in a selected browser.
- Each window has a **Clone** function if you want to have two views of the same information.
- You can search for different items, using **Workspace→Search**.
- You can find all code that has references to a selected type, using **Selected→References To.**

The Workbench Interfaces Page

The Interfaces page of the Workbench (Figure 24) is similar to the Classes page (Figure 23) except that it displays interfaces instead of classes. The Interfaces page consists of three panes: Interfaces, Methods, and Source.

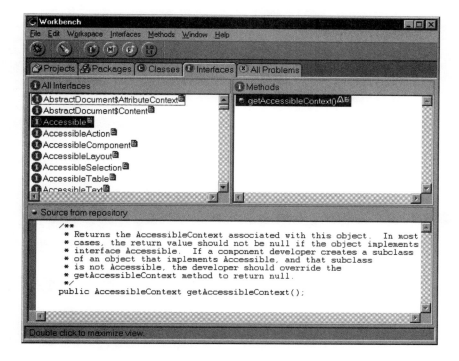

Figure 24. Workbench Interfaces Page

The Workbench All Problems Page

On the All Problems page you can find all incorrect code in the workspace. The incorrect code found within a method causes the method to be flagged with a red X, and the method's class will be flagged with a grey X (see Figure 25). If you have incorrect code in a class or interface declaration, the class or interface is flagged with a red X.

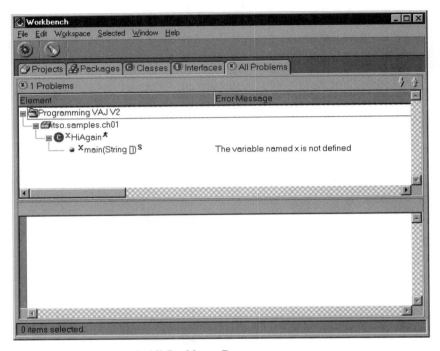

Figure 25. Workbench All Problems Page

In your version of VisualAge for Java you should not have any errors (not yet anyway). You can create an error to see the result:

❑ Select the **Projects** tab on the Workbench.

❑ Expand (click on the plus sign) the HiAgain class and then select the main(String)[] method.

❑ Add the line: x=2; before the closing brace (}) and save the method (using **Edit→Save** or Control-S).

Figure 27 on page 42 shows the Warning dialog box that appears when you attempt to save incorrect code. At this point you can cancel, return to the code and fix the error, or save the code with the error.

If VisualAge for Java can suggest corrections to the code, it displays them in the lower pane. You can select the entry under Suggested corrections and click the **Correct** button to correct your code.

❏ Click the **Save** button in the Warning dialog.

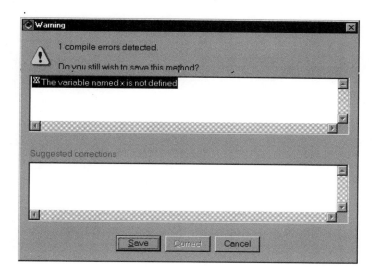

Figure 26. Warning Dialog: Undefined Variable

❏ Select the **All Problems** tab on the Workbench. Figure 25 on page 40 shows the error in the page. Select the main method, delete the line x=2;, and save the method. The problem should disappear.

In most cases when you type incorrect code, you get the Warning dialog shown in Figure 26 on page 41. In some cases when the VisualAge for Java compiler cannot parse the incorrect code, you get an Error dialog (Figure 27 on page 42). In this case you must return to the code and fix it before you can save it. If VisualAge for Java can suggest corrections to the code, it shows them in the lower pane.

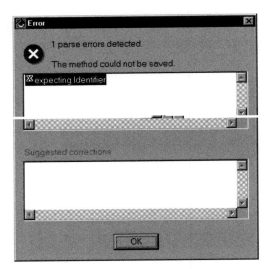

Figure 27. Error Dialog Box: Parse Errors Detected

Leaving Errors in Your Code

It may seem a little strange to leave errors in your code. However, in VisualAge for Java there is little risk. For example, if you forget to create a variable before you reference it, you can save the code that references the variable, go the All Problems page later, and add the variables to the class declaration.

In the worst case, where you are not sure what you should fix, you can just return to an earlier version of the code.

Importing and Exporting Java Code with VisualAge for Java

You have already learned that VisualAge for Java Professional stores your projects in a repository, not directly in the file system. To deploy your Java projects, or to share code with other developers, you have to import and export Java classes. If you are part of a development team you should look at VisualAge for Java Enterprise, which provides complete support for team development.

You can import and export Java classes and resources to and from the VisualAge for Java environment in several formats:

❑ Java source code

You can import Java source code from the file system. The code is compiled as it is imported, and package hierarchies are retained. You would export Java source code when you want to share it with developers who are using a different development environment or edit it using a different editor from that provided with VisualAge for Java.

❑ Java class files

Java class files are exported when you are ready for testing outside the VisualAge for Java environment or to deploy your program. Class files can also be imported into VisualAge for Java. However, the imported class cannot be modified, and the source code, as you would expect, is not visible.

❑ Java archive files

Java archive (JAR) is a platform-independent file format that enables you to compress a Java applet and its resources (such as .class files, images, and sounds) into a single file. JAR files are a good way of distributing Java applets, applications, and their supporting resources. You can install the files on a Web server where Web browsers can access them. You can export a complete VisualAge for Java project as a JAR file.

JAR files can also be imported into VisualAge for Java. The classes are compiled and placed in a project. Any supporting resource files are placed in a resource directory with the same name as the project under:

    \ibmvjava\ide\project_resources

❑ VisualAge for Java interchange files

Interchange files are used to exchange Java classes built with VisualAge for Java Professional among different VisualAge for Java Professional environments. The files maintain version information and comments as well as visual development information.

When you import an interchange file, it is loaded into your repository. You then have to load it into your workspace from the repository. Any program elements that you export by using an interchange file must be versioned first. Versions and the repository are fully explained in Chapter 5, "Managing and Fixing Your Code" on page 153.

Importing into VisualAge for Java

Note that importing code into the VisualAge for Java environment is not the same as using the import keyword in Java source code.

To import code into VisualAge for Java:

Improved in V2! 1. Open the Import dialog, using one of these methods:

- **File→Import** from the menu bar on any page.
- **Selected→Import** from the menu bar on the Projects page.
- **Packages/Types→Import** from the menu bar on the Packages page.
- **Classes→Import** from the menu bar on the Classes page.
- **Interfaces→Import** from the menu bar on the Interfaces page.

A SmartGuide prompts you for the source of import (Figure 28).

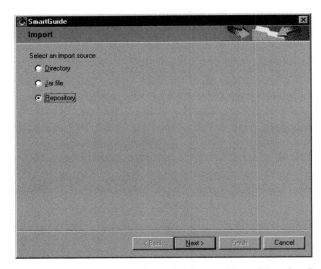

Figure 28. Importing Java Files into VisualAge for Java

2. Select the source of import:

- **Directory** - .java or .class files
- **Jar file**
- **Repository** - interchange files

For Directory and Jar file imports, select:

- The directory where the import files reside
- The specific classes (source or bytecode) and resources to be imported
- The project into which to import the classes
- Whether or not to overwrite existing resources

For Repository imports, select:

- The repository file to be imported
- The specific projects or packages to import (Figure 29 on page 45)

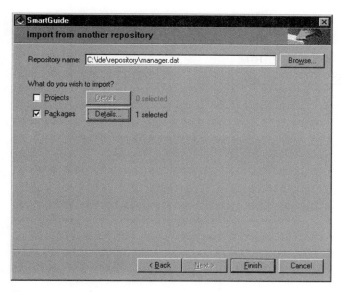

Figure 29. Importing from Another Repository

Exporting from VisualAge for Java

To export code from VisualAge for Java:

1. Optionally, select one or more projects, packages, or classes or interfaces.

   - When you select a package, all classes and interfaces in the package are exported.

   - When you select a project, all classes of all the packages within that project are exported.

2. Open the Export dialog (Figure 30), using one of these methods:

   - **File→Export** from the menu bar on any page

   - **Selected→Export** from the menu bar on the Projects page

   - **Packages/Types→Export** from the menu bar on the Packages page

   - **Classes→Export** from the menu bar on the Classes page

   - **Interfaces→Export** from the menu bar on the Interfaces page

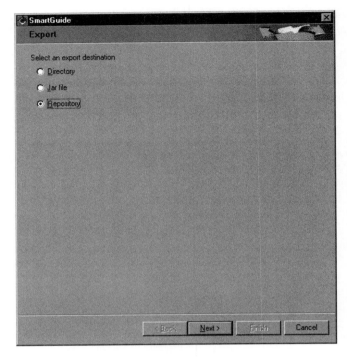

Figure 30. The Export SmartGuide

3. Select the export destination:

- **Directory** - .java or .class files
- **Jar file**
- **Repository** - interchange files

For Directory exports, select:

- The root directory where the export files will reside
- The specific classes (source or bytecode) and resources to be exported
- You can also set several options on the export:

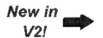
New in V2!

- Select referenced classes to export
- Deselect the BeanInfo and Property Editor classes from the export
- Whether to create HTML files to launch applets
- Whether to overwrite existing files
- Whether to open the created HTML files in a browser

For Jar file exports (Figure 31), the options include those for Directory exports as well as these:

- Selecting specific beans and classes to export
- Whether to compress the contents of the Jar file

For Repository exports, select:

- The repository file to be exported
- The specific projects or packages to export

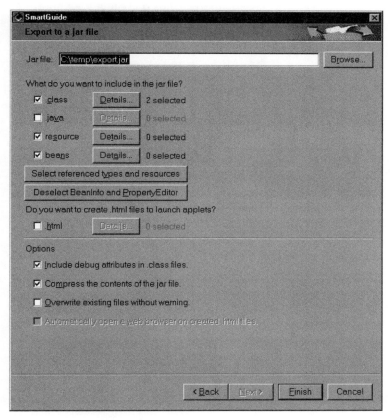

Figure 31. Exporting to a Jar File

New in V2!

Exporting Your Code

VisualAge for Java has some powerful new features for exporting code. The Deployment Wizard is invoked by selecting the **Select referenced types and resources** button. The Deployment Wizard automatically includes the types your code needs. Therefore your exported Jar files will only include the code they need.

When exporting a Jar file, you can select specific beans to export. This action forces the creation of a manifest file in your Jar file, enabling other environments to recognize the beans in your Jar file and other VisualAge for Java environments to automatically add beans from the JAR file to the palette.

If the JAR file is to be directly used in the Classpath for a Java application or applet, do not compress its contents.

You can also now export visual builder information in Java source and class files. Select the **Generate meta data method** checkbox in the Design Time section of the Options dialog. VisualAge for Java will generate a getBuilderdata method that contains the visual builder information for the class.

3 Beginning the ATM Project

Although Java was originally marketed as a language for creating applets, many Java development efforts focus on building Java applications. The object-oriented nature, portability and security of the Java language make it a good choice for application development.

In this chapter you will be introduced to the basic design of the ATM application that is used in this book. You will learn about JavaBeans, and you will create your first JavaBeans for the ATM application.

ATM Application

The ATM application emulates a simple automated teller machine to explain how to build Java applications and applets using VisualAge for Java. Yes, we know that most of you do not have card readers on your PC, so you could not actually emulate a real ATM, but this could be the basis for software running in a real ATM machine built around a Java chip!

The requirements for the ATM are simple. It should:

- Handle two types of accounts:
  - Savings
  - Checking
- Perform withdraw and deposit transactions for each of the accounts
- List a transaction history log for each of the accounts
- Restrict withdrawals beyond a minimum overdraft amount or minimum balance

Figure 32 shows a prototype of the ATM screen panels and the flow of events. When a person uses an ATM, the ATM must:

- Receive a valid card ID
- Display the card ID with a greeting and ask for a PIN to match the card ID entered
- Validate the PIN with the matching card ID
- Let the user reenter the card ID or PIN if necessary
- Let the user choose an account and display the appropriate account information panel
- Display a transaction history log in a list at the user's request

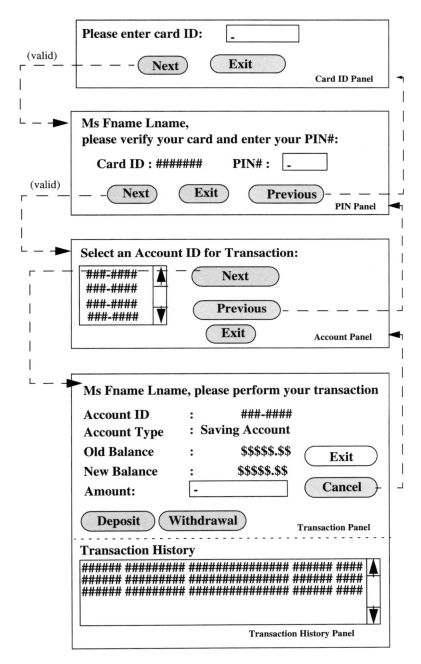

Figure 32. Prototype ATM Application Panels and Flow

ATM Object Model

Figure 33 shows the object model of the ATM application.

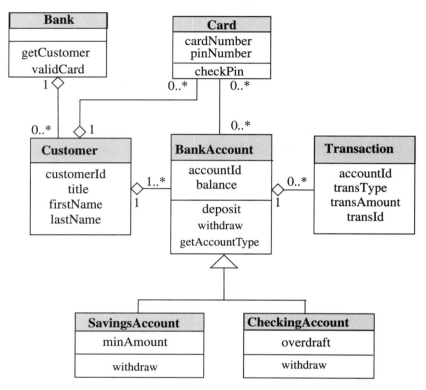

Figure 33. Object Model of the ATM Application

The model uses Unified Modeling Language (UML) notation. If you are not familiar with the notation, check the UML documentation at www.rational.com. Even if you are not familiar with UML you should be able to follow the diagram and this description:

☐ The Bank class holds all customers of the bank. In addition, the bank will validate cards and supply a customer object given a valid card.

☐ The Customer class stores the customer information and holds all of the customer's accounts and cards.

☐ The Card class stores the card number and personal identification number (PIN) and references all the accounts that are valid for the card.

☐ The account classes — BankAccount, the abstract superclass; CheckingAccount; and SavingsAccount — hold individual account information as well as a list of account transactions.

- BankAccount, SavingsAccount, and CheckingAccount are closely related. The BankAccount class represents the generic bank account, with all of the features of a bank account, such as account ID, balance, and customer ID. SavingsAccount and CheckingAccount inherit from BankAccount, but each of them has additional information and behavior. The SavingsAccount class contains the information related to the minimum amount, and the CheckingAccount class contains an overdraft value that has to be less than a specified amount. In other words, the instances of the SavingsAccount and CheckingAccount classes represent the real accounts of the customer.

- Transaction objects are needed to store customer information and transaction history.

- Although not shown in Figure 33 on page 52, each class also implements a toString method.

JavaBeans

Software components are standard and reusable building blocks for software development. Basically, they encapsulate function and provide services based on a strict specification of their interface. Because of this specification, they can be used as "black boxes" (components whose internal state is hidden) and, combined with other software components, to build a complete application.

The *JavaBeans* specification is the standard component model for the Java language and is the component model used by VisualAge for Java. It describes how Java classes should appear and behave in order to be treated as JavaBeans. Beans can be visual components, such as a button or a list, that you use to build the user interface or *view* of your application. They can also be nonvisual components, such as a bank account, that typically represent the business logic or *domain model* of your application. To build an application or an applet with a bean manipulator tool, such as the VisualAge for Java Visual Composition Editor, you typically drag and drop the beans you want to use into a working area and wire, or connect, them together. This visual programming approach is an extremely productive way to create applications.

JavaBeans provide support for:

- *Portability*: Beans can be created and run on any Java platform.

- *Introspection*: The tool that you use to combine beans can automatically discover how a bean works.

❏ *Properties and customization*: Properties are a bean's attributes. A developer using a bean can customize the appearance and behavior of a bean by changing its properties.

❏ *Persistence*: The state of a bean can be saved and then reloaded through the serialization function of the JDK 1.1.

The key to understanding and using a bean is to understand its features, that is, the *events*, *properties*, and *methods* that it exposes. A bean exposes a feature by making it available to other beans. The features a bean exposes constitute its interface, and you can use this interface to combine beans with each other, through a tool such as the Visual Composition Editor.

Event Features

Events are *fired* by a bean to indicate that there has been some change in its state. For example, a bank account bean could fire an event when the balance changes. Other beans can register their interest in these events and be notified of their occurrence. Beans can both fire and listen for events. Beans expose the events that they fire in their bean interface.

The JDK 1.1 defines an event specific to JavaBeans: the property change event. This event allows beans to notify each other when one of their properties changes (see "Property Features" on page 55).

Figure 34 shows the sequence of calls or method invocations to support property change notification:

❏ The Event Listener, or target bean, implements the PropertyChangeListener interface, consisting of the propertyChange method. This method contains the behavior to be executed when the event is fired.

❏ The addPropertyChangeListener method is invoked on the Event Source (the bean that fires the property change) with the Event Listener as the parameter.

❏ When the value of the property changes, the Event Source fires a property change event resulting in the *propertyChange* method, with a PropertyChangeEvent object as the parameter, being executed on each Event Listener.

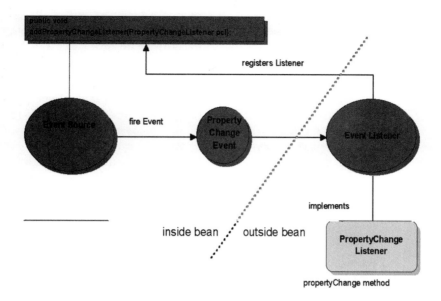

Figure 34. Property Change Event

Property Features

The attributes exposed by a bean are called *properties*. Properties can be *read*, *written*, *bound, indexed*, and *constrained*. The properties exposed by a bean are typically a subset of its attributes.

The properties exposed by a bean are the data that it knows and whose value it wants other components to be able to get and/or set. The values are always accessed and manipulated through accessor (getter) and mutator (setter) methods that follow a default design pattern, which is in fact a simple naming convention defined by the JavaBeans specification:

❑ For a readable and writeable property named xxx, there are two methods, getXxx and setXxx, to access and change the value of the property. The type returned by the get method is the same type as the argument passed to the set method. Because of this specification, bean properties typically begin with a lower-case letter.

❑ You can also define get and set methods for a boolean property by following the above convention. However, the prefix is can be used instead of get.

Properties can be categorized as *bound, indexed*, or *constrained*:

❑ *Bound properties* are properties that fire the property change event when their value is changed. A PropertyChangeEvent object includes the old and new values of the property. An example of a bound property might be the balance property of a bank account. The setBalance method would fire a property change event so that the balance can be updated in a listener object.

❑ *Indexed properties* are simply properties that support a range of values. They are implemented through arrays and have four accessor and mutator methods to access the arrays of values by either a single element or the entire array. For example, the indexed transactions property could represent a list of transactions of a bank account. The following methods would be defined to access the transactions:

```
void setTransactions( int index, Transaction aTransaction)
Transaction getTransactions( int index)
void setTransactions( Transaction[] transactions)
Transaction[] getTransactions()
```

❑ *Constrained properties* are properties that allow other beans to decide whether a change in the property's value is to be accepted. The other beans are notified through a vetoable change event, and they can throw a PropertyVetoException to veto the changes and have the property changed back to its original value.

According to the JavaBeans specification, a property should probably be both bound and constrained because a listener may want to know when the property was actually changed.

Properties can also be designated as *hidden*, where they are not visible in the development environment, and *expert*, where they should be manipulated only by expert users.

Special property editors can also be created to change the value of the properties when the beans are being used in the development environment. A special Customizer class can also be created to control the customization of the complete bean at development time.

Method Features

Method features are the actions that a bean exposes for invocation by other components. The bean methods, by default, are the set of public methods of the class underlying the bean.

Be aware of the naming convention used by JavaBeans when you write methods. For example, accessor and mutator methods should follow the naming convention described in "Property Features" on page 55 for each bean property.

Introspection and the BeanInfo Class

The power of JavaBeans is evident when you use VisualAge for Java and drag a bean off its palette and drop it on the free-form surface. At this time, VisualAge for Java creates the bean by calling its default constructor (all JavaBeans should have a default constructor defined) and extracts all information necessary to create a property sheet and event handlers for the bean without accessing its source code.

The magic lies in the *introspection* mechanism, which allows an application builder, like VisualAge for Java, to interrogate a bean to discover its properties, methods, and events.

Each bean can optionally be associated with a BeanInfo class which gives all information regarding the bean. An Introspector class queries the bean by using a getBeanInfo method that returns a BeanInfo object. A BeanInfo class can be used to define bean features that do not follow the default specification. For example, the getter method for a property named address could be address rather than getAddress as defined by the bean specification. In addition, some things, such as setting the icon for a bean, must be specified in the BeanInfo class.

If a bean is not associated with a BeanInfo class, the application builder uses a *reflection* mechanism to study the public methods of the bean and then applies the simple naming conventions defined by the JavaBeans specification for properties and events to deduce from those methods which properties, events, and public methods are exposed.

All Java classes are beans, because there is no separate specification language and no BeanInfo class is required. However, some classes are not intended to be used as beans; they are intended as strictly programmatic interfaces. For example, in this book the Transaction class is not intended to be used as a bean. Transaction objects will only be created and then displayed in a list.

For the remainder of this book, when you see the term *bean*, it refers to a Java class that was designed to be used as a bean, that is, it is intended to be used in a visual development environment: VisualAge for Java in this case.

Using VisualAge for Java to Create JavaBeans

Now that you know a little about beans, you will see how easily you can create and combine them in VisualAge for Java. You will use VisualAge for Java to create all of the beans for the ATM model, but first you have to know something about the Class Browser and its BeanInfo page.

The Class Browser

You will spend a lot of time using the class browser to create and assemble beans. The class browser consists of five views, or pages:

❑ Methods: A two-pane view of all methods defined on the class as well as the source for the selected method

❑ Hierarchy: A three-pane view of the class hierarchy, methods and source

❑ Editions: A three-pane view of all the editions of the class, the methods, and source

❑ Visual Composition Editor: A visual builder where you assemble composite JavaBeans

❑ BeanInfo: A three-pane view of the bean features, feature definitions, and reflection information for a selected feature. The BeanInfo page also shows the source for methods associated with features

When you use the Class Browser you typically only browse or edit one class. For example, in this book if the BankAccount class is opened in the Class Browser, that instance of the Class Browser is referred to as the BankAccount Class Browser and the BankAccount is referred to as the primary bean or class. You may also see references in other publications to the *primary part* which also refers to the class opened in the Class Browser when you are working in the Visual Composition Editor.

Methods

The Methods page is used for coding Java methods in the class being browsed (Figure 35). It is a matter of personal preference where you want to work when you are coding Java in VisualAge for Java. The Methods and Hierarchy pages of the Class Browser are similar. You can also code in the Source panes of the Workbench windows.

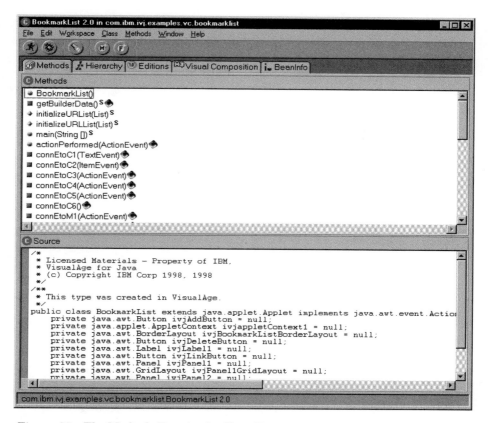

Figure 35. The Methods Page in the Class Browser

Hierarchy

The Hierarchy page is similar to the Methods page except that there is an additional pane where you can quickly edit the class declaration and view (and edit, if you want) the class declarations of superclasses (see Figure 36 on page 60). The Hierarchy page is a very productive place to edit Java code.

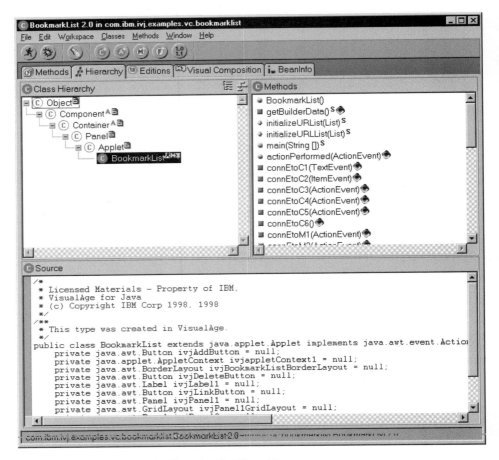

Figure 36. The Hierarchy Page in the Class Browser

Editing a Superclass

The ability to edit the superclasses of the class you have opened in the class browser is very powerful. Be careful about changing the code of a superclass because other code may be dependent on the superclass.

On the Methods page you can also set the visibility so that you can edit methods that are inherited from superclasses. Again you should be careful when changing inherited methods.

Editions

Use the Editions page when you want to compare and replace different editions of the class and its methods (see Figure 37 on page 61). Although you can use other windows, the Editions page provides an **Editions→Add to Workspace** function for each edition of the class and method, an **Editions→Go To Current Edition** function, and the ability to quickly view each different edition.

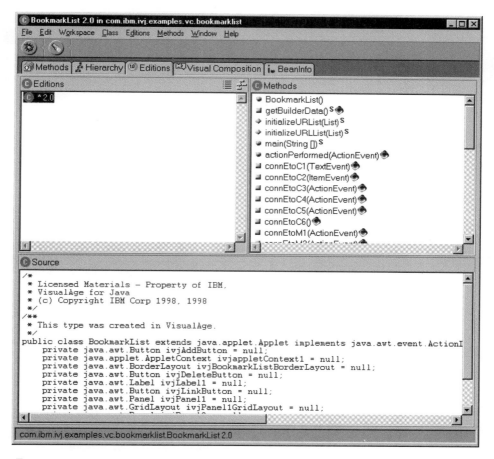

Figure 37. The Editions Page in the Class Browser

Visual Composition Editor

The Visual Composition Editor (Figure 38) is the main topic of Chapter 4, "Building User Interfaces" on page 99. You will spend most of your time with this window while learning VisualAge for Java and may continue to use it frequently as you develop your own projects.

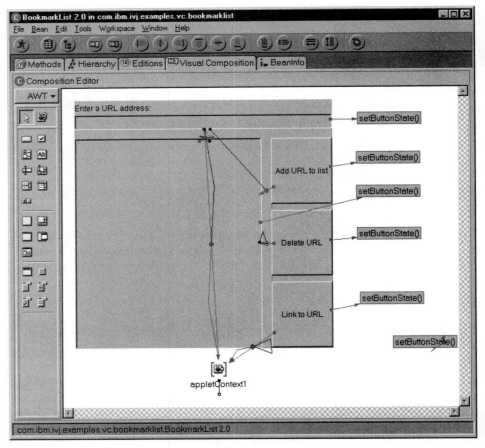

Figure 38. The Visual Composition Editor Page in the Class Browser

BeanInfo

You now know that the features of a bean interface consist of properties, events, and methods. These features represent the properties and behavior of your class.

The BeanInfo page (Figure 39) is accessed from the **BeanInfo** tab in the Class Browser or by selecting **Selected→Open To** in the Workbench. The BeanInfo page is where you create and view the events, methods, and properties of a bean. From the BeanInfo page, you use the Features menu to manage bean features. You access the Features menu by either selecting **Features** or opening it as pop-up menu from the Features pane.

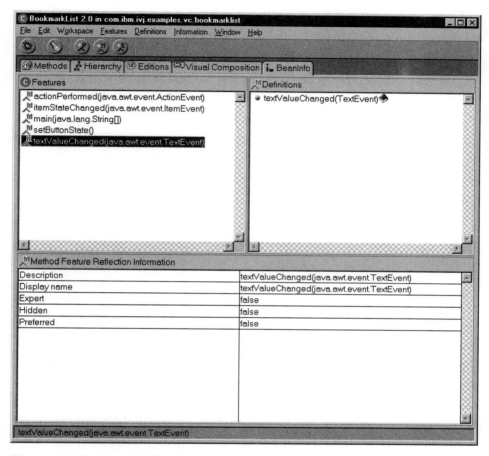

Figure 39. The BeanInfo Page in the Class Browser

Using the BeanInfo Page

You can add new features using either tool bar buttons (the buttons labeled P, M, and E) or Features menu choices. When you add new bean features, VisualAge generates methods and BeanInfo information for the features. The methods correspond to the JavaBean specification for that type of feature.

Each bean and each feature of the bean have a set of attributes that you can specify in the Information pane.

Working with the Class
To return to the information for the class when you have selected a feature in the BeanInfo page or a method in the Methods or Hierarchy pages, press the Control key and select the currently selected property or feature to deselect it.

The Bean or Feature Information pane fields include:

Customizer class

The name of the optional Customizer class that can be used to customize the bean at design time

Hidden-state

Defines whether the property settings of a bean will be generated as Java code or whether the state of the bean will be saved to a file as a serialized bean

Icons

The icon that will be shown when the bean is on the palette or dropped on the free-form surface

All property, method, and event features on the BeanInfo page share the following features:

Description

The description shown in the Visual Composition Editor when the property is shown or selected in a Connection Property dialog box, Connection dialog box, or Tear-off dialog box

Display name

The feature name shown in the Visual Composition Editor (or on the palette when applied to a bean)

Expert

Whether the property will be shown only in the Visual Composition Editor when the **Expert** checkbox is selected

Hidden

Whether the property will be visible in the Visual Composition Editor

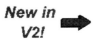
Preferred

Whether the feature will be displayed on the Preferred Connections list of the bean

Property Features

When you create a property feature on the BeanInfo page, the property feature is shown with a set of letters in superscript at the right side of the property name. The letters identify the attributes of the property as indicated in Table 4.

Table 4. Property Identifiers

Identifier	Property Attribute
R	Readable
W	Writeable
B	Bound
C	Constrained
H	Hidden
I	Indexed
E	Expert

Property features can be designated whether or not they are visible in the property sheet at design time. You can explicitly set the Property Editor, get method, and set method in the Property Feature Information pane.

The internal attribute name for a property has the prefix field, followed by the property name with the first letter in upper-case. For example, a property named accountId is represented by the private fieldAccountId attribute, and the get and set methods are called getAccountId and setAccountId.

Method Features

For each method feature you create in VisualAge for Java, a public Java method stub is created with a method signature corresponding to the values you enter in the SmartGuide.

The BeanInfo page lists only those method features defined on the bean you are working with, not features of the ancestors of this bean class. However, the features defined on an ancestor bean are accessible when you work with the bean in the Visual Composition Editor.

Event Features

You can add two types of event features through the BeanInfo page:

Event Set

You add a new event set to a bean when you want it to fire existing events. The event will be added as a feature in the BeanInfo page. In the Event Feature Information pane you can designate whether the event will be a *unicast* (only one listener supported) or *multicast* event.

For the event to be fired you must manually add the Java code to fire the event.

Listener Interface

When you add a new Listener interface you actually create a whole new event that your bean will fire. You enter the event name and the methods that will be called when the event is fired.

In the Event Feature Information pane you can designate whether the event will be unicast (only one listener supported) or multicast.

Again, you must write the code to fire the event. VisualAge for Java provides you with a convenience method that allows you to fire the event with one method call (see "Creating a New Event Interface" on page 78).

To learn how to create a new Listener interface see "Creating the pinChecked Event" on page 87.

What about the BeanInfo Class?

A JavaBean can optionally be associated with a BeanInfo class, named by appending BeanInfo to the name of the bean. VisualAge for Java generates a BeanInfo class when you are working in the BeanInfo page and you perform an action that necessitates the creation of a BeanInfo class. Such actions include promoting a feature, creating a bound property or modifying information in the Bean Information pane (for example, you set an icon for the bean). You can explicitly save this information by selecting the **Information→Save** menu item or, when you select another property or close the window, you are prompted with the Bean Information dialog: Information has been modified - save changes?.

When you are initially working with your bean, public methods that you create with the Methods page are automatically added as method features until the BeanInfo class is created. After a BeanInfo class exists, public methods are not automatically added as method features. You must add them using **Features→Add Available Features**.

You can explicitly create a BeanInfo class before you add any features by selecting **New BeanInfo Class** from the Features menu. This selection opens the SmartGuide for the BeanInfo Class (Figure 40), which you use to define bean information for the bean as a whole.

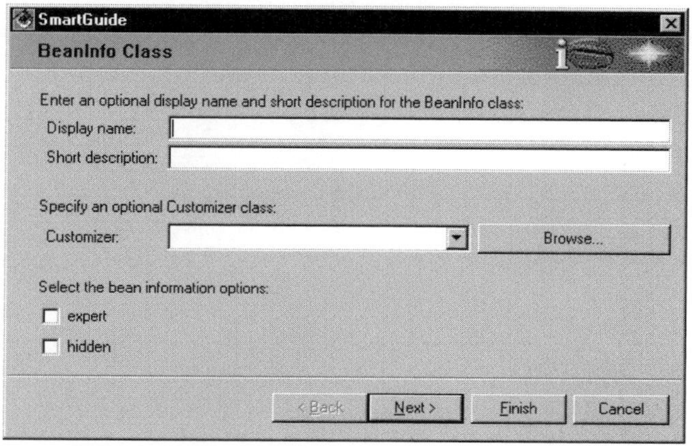

Figure 40. The BeanInfo Class SmartGuide

In the BeanInfo Class SmartGuide, you can specify a display name and short description to use for the bean. You can also mark the bean as expert or hidden to limit or prevent accessibility to it in the Visual Composition Editor. If you want to provide customized initialization of bean properties, you can specify a Customizer class.

The Bean Icon Information SmartGuide (Figure 41) follows the BeanInfo Class SmartGuide. Use the Bean Icon Information SmartGuide to specify files containing icons for the bean. These icons will be displayed if you add the bean to the palette or when you drop the bean on the free-form surface.

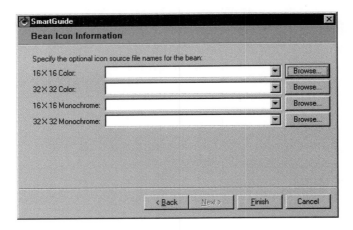

Figure 41. The Bean Icon Information SmartGuide

Building the ATM Model

In this section you will learn how to use VisualAge for Java to implement the business logic classes that the ATM application uses.

As shown in the object model of the ATM application (see Figure 33 on page 52), the ATM requires the following objects:

❑ Transaction

❑ BankAccount

❑ SavingsAccount

❑ CheckingAccount

❑ Card

❑ Customer

❑ Bank

You will create the beans in the above order so that the types that a bean has as properties will already be created. With VisualAge for Java you could create beans that contain references to undefined types, but it is good practice to define types before you use them! In VisualAge for Java you cannot create property features of undefined types.

Create all these beans in the itso.atm.model package.

Building the Transaction Class

Transaction
accountId
transId
transType
transAmount
Transaction(String,int,BigDecimal)

As indicated in "Introspection and the BeanInfo Class" on page 57, the Transaction class would not be used as a JavaBean. That will affect the way you build the class in VisualAge for Java:

❑ A default constructor is not required.

❑ JavaBean properties will not be created, so the BeanInfo page will not be used.

The Transaction class has four attributes and a constructor that takes three parameters. You build the itso.atm.model.Transaction class by using the Workbench to create the class and then use the Class Browser Hierarchy page to add the attributes and the new constructor.

Creating the Transaction Class

On the Projects page of the Workbench, select the **itso.atm.model** package in the Programming VAJ V2 project, then select **Selected→Add→Class**. Fill in Transaction for the *Class Name*. Make sure the *Superclass* field is java.lang.Object and that the **Browse the class when finished** checkbox is selected and the **Compose the class visually** is not selected and click **Next**. Select the **toString()** checkbox in the *Which method stubs would you like to create* section. Click **Finish**.

The toString Method
Creating a toString() method for each class makes it easy to unit test each class. Use the toString method to print out the state of each class when you are testing. In many cases you will reuse the toString method somewhere else in your user interface.

If you did not create the itso.atm.model package in "Creating Packages" on page 35, you are prompted to create it now.

Adding attributes to the Transaction class

Follow these steps to add the accountId, transType, transAmount, and transId attributes to the Transaction class:

1. In the Class Browser, switch to the Hierarchy page.

2. Select **Transaction** in the Class Hierarchy pane.

3. Modify the class declaration in the Source pane to match the following code:

```
public class Transaction {
    private int transType;
    private java.math.BigDecimal transAmount;
    private java.sql.Timestamp transId;
    private String accountId;
    static final String transTypes[] = {
        "Deposit Transaction", "Withdrawal Transaction"
    };
    static final int DEPOSIT_TRANS_TYPE = 0;
    static final int WITHDRAWAL_TRANS_TYPE = 1;
}
```

Note: Throughout the book the sample code may not show the comments that VisualAge for Java places in the generated code.

The transTypes string and two static integers, DEPOSIT_TRANS_TYPE and WITHDRAWAL_TRANS_TYPE, are used to define the two transaction types: withdraw and deposit.

Adding the New Constructor to the Transaction Class

Follow these steps to add the new constructor to the Transaction class:

1. In the Hierarchy page, select **Transaction** in the Class Hierarchy pane.

2. Select **Methods→Add Method**.

3. Select the **Create a new constructor** radio button.

4. Change the entry field from Transaction() to: Transaction(String accountId, int transType, java.math.BigDecimal amount).

5. Click **Finish**.

6. In the Source pane, modify the constructor to match the following code:

```
public Transaction( String accountIdParam, int transTypeParam,
        java.math.BigDecimal transAmountParam)
{
    accountId = accountIdParam;
    transType = transTypeParam;
    transAmount = transAmountParam;
    transId = new java.sql.Timestamp( System.currentTimeMillis());
```

}

Notice that the transId is set to a timestamp that is constructed using the current system time.

Hiding the Default Constructor
In the Transaction class the default constructor is not needed. In fact it should never be called. One way to ensure that the default constructor is not called is to make it private. A private constructor cannot be called outside the class, and it can never be subclassed with a more lenient access modifier.

Completing the toString Method

Select the **toString** method in the Methods pane on the Methods or Hierarchy page of the Class Browser. Modify the code to look like this:

```
public String toString()
{
    return transTypes[ transType] + ": $" + transAmount +
            " [" + transId + "]";
}
```

Congratulations! You have created your first class of the ATM model.

Building the BankAccount Bean

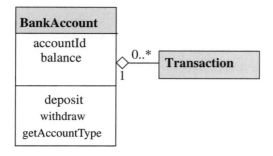

You will implement the BankAccount as a JavaBean, that is, you will create features that will be used to connect to the bean. As indicated in Figure 33 on page 52 the BankAccount is abstract, so you will implement the itso.atm.model.BankAccount bean as an abstract class.

Creating the Abstract BankAccount Class

On the Projects page of the Workbench, select the **itso.atm.model** package in the Programming VAJ V2 project, then select **Selected→Add→Class**. Fill in BankAccount for the *Class Name*. Make sure the **Browse the class when finished** checkbox is selected and the **Compose the class visually** is not selected, and click **Next**.

Compose the Class Visually Checkbox
Selecting the **Compose the class visually** checkbox disables the **Next** button on the dialog box and causes the new class to open to the Visual Composition Editor page of the Class Browser. If you select the checkbox by mistake for a nonvisual class or vice versa, no harm is done.

Select the **abstract** checkbox in the *Select the modifiers for the new type* section and the **toString** checkbox. Click **Finish**.

You will create the following properties on the BankAccount class:

❑ accountId, of type java.lang.String

❑ balance, of type java.math.BigDecimal (This will be a bound property.)

❑ transactions, of type java.util.Vector

Bound and Constrained Properties
If possible, in the design phase of your project you should define which properties are bound or constrained. Not all properties will need to fire these events.
If properties only fire events that are expected on the basis of the design, the system will be easier to understand.
Using bound properties too frequently can also lead to a system whose performance degrades because so many events are firing.

Adding Property Features to the BankAccount

Follow these steps to add the accountId property to the BankAccount class:

1. In the Class Browser, switch to the BeanInfo page.

2. From the menu bar select **Features→New Property Feature** to create the property that will store the accountId.

3. Enter accountId in the *Property name* field and make sure that java.lang.String is in the *Property type* field. Make sure the **Readable** and **Writeable** check boxes are selected and that the **Indexed, bound,** and **constrained** checkboxes are not selected (Figure 42 on page 73). Click the **Finish** button to create the accountId property.

Creating Properties in the Examples
As you work through the examples in this book you can assume that properties are not bound unless the example explicitly states that they are bound.

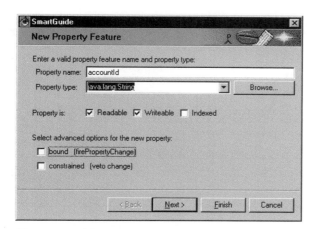

Figure 42. New Property Feature SmartGuide

The feature name will appear in the Features pane, and the accessor and mutator methods as well as the property type will appear in the Definitions pane.

4. Repeat Steps 2 and 3 for the other properties:

Property name	Property type	Indexed	bound
balance	java.math.BigDecimal	false (not selected)	true (selected)
transactions	java.util.Vector	false	false

Creating the accountType Method and Feature

The account type method is implemented in the concrete subclasses of the BankAccount class, not in the BankAccount class itself. The BankAccount class defines an abstract getAccountType method. You cannot use the **New Method Feature** item to create an abstract method feature. You must create the getAccountType method and then add it as a feature. In "Creating the Deposit Method Feature" on page 76, you will use the **New Method Feature** item to create a method feature.

Follow these steps to create the getAccountType method:

1. In the BankAccount Class Browser go to the Methods page. Create a new method: public abstract String getAccountType(). Specifically

   a. Open the Create method SmartGuide, using **Methods→Add→Method**.

   b. Enter String getAccountType() in the first entry field.

   c. Click **Next**.

   d. Select the **public** radio button and the **abstract** checkbox.

   e. Click **Finish**.

   f. Switch to the BeanInfo page.

   g. Select **Features→Add Available Features**

   h. Select **accountType** from the list.

   Note: This actually adds the accountType **property** to the bean features (as shown in Figure 43). If you select the getAccountType() method from the list then the getAccountType method feature is added. You can also add both features. The code will work exactly the same way because a readable property implies the getter method.

   i. Click **OK**.

Now when you create the CheckingAccount and SavingsAccount beans, VisualAge for Java will automatically create the concrete version of the getAccountType method.

The BankAccount BeanInfo page should now look like the page shown in Figure 43.

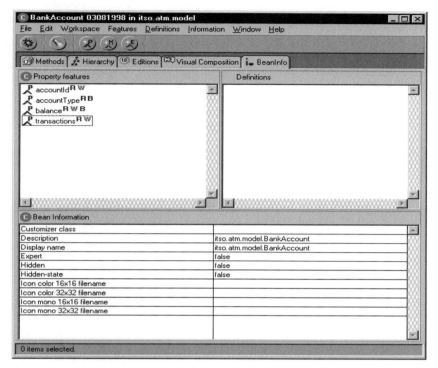

Figure 43. BankAccount Bean with Property Features

The Deposit and Withdrawal Functions
Withdraw and deposit on the bank account are implemented through two methods for each function. One method takes a String and calls a second method, which takes a BigDecimal. The actual property is a BigDecimal, but the user interface text fields work with strings. When two different methods are used, the user interface is separated, or uncoupled, from the property. For example, using two methods would allow the first method to check for a valid number before calling the second method.

Adding the Deposit Function to the BankAccount

Because the deposit function is not dependent on the account type, you can implement the deposit method in the BankAccount class and use the same implementation for SavingsAccount and CheckingAccount. The deposit method adds the amount entered by the user to the current balance and then creates a new transaction record.

Create the deposit method as protected, using **Methods→Add→Method** on the Methods page. The protected deposit method will rely on public deposit methods to pass it a BigDecimal parameter. Only the public deposit method will be exposed in the bean interface.

The source for the deposit method is:

```
protected void deposit (java.math.BigDecimal amount) {
    setBalance( getBalance().add( amount));
    getTransactions().addElement( new Transaction( getAccountId(),
            Transaction.DEPOSIT_TRANS_TYPE, amount) );
    return;
}
```

Creating the Deposit Method Feature

Follow these steps to create the deposit method feature:

1. From the BeanInfo page menu bar select **Features→New Method Feature** to get to the New Method Feature SmartGuide (Figure 44).

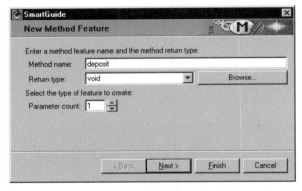

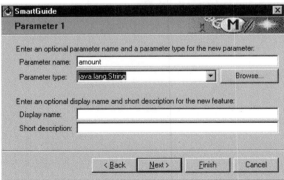

Figure 44. New Method Feature SmartGuides

2. Enter deposit in the *Method name* field and void in the *Return type* field. Set the *Parameter count* field to 1. Click **Next** and enter amount in the *Parameter name* field. Select java.lang.String from the pull-down in the *Parameter type* field. Click **Finish** to create the deposit method.

Adding Parameters to Method Features

When you add property features or set parameters in the New Method Feature SmartGuide, there are several ways to enter the property or parameter types:

- Enter the type directly.
- If the type is a primitive or an array of primitives (such as float or int) or a String, select it from the pull-down list.
- Select the type, using the **Browse** button.

Select the **deposit** method feature in the Features pane and then select the **deposit** method in the Definitions pane to show the source code in the Source pane. Modify the code:

```
public void deposit( String amount) {
    if ( !(amount.trim().equals("")) )
    {
        deposit( new java.math.BigDecimal(amount));
    }
}
```

The public deposit method invokes the previously defined deposit method. It first checks to make sure that the parameter is a valid number. It has a return type of void and one parameter, amount, of type java.lang.String.

Adding the Withdraw Function

The withdraw function is also divided into public and protected methods. The actual withdrawal is dependent on the account type. Therefore, you will define the protected withdraw method feature in the BankAccount class as abstract and provide the implementation in the SavingsAccount and CheckingAccount subclasses.

Create the protected withdraw method, using **Add→Method** in the Methods page (or simply typing over another method and saving the new code). The complete method definition for withdraw is:

```
protected abstract void withdraw(java.math.BigDecimal amount);
```

The public withdraw method is not dependent on the account type and can be defined on the BankAccount class. Create it using the BeanInfo **New**

Method Feature item. It has a return type of void and one parameter, amount, of type java.lang.String. Add the method feature and modify the source:

```
public void withdraw( String amount) {
    if ( !(amount.trim().equals("")) ){
        withdraw( new java.math.BigDecimal(amount));
    }
}
```

If you forgot to add the public withdraw method as a method feature, you can use **Add Available Features** to add it.

Creating a New Event Interface

The BankAccount object fires a limitExceeded event if there are not enough funds for a withdrawal. If the withdrawal is not allowed, the ATM application can display a message to the user.

To define and fire the event, perform the following steps:

1. Create a new event listener interface, using the New Event Listener SmartGuide (select **New Listener Interface** in the **Features** pull-down; see Figure 45 on page 79).

2. On the first page of the SmartGuide, enter limitExceeded in the *Event name* field, and click **Next**. Notice how VisualAge for Java filled in the other fields for you.

3. On the second page, enter the name of the method that the listener class has to implement, handleLimitExceeded, click **Add**, then **Finish**.

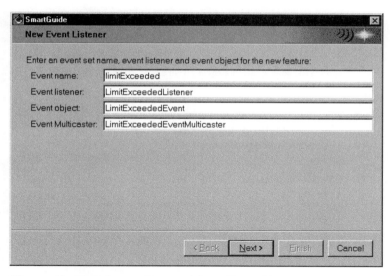

Figure 45. Defining an Event with an Event Listener

VisualAge for Java automatically generates the event and interface classes and the supporting methods for you:

❑ limitExceededEvent class
❑ limitExceededListener interface
❑ fireHandleLimitExceeded method
❑ addlimitExceededListener method
❑ removelimitExceededListener method

After code generation, you will find the fireHandleLimitExceeded method in the BankAccount class. The SavingsAccount and CheckingAccount classes will use this method in their own withdraw method to fire the event.

Once the event has been added, the BankAccount Bean is complete (Figure 46).

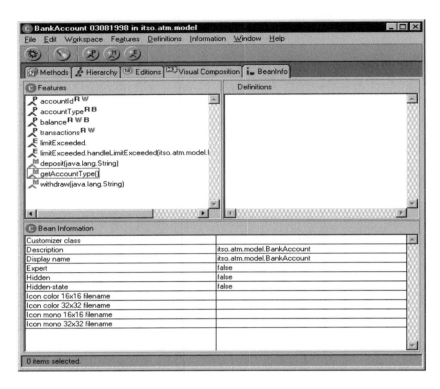

Figure 46. BankAccount Bean with Properties, Events, and Methods

Completing the toString Method

Select the **toString** method in the Methods pane on the Methods page of the Class Browser. Modify the code:

```
public String toString()
{
   java.util.Enumeration allTransactions = getTransactions().elements();
   String returnString = getAccountType() + ": " + getAccountId() +
         " Balance: " + getBalance():
   // remove code below for Chapter 6, otherwise it does not work
      while( allTransactions.hasMoreElements()){
         returnString += "\n\t" + allTransactions.nextElement();
      }
   return returnString;
}
```

Building the CheckingAccount Bean

CheckingAccount
overdraft
withdraw

CheckingAccount is a subclass of the BankAccount class. In addition to the function of the basic account class, the CheckingAccount class provides overdraft protection. To create the CheckingAccount class, select the BankAccount class in the Workbench and then select **Selected→Add Class**. In the Create Class SmartGuide, enter CheckingAccount in the *Class name* field. Notice how all of the other fields are filled (make sure that the *Superclass* field is set to BankAccount). Click **Finish** to create the class.

Next you will create a new property on CheckingAccount, called overdraft, as a java.math.BigDecimal value. The bank has decided that the overdraft property must be between $0 and $1000. To enforce this you can implement a custom property editor for the overdraft:

1. In the itso.atm.model package, create a class called OverdraftEditor that inherits from sun.beans.editors.FloatEditor.

> **Shortcut: Creating a New Method**
> Try this easy way of creating a new method: Select the new OverdraftEditor class and select **Selected→Method Template** in the Workbench (in the Class Browser the Method Template menu item is in the Class, Classes, and Methods menus). Replace the generated source with the source for the method and replace the method using Shift-Control-S.

2. Add a void setAsText(java.lang.String text) method to OverdraftEditor with the following code:

```
public void setAsText( String text)
            throws java.lang.IllegalArgumentException
{
    java.math.BigDecimal value = null;
    float floatValue;
    try{
        value = new java.math.BigDecimal(text);
        floatValue = value.floatValue();
```

```
            if( floatValue >= 0. && floatValue <= 1000.){
                setValue( value);
            }
            else{
                throw new java.lang.IllegalArgumentException(text);
            }
        }
        catch( NumberFormatException e){
            throw new java.lang.IllegalArgumentException(e.getMessage());
        }
    }
}
```

Now create the overdraft property of type java.math.BigDecimal on the CheckingAccount class, using the BeanInfo page, and set the property editor to itso.atm.model.OverdraftEditor as shown in Figure 47 on page 83.

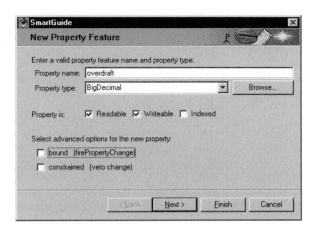

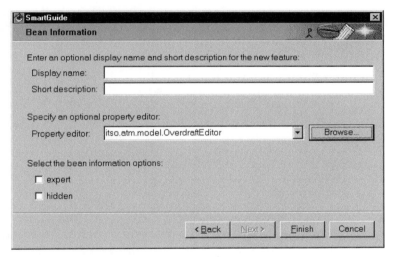

Figure 47. Adding the Overdraft Property and Property Editor

Attribute Initialization
When VisualAge for Java creates the attribute to hold the overdraft, it creates the following code:
private java.math.BigDecimal fieldOverdraft =
new java.math.BigDecimal(0);
This way you do not have to worry about the initial value of the overdraft or the initial minimum balance value in the Savings account.

The CheckingAccount class has to implement its own withdraw method. This method checks whether the account balance can be updated on the basis of the balance and overdraft properties. It notifies other interested objects of the result of the withdrawal transaction, using the LimitExceeded event defined in the BankAccount class:

```
protected void withdraw(java.math.BigDecimal amount)
{
    if ( getBalance().add( getOverdraft()).compareTo( amount) > 0.0)
    {
        setBalance( getBalance().subtract(amount));
        getTransactions().addElement( new Transaction(
            getAccountId(),Transaction.WITHDRAWAL_TRANS_TYPE, amount));
    }
    else
    {
        fireHandleLimitExceeded( new LimitExceededEvent( this));
    }
}
```

This is a good time for you to see the Code Assist and Fix on Save functions. To see the Code Assist function, in the Source pane of the withdraw method delete WITHDRAWAL_TRANS_TYPE from Transaction.WITHDRAWAL_TRANS_TYPE. Position your cursor at the end of Transaction. and press Control-Spacebar. Figure 48 shows the list of possible fields and methods you can choose from in the context of a Transaction object. Code Assist will prompt you with types, fields, and methods, depending on the context. Select WITHDRAWAL_TRANS_TYPE by double-clicking or using the cursor and the return key.

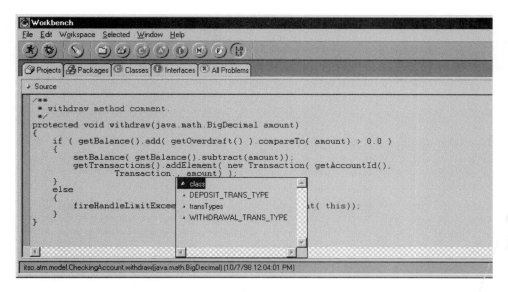

Figure 48. Code Assist

To see the Fix on Save function, change WITHDRAWAL_TRANS_TYPE to WITHDRAWAL_TYPE and save the code. You should see the dialog shown in Figure 49 on page 85. Select **Correct** to correct and save the code.

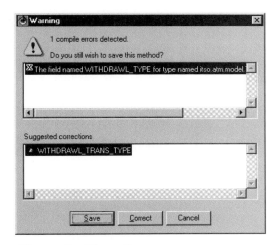

Figure 49. Fix on Save

One last thing and you are finished with the CheckingAccount class. Remember the getAccountType method? You created it as an abstract method on the BankAccount class (see "Creating the accountType Method Feature" on page 74). Now you must fill in the source for the getAccountType method.

Select the **getAccountType** method and modify it:

```
public String getAccountType() {
    return "Checking Account";
}
```

Building the SavingsAccount Bean

SavingsAccount
minAmount
withdraw

SavingsAccount is also a subclass of the BankAccount class. In addition to the function of the basic BankAccount class, it has to maintain a minimum balance.

Create the SavingsAccount class the same way you created the CheckingAccount class. Add a new property feature, minAmount, as a BigDecimal value. Implement the withdraw method:

```
protected void withdraw(java.math.BigDecimal amount) {
    if ( getBalance().subtract(amount).compareTo( getMinAmount() ) >= 0)
    {
        setBalance( getBalance().subtract( amount)) ;
        getTransactions().addElement( new Transaction( getAccountId(),
            Transaction.WITHDRAWAL_TRANS_TYPE, amount));
    }
    else
    {
        fireHandleLimitExceeded( new LimitExceededEvent( this));
    }
}
```

Now modify the getAccountType method in SavingsAccount:

```
public String getAccountType() {
    return "Savings Account";
}
```

Building the Card Bean

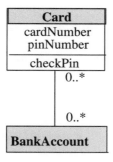

Create a new class, itso.atm.model.Card, that extends Object. Click **Next** in the Create Class SmartGuide and select the **toString()** checkbox in the *Which method stubs would you like to create* section.

Now create the following property features on the Card class:

Name	Type	Bound
accounts	java.util.Vector	false
cardNumber	java.lang.String	false
pinNumber	java.lang.String	false

Modify the toString method:

```
public String toString()
{
    java.util.Enumeration allAccounts = getAccounts().elements();
    String returnString = "Card: " + getCardNumber() + " PIN: " + getPinNumber();
    while( allAccounts.hasMoreElements()){
        returnString += "\n\t" + allAccounts.nextElement();
    }
    return returnString;
}
```

Creating the pinChecked Event

The Card bean has to send messages to other objects about the result of the PIN validation. This behavior is implemented as one event, pinChecked, in the ATM application. The pinChecked event is slightly different from the limitExceeded event. The pinChecked event will use one event object, PinCheckedEvent, but will define two methods to handle the event:

handleValidPIN
handleInvalidPIN

To define and fire the event, perform the following steps:

1. Create a new event listener interface (similar to the listener interface created in "Building the BankAccount Bean" on page 71), using the New Event Listener SmartGuide (select **New Listener Interface** in the **Features** pull-down).

2. On the first page of the SmartGuide, enter the name of the event, pinChecked, and click **Next**.

3. On the second page, enter the name of the methods that the listener class has to implement. Enter handleValidPin, then click **Add**. Enter handleInvalidPin, click **Add** again, then **Finish**.

Now, all you have to implement is the logic to fire the events:

1. On the BeanInfo page, add a new method feature to the Card class and call it checkPin, with a *Return type* of void. Enter 1 in the *Parameter count* field. On the next page, enter pinEntered in the *Parameter name* field and java.lang.String in the *Parameter type* field (Figure 50 on page 89). Click the **Finish** button. The checkPin method compares the pinEntered parameter with the pinNumber property and notifies listeners by firing the pinCheckedEvent, using the handleValidPIN or handleInvalidPIN method as appropriate.

2. Change the checkPin method stub to match the following code:

```
public void checkPin( String pinEntered){
    if ( getPinNumber().trim().equals( pinEntered.trim()) ){
        fireHandleValidPin( new PinCheckedEvent( this));
    }
    else{
        fireHandleInvalidPin( new PinCheckedEvent( this));
    }
}
```

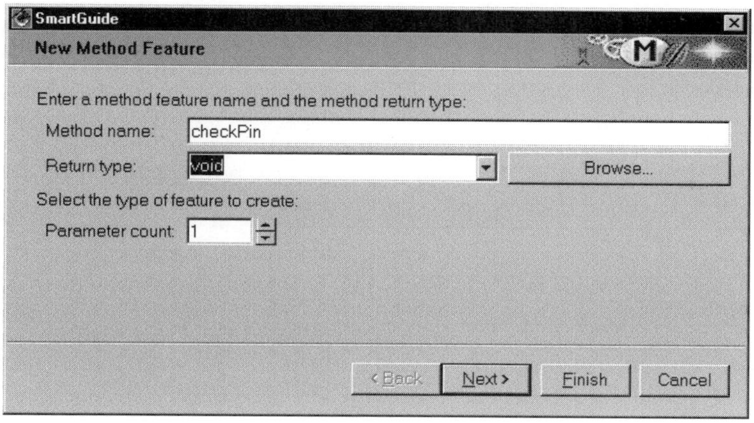

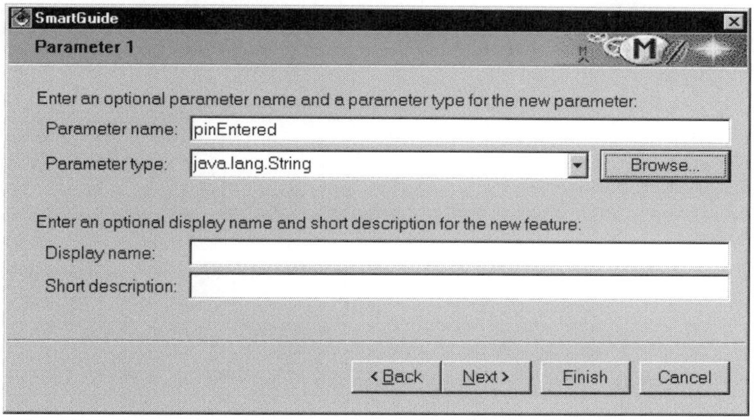

Figure 50. Adding the checkPin Method Feature

The Card bean needs one more method feature, getAccount, returning a BankAccount object and taking one parameter, index of type int. Add the method and modify it:

```
public BankAccount getAccount( int index) {
    return (BankAccount)getAccounts().elementAt( index);
}
```

The accounts property was not created as an indexed property because it uses a Vector rather than an array to store the values. Therefore you do not have to know anything about the number of elements beforehand. If an array had been used, accounts could have been created as an indexed property.

Once you have added these methods features, the Card Bean should look like that shown in Figure 51.

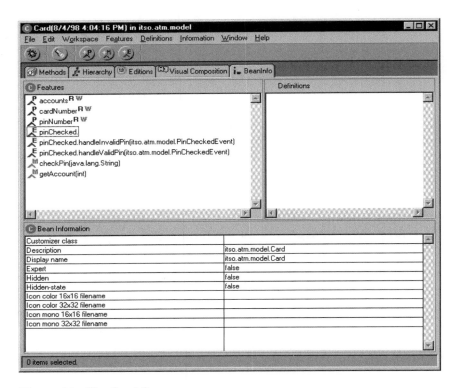

Figure 51. The Card Bean

Deleting Features

Now that you have created features, you probably want to know how to delete them (especially when you create one incorrectly). It is simple: You select the features you want to delete and then select **Features→Delete**. You are presented with a dialog that confirms the deletion of the feature and asks you to select the methods to delete. Select any methods that will not be used.

Once you have deleted the feature and the selected methods, you have other code to clean up, depending on the type of feature:

❑ Property

The attribute holding the property value must be deleted. For example, the string property, accountId, is represented by this attribute declaration:

private fieldAccountId = new String();

You must delete this declaration manually from the class declaration.

❑ Event listener interface

When deleting an event, you must manually delete:

- Any of the convenience methods that fire the event; for example, if you were deleting the PinChecked event you would have to delete the following methods from the Card class:

  fireHandleInvalidPin(itso.atm.model.PinCheckedEvent event)
  fireHandleValidPin(itso.atm.model.PinCheckedEvent event)

- The event, event multicaster, and listener classes created. For the PinChecked event, you would delete:

  PinCheckedEvent
  PinCheckedEventMulticaster
  PinCheckedListener

- The listener attribute created in the class declaration that fires the event. For the PinChecked event:

  protected transient itso.atm.model.PinCheckedListener aPinCheckedListener = null;

Building the Customer Bean

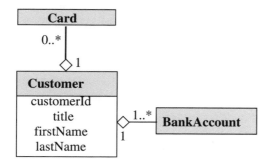

To create the Customer class, select the itso.atm.model package in the Workbench and then select **Selected→Add→Class**. Enter Customer in the *Class Name* field and click **Next**. Select the **toString()** checkbox in the *Which method stubs would you like to create* section. Click **Finish**.

Now create the following property features on the Customer class:

Name	Type	Bound
accounts	java.util.Vector	false

Name	Type	Bound
customerId	java.lang.String	false
firstName	java.lang.String	false
lastName	java.lang.String	false
title	java.lang.String	false
cards	java.util.Vector	false

Select the toString method in the Source pane and modify the code:

```
public String toString() {
    java.util.Enumeration allCards = getCards().elements();
    String returnString = getTitle().trim() + " " +
            getFirstName().trim() + " " +
            getLastName().trim();
    while( allCards.hasMoreElements()){
        returnString += "\n\t" + allCards.nextElement();
    }
    return returnString;
}
```

The trim method just trims extra whitespace from a string. Save the code by selecting **Save** from the Source pane pop-up menu.

Adding a Custom Property Editor to the Customer Bean

Custom property editors are used in JavaBean development environments to customize a JavaBean at development time. They are defined in the BeanInfo class or found through JavaBean naming patterns. When the property sheet for a bean is displayed in the Visual Composition Editor, any custom property editors that are defined for the bean's properties are instantiated and used to change the properties in the property sheet.

The following is a simple (but not particularly useful) example of a custom property editor. The title property for the Customer bean has three valid values: Mr., Mrs., and Ms. You can create a custom property editor so that only these choices are available for setting the property in the development environment. To create the custom property editor for the title property, follow these steps:

1. Create a class called CustomerTitleEditor that inherits from java.beans.PropertyEditorSupport in the Programming VAJ V2 project and itso.atm.model package.

2. Add a public method to CustomerTitleEditor named String[] getTags() with the following code:

```
String result[] = {"Mr.", "Mrs.", "Ms."};
return result;
```

The getTags method is used when the property value must be one of a set of known values.

3. Open the Customer bean in the Class Browser and switch to the BeanInfo page. Select the title property and click in the entry field to the right of *Property editor*. Click on the drop-down list arrow and then select itso.atm.model.CustomerTitleEditor. Select **Information→Save**.

Now when you use the Customer bean in the Visual Composition Editor, you will be able to choose the title property rather than type it in.

It is always a good idea to test each class you create when coding. In this case, you could type the following into the Scrapbook and run it to begin testing to see that your class is functioning properly:

```
itso.atm.model.Customer c = new itso.atm.model.Customer();
c.setCustomerId( "1234567");
c.setFirstName("John");
c.setLastName("Doe");
c.setTitle("Mr.");
System.out.println( c);
```

You can create test scripts for each of the classes you create to ensure they are working as designed. Alternatively you can add a main method to each class and put the test code within the main method. Then you can simply run each class to test it.

Building the Bank Bean

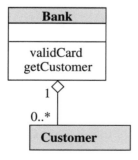

The itso.atm.model.Bank bean is fairly simple. Create the Bank class and again add the declaration for the toString() method. Add one property feature: customers of type java.util.Vector. Create two method features: Customer getCustomer(Card cardParam), which returns a customer given a valid card, and Card validCard(String cardParam), which checks whether a card is valid based on its number.

The method bodies should match the following code:

```
public Customer getCustomer( Card cardParam) {
    java.util.Enumeration allCustomers = getCustomers().elements();
    while( allCustomers.hasMoreElements()){
        Customer customer = (Customer)allCustomers.nextElement();
        java.util.Enumeration customerCards = customer.getCards().elements();
        while( customerCards.hasMoreElements()){
            Card card = (Card)customerCards.nextElement();
            if( card.getCardNumber().equals( cardParam.getCardNumber())){
                return customer;
            }
        }
    }
    return null;
}

public Card validCard( String cardParam) {
    java.util.Enumeration allCustomers = getCustomers().elements();
    while( allCustomers.hasMoreElements()){
        Customer customer = (Customer)allCustomers.nextElement();
        java.util.Enumeration customerCards = customer.getCards().elements();
        while( customerCards.hasMoreElements()){
            Card card = (Card)customerCards.nextElement();
            if( card.getCardNumber().equals( cardParam)){
                return card;
            }
        }
    }
    return null;
}

public String toString()
{
    java.util.Enumeration allCustomers = getCustomers().elements();
    String returnString = "Bank Information";
    while( allCustomers.hasMoreElements()){
        returnString += "\n\t" + allCustomers.nextElement().toString();
    }
    return returnString;
}
```

Whew! You have completed the model for the ATM application. It may have seemed like a lot of work, but the early work of designing and implementing a robust model pays off later.

Before you congratulate yourself, however, take a moment to test your new ATM model. In the Scrapbook you can exercise the model by typing in the code listed below. Alternatively, you can use the Scrapbook to open the ExerciseModel.txt file. This file is included with the sample code and contains the code listed below.

Select this code in the Scrapbook and then select **Edit→Run**:

```
/* First create the bank */
itso.atm.model.Bank bank = new itso.atm.model.Bank();
/* Create the customers */
itso.atm.model.Customer customer1 = new itso.atm.model.Customer();
itso.atm.model.Customer customer2 = new itso.atm.model.Customer();
/* Add the customers to the bank */
bank.getCustomers().addElement(customer1);
bank.getCustomers().addElement(customer2);
/* Create the ATM cards */
itso.atm.model.Card customer1Card = new itso.atm.model.Card();
itso.atm.model.Card customer2Card = new itso.atm.model.Card();
customer1Card.setCardNumber("100001");
customer1Card.setPinNumber("3405");
customer2Card.setCardNumber("100002");
customer2Card.setPinNumber("0033");
/* Add the cards to the customers */
customer1.getCards().addElement(customer1Card);
customer2.getCards().addElement(customer2Card);
/* Set the customer information */
customer1.setCustomerId("3056978");
customer1.setLastName("Doe");
customer1.setFirstName("John");
customer1.setTitle("Mr.");
customer2.setCustomerId("6979304");
customer2.setLastName("Smith");
customer2.setFirstName("Anne");
customer2.setTitle("Ms.");
/* Create the accounts */
itso.atm.model.CheckingAccount checkingAccountCustomer1 = new
itso.atm.model.CheckingAccount();
checkingAccountCustomer1.setAccountId("34759023");
checkingAccountCustomer1.setBalance(new java.math.BigDecimal(1000.));
itso.atm.model.SavingsAccount savingsAccountCustomer1 = new
itso.atm.model.SavingsAccount();
savingsAccountCustomer1.setBalance(new java.math.BigDecimal(100.));
savingsAccountCustomer1.setAccountId("34759023");
itso.atm.model.CheckingAccount checkingAccountCustomer2 = new
itso.atm.model.CheckingAccount();
checkingAccountCustomer2.setAccountId("34744442");
checkingAccountCustomer2.setBalance(new java.math.BigDecimal(10000.));
/* Add the accounts to the customers and the cards */
```

```
customer1.getAccounts().addElement(checkingAccountCustomer1);
customer1.getAccounts().addElement(savingsAccountCustomer1);
customer2.getAccounts().addElement(checkingAccountCustomer2);
((itso.atm.model.Card)
customer1.getCards().firstElement()).getAccounts().addElement(checkingAccountCustomer1);
((itso.atm.model.Card)
customer1.getCards().firstElement()).getAccounts().addElement(savingsAccountCustomer1);
((itso.atm.model.Card)
customer2.getCards().firstElement()).getAccounts().addElement(checkingAccountCustomer2);
/* Make some transactions  and look at the model */
checkingAccountCustomer1.deposit("23455.33");
System.out.println(bank.toString());
checkingAccountCustomer1.deposit("533.");
System.out.println(bank.toString());
savingsAccountCustomer1.withdraw("5.");
System.out.println(bank.toString());
checkingAccountCustomer2.withdraw("533.");
System.out.println(bank.toString());
```

The output in the Console should match the following text (except for the time stamps, of course):

```
Bank Information
Mr. John Doe
Card: 100001 PIN: 3405
Checking Account: 34759023 Balance: 24455.33
Deposit Transaction: $23455.33 [1998-09-16 15:42:28.818]
Savings Account: 34759023 Balance: 100
Ms. Anne Smith
Card: 100002 PIN: 0033
Checking Account: 34744442 Balance: 10000
Bank Information
Mr. John Doe
Card: 100001 PIN: 3405
Checking Account: 34759023 Balance: 24988.33
Deposit Transaction: $23455.33 [1998-09-16 15:42:28.818]
Deposit Transaction: $533 [1998-09-16 15:42:32.562]
Savings Account: 34759023 Balance: 100
Ms. Anne Smith
Card: 100002 PIN: 0033
Checking Account: 34744442 Balance: 10000
Bank Information
Mr. John Doe
Card: 100001 PIN: 3405
Checking Account: 34759023 Balance: 24988.33
Deposit Transaction: $23455.33 [1998-09-16 15:42:28.818]
Deposit Transaction: $533 [1998-09-16 15:42:32.562]
Savings Account: 34759023 Balance: 95
Withdrawal Transaction: $5 [1998-09-16 15:42:32.589]
```

Ms. Anne Smith
Card: 100002 PIN: 0033
Checking Account: 34744442 Balance: 10000
Bank Information
Mr. John Doe
Card: 100001 PIN: 3405
Checking Account: 34759023 Balance: 24988.33
Deposit Transaction: $23455.33 [1998-09-16 15:42:28.818]
Deposit Transaction: $533 [1998-09-16 15:42:32.562]
Savings Account: 34759023 Balance: 95
Withdrawal Transaction: $5 [1998-09-16 15:42:32.589]
Ms. Anne Smith
Card: 100002 PIN: 0033
Checking Account: 34744442 Balance: 9467
Withdrawal Transaction: $533 [1998-09-16 15:42:32.724]

4 Building User Interfaces

Support for developing Java user interfaces has been limited. The user interfaces of Java programs are not as sophisticated as those created in other development environments. With the new graphical user-interface (GUI) toolkit that Java Foundation Classes (JFC) provide, Java developers can now create user interfaces that provide the level of sophistication that users expect.

This chapter introduces the JFC and shows you how to use them in the VisualAge for Java Visual Composition Editor. You will learn how to visually compose the user interface of your Java program and let the Visual Composition Editor generate the code automatically for you.

As you use the JFC to create more complex user interfaces, you will want to learn more about it from other resources, such as those listed in "Related Publications" on page 365.

An Abstract Windowing Toolkit Refresher

In the JDK there is a set of classes called the Abstract Windowing Toolkit (AWT). Before the JFC, the AWT was the only standard API for providing GUIs for Java programs. The initial goal was to provide developers with a rudimentary library for building applications and applets. Important features of the AWT are:

❑ 100% portability from a single set of source code

❑ A native look and feel on the deployment platform

The AWT uses a layered toolkit model where each Java component creates a native component. It is referred to as the *peer* model. Each Java component class 'wraps' the peer or native implementation. The peer model can increase complexity because many native components maintain their own state.

The first version of AWT included in JDK 1.0 had many limitations and a programming model that was awkward to use. The AWT version provided with JDK 1.1 removes many of those limitations and introduces a new component programming model based on JavaBeans. The programming model eases the creation of GUIs by using visual programming tools such as the Visual Composition Editor of VisualAge for Java.

What Is the JFC?

The JFC is also known by its code name *Swing* (derived from the music demo given at the 1997 JavaOne convention in San Francisco). The JFC component set is a new GUI toolkit that provides a rich set of windowing components, the visual components used in GUI-based programs.

With the JFC, you can develop efficient GUI components that have exactly the "look and feel" that you specify. For example, a program that uses JFC components can be designed such that it will execute without modification on any kind of computer and can always look and feel just like a program written specifically for the particular computer on which it is running.

The JFC provides:

❑ Improved runtime performance for GUI applications

❑ Improved "time to load" for applets with fewer classes to download than the AWT

❑ Easy conversion of existing AWT components to JFC lightweight components

The JFC and the AWT

Almost all JFC components are said to be *lightweight* because they do not rely on user interface code that is native to the operating system on which they are running; they "borrow" the screen resource of an ancestor.

The JFC contains far more components than the AWT toolkit. Many of the components in the JFC are 100% Pure Java versions of pre-JFC AWT components such as Button, Scrollbar, and List. But the JFC also includes a pure Java set of higher-level components (such as trees and tabbed panes) that were not available in the AWT API.

Like the AWT, JFC components follow the JavaBeans specification. JavaBean support is built into the JFC, so it makes it easy to use JFC components in application-builder programs that use JavaBeans.

The major differences between the AWT and the JFC are:

❑ The JFC uses the model-view-controller (MVC) paradigm to separate the data from the user interface. This changes both the events that the user interface uses and the way you interact with the components.

❑ The JFC has different *look and feel* settings that specify how the whole user interface looks and behaves.

Some other differences:

❑ JFC components often have an inner element or *content pane* where you add child components. In the AWT you add child components directly to a subtype of Frame or Applet, for example.

❑ The AWT has only two types of buttons; Button and CheckBox, which inherit directly from the component class. In the JFC, the button hierarchy provides much more functionality (Figure 53).

❑ In the AWT, the Menu class descends from the Object class, not the Component class. In the JFC, the JMenu class descends from JComponent, in a more complex tree that also encompasses the button tree. Thus it is easy to coordinate button events and menu events. The JFC has a new interface, Action, that allows several controls to be associated with the same function. For example, a single mouse click can activate or deactivate both a menu item and a corresponding toolbar button.

Mixing AWT and JFC components in the same program is possible but not recommended. Not only will you have problems (especially with overlapping elements) but you will also have to maintain code with two separate GUI toolkits, and the AWT classes may not always be part of the JDK.

JFC Components

The JFC is huge and consists of 20 packages (Figure 52 on page 102) containing more than 250 classes and 75 interfaces. Although some JFC components are similar to their AWT predecessors, in most cases there are important differences.

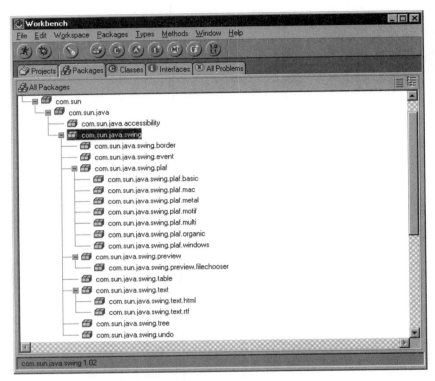

Figure 52. JFC Packages

Figure 53 on page 103 shows many of the user interface components of the JFC component hierarchy and how they relate to each other. Notice how many JFC components have the same name as AWT components, but with a J added at the beginning of the name. Some of these components, for example, JApplet, JFrame, and JDialog, extend their AWT counterparts, but most do not, for example, JPanel, JButton, JMenu, and JTextField.

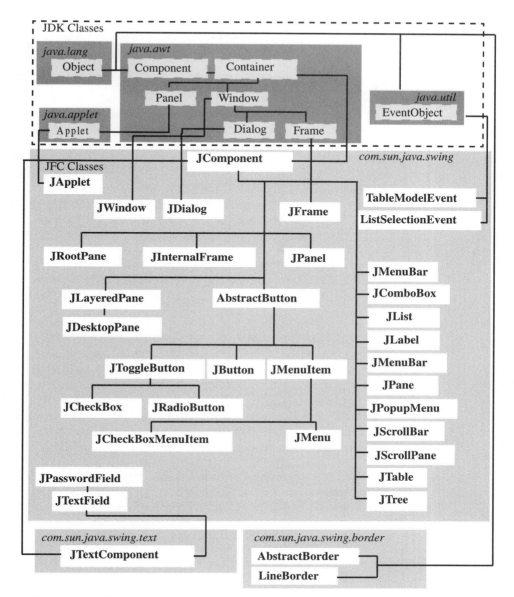

Figure 53. JFC Component Hierarchy

Figure 53 shows only a part of the JFC component hierarchy. There are separate hierarchies for models, tables, text, actions, events, trees, and undo. Notice the JApplet and JFrame. These are the initial components you subclass when building new applications or applets.

The JFC and the MVC Architecture

The MVC architecture separates your application into three parts:

Model

> The model part is the business model or set of classes representing the domain of the application. This part is where business rules or domain logic are encapsulated. The model part can also (indirectly or directly) contain the data your application needs.

View

> The view is the user interface of your application.

Controller

> The controller handles the interaction between the user and the view and can also control the interaction between the model and the view.

MVC was originally created in Smalltalk development but is now recognized as a valid architecture for many different environments. For a simple example of a controller, see "Building the BookmarkListController" on page 126.

The JFC has introduced MVC to Java developers. In the AWT, components do not expose an association with the data they display. For example, a list simply has methods to add and remove elements. A text field has methods to set or get the string being displayed. The JFC now associates models with each user interface element that displays data. For example a list is associated with a list model, and a text field is associated with a document model. Lists and other more complex components are also associated with selection models that handle the selection interaction of the component.

To use JFC components you must be aware of the models that each component uses. In most cases, however, you do not have to explicitly use a model. If you do use a model, it will probably be the default supplied by the JFC for the component. In "Visual Programming in Action" on page 124 you will learn how to use the list model to instantiate and manipulate a list.

The JFC Implementation of MVC
In the JFC implementation of MVC, the view and controller are combined into one class. The primary component class (for example, JList) contains the view and the controller, and the model class (for example, DefaultListModel) contains the model.

Look and Feel

The JFC can assume several platform independent look and feels. The look and feel packages are located under the com.sun.java.plaf package (plaf stands for *pluggable look and feel*). They include:

Metal

The Metal look and feel, officially called the Java Look and Feel, is the default and the only look and feel available at design time in the Visual Composition Editor. Metal is a good look and feel for applications that run on many different platforms.

Windows

The Windows look and feel emulates an application running in the Windows NT, Windows 95, and Windows 98 environments. It is designed to work only in these environments.

Motif

The Motif look and feel emulates the Motif desktop found on many UNIX systems.

Multi

The Multi look and feel allows a component to be associated with several different look and feels at the same time.

Two other look and feels are not included in the standard JFC 1.02 packages:

Organic

The Organic look and feel was the original goal of Project Metal (a development effort at Sun MicroSystems). The actual result of Project Metal was the Java Look and Feel.

Mac

The Mac or MacOS look and feel emulates the look and feel of a Macintosh. It is designed to work only on Macintosh computers.

The look and feels are truly pluggable so it is easy to create an application that allows a user to switch look and feels by using com.sun.java.swing.UIManager.getInstalledLookandFeels() to see which look and feels are available on the workstation and then calling com.sun.java.swing.UIManager.setLookandFeel(). Use the UIManager to query and set most aspects of the user interface. If you have to be different, it is also possible to create your own look and feel.

Layout Managers

Java uses layout managers to decide how components are positioned within their container. The choice of a layout manager for your container directly affects the size, shape, and placement of your components within that container. In addition, layout managers adapt dynamically to the dimensions of the container, solving many problems related to display resolution or font changes.

You have five layout managers to choose from in JDK 1.1, ranging from the very simple FlowLayout and GridLayout, to the special-purpose BorderLayout and CardLayout and the flexible GridBagLayout. You can also choose not to have any layout manager by using the null layout.

The classes implementing the layout managers in JDK 1.1 are:

❑ FlowLayout

❑ BorderLayout

❑ CardLayout

❑ GridLayout

❑ GridBagLayout

In the IBMJavaExamples project, the com.bim.ivj.example.examples.vc.swing.layoutmanagers package shows you samples of the different layout managers.

The JFC defines two new layout managers:

❑ BoxLayout

❑ Overlay Layout

FlowLayout

FlowLayout lays out components from left to right, starting new rows if necessary (Figure 54).

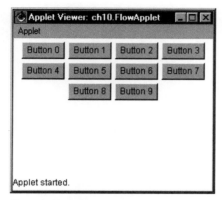

Figure 54. FlowLayout

BorderLayout

BorderLayout organizes components, using constraints based on the compass directions: North, East, South, and West. The fifth direction is Center. You do not have to use all directions in your programs if you do not need them (Figure 55). A component in the Center will expand to fill any space in the container.

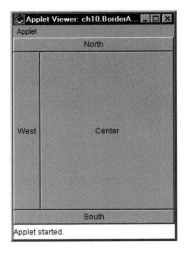

Figure 55. BorderLayout

BoxLayout

Use the BoxLayout to arrange components along either an x-axis or y-axis. In a y-axis Boxlayout, components are arranged from top to bottom in the order in which they are added. Unlike GridLayout, BoxLayout allows components to occupy different amounts of space along the primary axis.

Along the nonprimary axis, BoxLayout attempts to make all components as tall as the tallest component (for left-to-right BoxLayouts) or as wide as the widest component (for top-to-bottom BoxLayouts). If a component cannot increase to this size, BoxLayout looks at its y-alignment property or x-alignment property to determine how to place it.

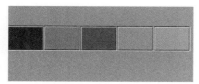

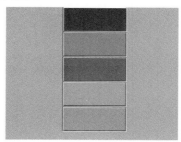

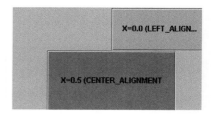

Figure 56. BoxLayout

CardLayout

CardLayout simulates a deck of cards, or a notebook, in that you can put a number of pages on top of each other, and you can traverse the pages in several ways. In other words you can have an area that can contain different components at different times. Figure 57 shows an example with two cards.

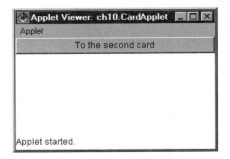 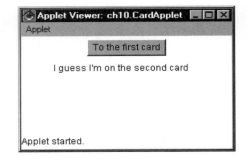

Figure 57. CardLayout

GridLayout

GridLayout organizes components, using a predefined number of rows and columns. It simply makes a number of components have equal size, displaying them in the requested number of rows and columns. It is possible to have a gap between cells. The components are added to cells starting from the top left corner, then going to the right. When a row is full, the next row is started from the left. Figure 58 shows an example of a simple calculator that uses the GridLayout manager for its digits buttons.

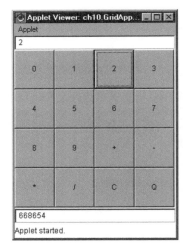

Figure 58. GridLayout

GridBagLayout

GridBagLayout is the most sophisticated and flexible but also most complex of the layout managers. The advantage of using GridBagLayout instead of GridLayout, which it resembles, is that the components do not have to be of the same size. You can use several types of constraints when attaching components to a container, including whether a component expands horizontally or vertically. In Figure 59 you can see that the entry field expands horizontally and the **Clear** button and list expand vertically.

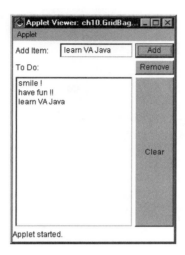

Figure 59. GridBagLayout

OverlayLayout

OverlayLayout (Figure 60) places each added component on top of one another and sizes the container large enough to hold the largest of its components.

The OverlayLayout class does not have a default constructor, so you cannot use it directly in the Visual Composition Editor. You must create it dynamically at runtime.

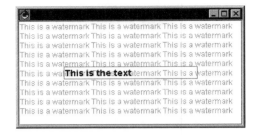

Figure 60. OverlayLayout

Using Layout Managers in VisualAge for Java

In the Visual Composition Editor you can select which layout manager a container will use from the Property sheet for the component. Once you have selected the layout manager, each component in the container will have a set of constraints on its Property sheet appropriate to that layout manager. The exception is the OverlayLayout, which cannot be selected from the Property sheet.

When you drop components onto the container, VisualAge for Java provides visual clues about the location of the component. Throughout this book you will learn how to use several of the layout managers in VisualAge for Java.

Visual Composition Editor

The Visual Composition Editor (Figure 61 on page 113) is a powerful GUI builder as well as a visual programming tool. Not only can you compose the user interface of your application visually but you also can specify the logic of your application by connecting together visual or GUI beans with nonvisual or invisible beans. You build composite beans or applets and applications by connecting beans together.

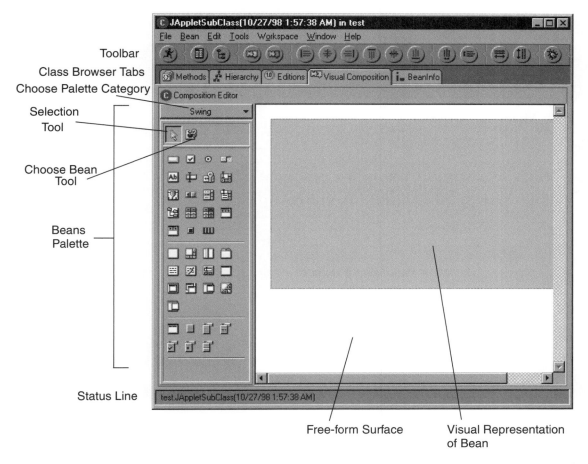

Toolbar
Class Browser Tabs
Choose Palette Category
Selection Tool
Choose Bean Tool
Beans Palette
Status Line
Free-form Surface
Visual Representation of Bean

Figure 61. The Visual Composition Editor

The Visual Composition Editor can manipulate two types of beans:

❏ Visual beans, which are subclasses of the AWT Component class (which includes the JFC). Examples are List, JList, Button, JButton, and TextField. Visual beans have a visual representation at design time that is similar to their appearance at runtime. The design-time appearance of JFC beans is their default appearance using the Metal Look and Feel; at runtime they have the look and feel that your application specifies.

❏ Nonvisual beans usually represent the business logic in your programs, for example, a BankAccount bean. At design time nonvisual beans appear by default as a puzzle icon, or they may have a specific icon associated with them (Figure 62). They do not have a visual representation at runtime.

Figure 62. Nonvisual Bean Icons

The Beans Palette

When you first start VisualAge for Java, the Beans Palette contains all of the user interface beans in the AWT and JFC as well as some "helper" beans. There are three categories of beans originally on the palette (Figure 63); you select them using the Choose Palette Category drop-down list. The selections are:

New in V2! ➡

- ❑ **Swing**
- ❑ **AWT**
- ❑ **Other** (the helper beans)

There is also an **Available** selection on the Choose Palette Category that you use to load additional features into the workspace.

Each category is further separated into subcategories by function. For the JFC and AWT, there are three major subcategories:

- ❑ Button and data entry
- ❑ Containers
- ❑ Menus

Within each sub-category you can identify individual beans, using *hover help* (explanations that appear at the cursor when you leave the cursor over an element on the screen).

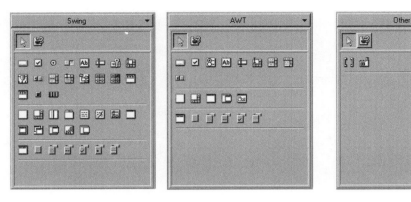

Figure 63. The Beans Palette with Swing, AWT, and Other Bean Categories

Always available directly below the **Choose Palette Category** button are the **Selection** and **Choose Bean** tools:

Selection
> Use the Selection tool to select and move beans and connections on the free-form surface.

Choose Bean
> Use the Choose Bean tool to add beans to the free-form surface that are not on the Beans Palette.

Improved in V2! ➡️

Beans Palette Modification

You can modify the palette by resizing it, changing the icon size, or adding or removing categories, separators, beans you have constructed yourself, or beans supplied by a vendor.

To modify the Beans Palette use the popup menu from the palette as shown in Figure 64 or select **Bean→Modify Palette**. After you invoke the function, the Modify Palette dialog appears (Figure 65) where you can choose the bean to modify on the palette.

If you import beans from a JAR file, VisualAge for Java automatically prompts you with the Modify Palette dialog.

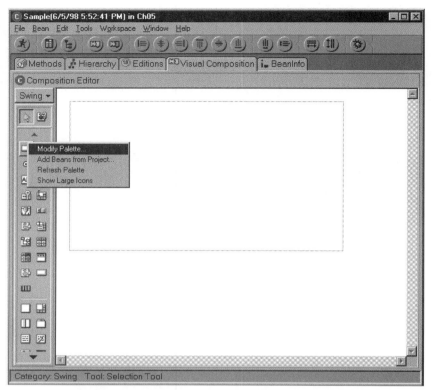

Figure 64. Modifying the Beans Palette

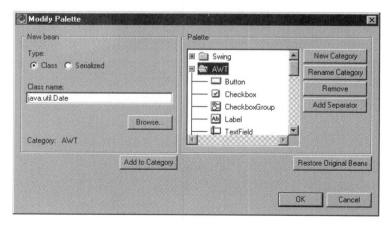

Figure 65. Modify Palette Dialog Box

Free-Form Surface

The free-form surface is where you do all of your visual programming. You select a bean from the Beans Palette or use the Choose Bean tool and then drop the bean on the free-form surface.

If the bean you are editing (the bean opened in the class browser) is a GUI bean, that is, it descends from java.awt.Component, it will have a visual representation (the large grey box shown in Figure 61 on page 113) on the free-form surface. This representation is where you add other GUI components to the bean. When you place beans onto any empty part of the free-form surface, you are adding them to the bean and not to the visual representation of the bean.

The empty part of the free-form surface is where you add invisible beans to the bean you are editing. For example, in the ATM application you will add buttons and text fields to the visual representation of the bean but you will add the model beans (for example, Bank and CheckingAccount) to the free-form surface outside the visual representation of the bean.

Adding Beans in the Visual Composition Editor
A bean that is added to the visual representation of another Container bean must be a subtype of java.awt.Component. When you add a bean to the visual representation of a bean, a declaration of the bean is added to the class declaration of the primary bean, and the add method is called on the GUI bean to which you added the bean.
When you add a bean anywhere else on the free-form surface, only the attribute is added to the class declaration. You can add other Container beans to the free-form surface and add GUI beans to them.

The Toolbar

The Visual Composition Editor's toolbar (Figure 66 on page 118) provides you with many useful shortcuts to menu actions.

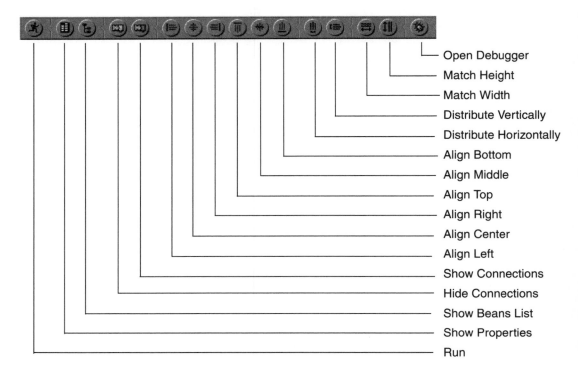

Open Debugger
Match Height
Match Width
Distribute Vertically
Distribute Horizontally
Align Bottom
Align Middle
Align Top
Align Right
Align Center
Align Left
Show Connections
Hide Connections
Show Beans List
Show Properties
Run

Figure 66. The Visual Composition Editor Toolbar

Using the Visual Composition Editor Alignment Tools
The toolbar has several controls to align, distribute, and size the components in the Visual Composition Editor. The controls only work with a null layout. Because using a null layout is not recommended for writing portable programs, you are better off not using the null layout and alignment tools unless you know the displays on which your programs will run or you are creating a quick prototype.
You can also use the alignment and distribution tools to arrange the nonvisual beans on the free-form surface. Using these tools and rearranging connections can facilitate visual development.

Working with Beans in the Visual Composition Editor

In this section you learn how to add beans to the free-form surface and customize beans through their Property sheet.

Adding Beans

The free-from surface is like a blank sheet of paper or work area where you can add, manipulate, and connect the beans that you work with to create your composite bean.

When you select a bean from the Beans Palette, the cursor is *loaded* with that bean and appears as a set of crosshairs. The bean can then be added to the free-from surface, the Beans List, or to an existing container bean (a bean that descends from java.awt.Container). When unloaded, the cursor reverts back to the Selection tool arrow (Figure 67).

Figure 67. Selection and Choose Bean Tools on the Palette

Improved in V2! ➡️ Select the **Choose Bean** tool (the right icon in Figure 67) to retrieve a bean that is not on the palette and drop it on the Beans List, the free-form surface, or an existing container bean.

After you invoke the **Choose Bean** tool, the Choose Bean dialog (Figure 68) appears. You can type the class name of your bean in the *Class name* field (remember to use the fully qualified name) or use the **Browse** button to find the class. In the *Name* field, type the name of the bean. Finally select whether you are creating a class, a variable, or a serialized bean read from a serialization file.

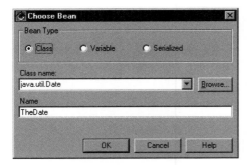

Figure 68. Choose Bean Dialog

The Sticky Function
To add multiple instances of the same bean, enable the *Sticky* function by holding down the Control key while selecting the bean. Selecting a new bean or the Selection tool disables *Sticky*.

Customizing Beans

Once you have dropped a bean on the free-form surface, you can customize it by double-clicking the bean to open its Property sheet. You can also open a bean's property sheet by selecting **Properties** from the bean's pop-up menu or selecting the **Show Properties** button on the tool bar. Using the Property sheet, you can change properties exposed by the bean as well as the bean name.

You can edit the properties for a single bean or select several beans and open a Property sheet for them. When you change a property on the Property sheet for multiple selected beans, the change affects all beans selected.

Figure 69 shows the property sheet of a JTextField bean. Select the **Show expert features** checkbox to access expert properties of the bean.

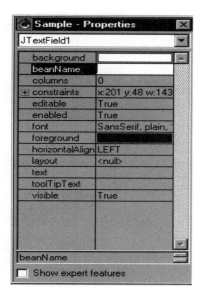

Figure 69. Property Sheet of a JTextField Bean

Each bean also has a pop-up menu (Figure 70 on page 122) that you access by clicking the right mouse button. The pop-up menu has the following selection items:

Properties
> Open the Property sheet for the bean.

Event to Code
> Start an event-to-code connection from this bean.

Open (class only)
> Open the bean's class in a class browser.

Promote Bean Feature
> Promote a feature of the bean as a feature on the primary bean.

Change Type (variable or factory only)
> Change the underlying type of the variable or factory.

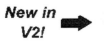
New in V2!

Morph Into
> Change the type of this bean or variable to another closely related type and update any conceitedness and properties. Morph Into can be used to change a class to a variable and vice versa or to change AWT components to JFC components.

Change Bean Name
> Change the name of the bean in the Visual Composition Editor.

The change will also affect the attribute name and the names of accessor and mutator methods.

Delete

Delete this bean from the free-form surface.

Layout

Position the bean on the free-form surface.

Connect

Start a connection from this bean.

Browse Connections

List all connections to and from this bean. You can also hide and show connections from the bean.

Reorder Connections From

Change the order in which connections from this bean are fired.

Tear-Off Property

Tear off a property from this bean so you can access it as a variable on the free-form surface.

Refresh Interface

If the BeanInfo interface has changed, use **Refresh Interface** to update the Visual Composition Editor environment with the changes.

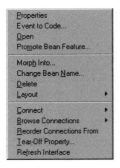 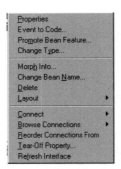

Figure 70. Bean Pop-up Menu for Class and Variable

Naming Beans

The Visual Composition Editor assigns default names to distinguish beans and connections when you generate the code to build programs. It assigns bean names on the basis of the class name and the number of beans of that type on the free-form surface or the name you specify when you use the

Choose Bean tool. You can give a bean a different name at any time. VisualAge for Java uses the bean name in two ways:

❑ The bean name is shown on the free-form surface and in the Property sheet. This name is not equivalent to the name property on objects of the Component class.

4. The bean name is also used as the basis for the attribute name in the Java source and the getter and setter methods generated for the bean. The attribute name is typically ivjBeanName, where BeanName is the name of the bean.

Give beans meaningful names if they will be accessed using Java code that you write yourself. If you do not give beans meaningful names it will be extremely difficult to write code that accesses the beans. For example, if you add an Exit button to an application, VisualAge for Java gives it a name based on the number of default button names currently in use. For example, the name might be ivjButton111. It will be much easier to write code that accesses the bean if you name the button ExitButton!

Properties created in the BeanInfo page use a similar naming convention. The attribute has the prefix field instead of ivj, however.

Beans List

Improved in V2! ➡

The Beans List is a very helpful tool. It shows all of the beans and connections on the free-form surface. From the Beans List you can:

❑ Select or delete any bean
❑ Access the pop-up menu and Property sheet for any bean
❑ Move a bean to a different container or position in the container
❑ Select or delete any connection
❑ Connect beans

Factory and Variable

Factory and Variable are helper beans. Typically, when you add JavaBeans to the free-form surface they are instantiated when your program starts or when the bean is first accessed. In many cases you do not want this behavior. For example:

❑ You may not know the specifics of a bean when the program starts.

❑ You may not want to use the resources when the program starts.

❑ You may only want a place holder or reference to an existing bean.

In these and other cases, you would use factories and variables instead of beans. Factories are visual tools that create other beans. Variables are visual place holders that reference other beans. Factories and variables are not really JavaBeans, they are helpers that cause code to be generated for you.

You can also use factories and variables to visually program the construction and manipulation of objects that are not beans, for example, objects that do not have a default constructor.

Visual Programming in Action

In this section you create a simple applet: the Bookmark List, which will keep track of your favorite URLs (Figure 71 on page 124). Along with the ATM application, the Bookmark List is used in examples throughout this book.

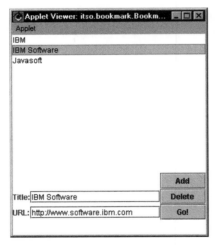

Figure 71. The Finished Bookmark List Applet

The Bookmark List will enable you to add or delete URLs and surf to those URLs. It will demonstrate the use of such features as creating a visual bean, using BorderLayout and GridBagLayout, tearing off a property, making event-to-method connections, and making event-to-code connections.

You will also build a controller for the Bookmark List. The controller will handle the interaction between the GUI and the actual list of URLs. While a controller is a bit of overkill for this example, it will let you expand the Bookmark List later to access a database and run as a servlet!

First you create two packages, itso.bookmark and itso.bookmark.applet, in the Programming VAJ V2 project to hold the Bookmark List classes.

Creating the Bookmark Classes

Create the following three classes for the Bookmark List (note the packages in which you create each class), using the Create Class SmartGuide:

1. itso.bookmark.Bookmark, which extends java.lang.Object. Make sure you deselect the **Compose the class visually** checkbox and select the **toString** method on the second page of the SmartGuide.

2. itso.bookmark.applet.BookmarkListController, which extends java.lang.Object

3. itso.bookmark.applet.BookmarkListView, which extends com.sun.java.swing.JApplet

---

Using the Create Applet SmartGuide
By default, the Create Applet SmartGuide creates a java.applet.Applet, not the JFC JApplet that you want. To create the BookmarkListView, using the Create Applet SmartGuide, click on Browse and select JApplet.

Building the Bookmark Class

The Bookmark class is very simple. It holds the title and URL for a bookmark and has a constructor that takes both the title and the URL and implements the toString method. Add the following properties:

Name	Type	Readable	Writeable	Bound
title	String	Yes	Yes	No
url	String	Yes	Yes	No

Add a new constructor to match the following code:

```
public Bookmark( String title, String url) {
    setTitle( title);
    setUrl(url);
}
```

Modify the toString implementation to return the title only:

```
public String toString() {
    return getTitle();
}
```

Building the BookmarkListController

The BookmarkListController class holds an instance of the DefaultListModel model and handles all interactions with the view. First add the following import statements to the top of the class declaration so you do not have to type those long package names:

```
import com.sun.java.swing.*;
import java.util.*;
import itso.bookmark.Bookmark;
```

Now add the model as a property feature:

Name	Type	Readable	Writeable	Bound
bookmarkList	DefaultListModel	Yes	No	No

Now you have to add the functionality of the list. You want to be able to:

❏ Add an entry to the list

❏ Delete an entry from the list

Adding an Entry

To add an entry, create a new method feature:

Name	Return Type	Parameters	Parameter 1	Parameter 2
addEntry	void	2	String title	String url

Fill in the method:

```
public void addEntry(String title, String url) {
    getBookmarkList().addElement( new Bookmark( title, url));
    return;
}
```

Deleting an Entry

To delete an entry, create a new method feature:

Name	Return Type	Parameters	Parameter 1
deleteEntry	void	1	String title

Fill in the method:

```
public void deleteEntry(String title) {
    Enumeration e = getBookmarkList().elements();
    Bookmark b = null;
    while( e.hasMoreElements()){
        b = (Bookmark)e.nextElement();
        if( b.getTitle().equals( title)){
            getBookmarkList().removeElement(b);
            return;
        }
    }
    return;
}
```

Initializing the BookmarkListController

To start off with some data, create the following method feature in the controller:

```
public void init( JApplet applet){
    StringTokenizer st = new StringTokenizer( applet.getParameter("Data"), ";");
    while (st.hasMoreTokens()) {
        addEntry( st.nextToken(), st.nextToken());
    }

}
```

Now you have a complete, if simple, model and controller!

Building the BookmarkListView Applet

First add the following import statement to the top of the BookmarkListView class declaration:

```
import itso.bookmark.Bookmark;
```

Setting the Applet Properties

1. Open the Visual Composition page of the BookmarkListView class browser.

2. Open the Beans List by selecting **Tools→Beans List**.

Notice that there are several beans in the list (Figure 72). The first BookmarkListView represents the complete bean you are editing and is really just a place holder. The second BookmarkListView is the subtype of JApplet that you created, and the JAppletContentPane is the content pane for the applet. Remember that the JFC now splits the functionality of many components between a pane and the component itself.

Figure 72. The Beans List

3. Select **BookmarkListView** in the Beans List and open the Property sheet for it by double-clicking with the left mouse button, or clicking with the right mouse button and selecting **Properties** or **Tools→Properties**. Expand the *constraints* item and set width =300, and height =300.

   It is a good idea to select the **Show expert features** checkbox now, so that you will always see all features. If you find that there are too many features and you do not use many of them, you can deselect the checkbox later.

4. Select **JAppletContentPane**. You can select it in the Beans List or by clicking anywhere within the visual representation of the applet. Open its Property sheet (Figure 73). Notice how many more properties this component has. Set *layout* to BorderLayout, then expand ***layout*** and set hgap=15 and vgap=15. Set the *background* to white by clicking on the color rectangle next to it, and then on the small button that appears. In the Background dialog box, select the **Basic** radio button and choose white.

BookmarkListView - Properties	✕

JAppletContentPane

alignmentX	0.5
alignmentY	0.5
autoscrolls	False
background	
beanName	JAppletContentPane
border	
constraints	<None>
cursor	DEFAULT_CURSOR
doubleBuffered	True
enabled	True
font	Dialog, plain, 12
foreground	
⊟ layout	BorderLayout
⌐— hgap	15
⌐— vgap	15
locale	en_US
maximumSize	0, 0
minimumSize	0, 0
nextFocusableComponent	
opaque	True
preferredSize	0, 0
requestFocusEnabled	True
toolTipText	
visible	True

beanName

☑ Show expert features

Figure 73. JAppletContentPane Property Sheet

The Beans List

The Beans List window displays an ordered list of the beans and connections on the free-form surface. The beans are initially listed in the order in which they were dropped, which also reflects the tabbing order. If we change the order of beans that have tabbing set, the Visual Composition Editor reflects the updated tabbing order.

Keeping the Beans List visible is a good idea most of the time. It will help you:

• Locate components that are under other components.

• Move or manipulate components when layout managers are in effect.

• Quickly see the names of various components and connections.

Adding the Invisible Beans

The only invisible bean you need is the controller. Click on the **Choose Bean** tool and then **Browse**. Start typing BookmarkListController until you can select it from the list (Figure 74 on page 130). Click **OK** and enter Controller in the *Name* field of the Choose Bean dialog and click **OK** again. Your cursor will change to crosshairs. Move the cursor over the free-form surface. If you move it over the visual portion of the applet, it changes to a circle with a line through it: You cannot drop this bean on the visual portion of a bean (it is not a subtype of Component). Move the cursor outside the visual portion of the applet and click the left mouse button to add the bean. Figure 75 on page 131 shows the free-form surface with the Controller added.

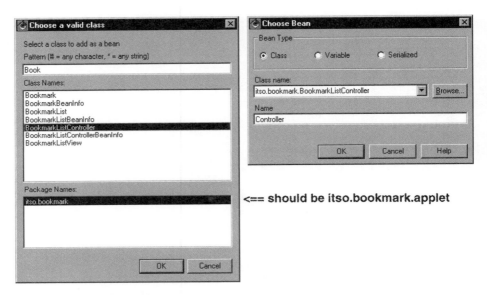

<== should be itso.bookmark.applet

Figure 74. Choosing the Controller

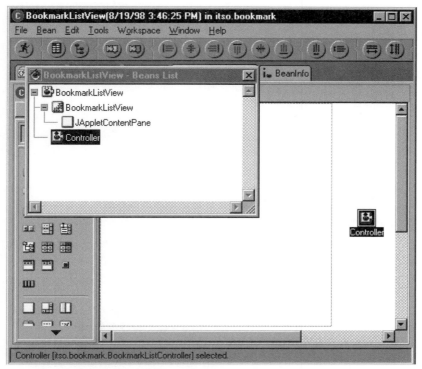

Figure 75. The Free-form Surface with the Controller

Adding the GUI Beans

Now you add the visual beans. To create an orderly interface, group the buttons and entry fields on a separate panel (Figure 76 on page 132):

1. Select **JPanel** from the Beans Palette and drop it on the free-form surface outside the visual applet. Dropping a GUI component outside the container is a way to work on the bean before it is influenced by the layout manager of the container. For example, if the panel is empty and is dropped on some areas of a border layout, its size becomes 0. Open the Property sheet and set the *layout* to GridBagLayout and the *background* to white.

   GridBagLayout is a very powerful layout manager but can be a little difficult to use at first. When you are placing GUI beans in a container using GridBagLayout, drop the first bean anywhere in the container. For subsequent beans, select the bean from the Beans Palette and then hold down the left mouse button as you move over the visual portion of the container. The cell where the component will be dropped is highlighted. Refer to Figure 76 on page 132 as you drop the beans.

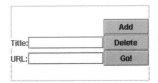

Figure 76. The GridBagLayout Panel with Components

If you absolutely cannot visually place the component where you want, open the Property sheet for the component and manually set the *gridX* or *gridY* property to the cell you want.

2. Drop 2 JLabels in JPanel1, one above the other, and set the *text* properties:
   JLabel1: Title:
   JLabel2: URL:

3. Drop a JTextField in JPanel1 to the right of each label. Set the *beanName* for each text field:
   TextField1: TitleTextField.
   TextField2: URLTextField.

   Set the *fill* property (expand the *constraints* property) to HORIZONTAL and the *weightX* property to 1.0 for both text fields. You can select multiple components and set the constraints at one time.

4. Drop three buttons to the right of the text fields and set their *beanName* and *text* properties:

Button	beanName	text
Top	AddButton	Add
Center	DeleteButton	Delete
Bottom	GoToButton	Go!

5. Set the *fill* property (expand the *constraints* property to see the layout constraints) to HORIZONTAL for all three buttons.

6. In the Beans List, move JPanel1 into the JAppletContentPane. Change the *constraints* property for Panel1 to South.

7. Drop a JList in the *center* portion of BookmarkList and set the *beanName* property for JList1 to URLList.

The free-form surface and the Beans List should now look similar to those in Figure 77.

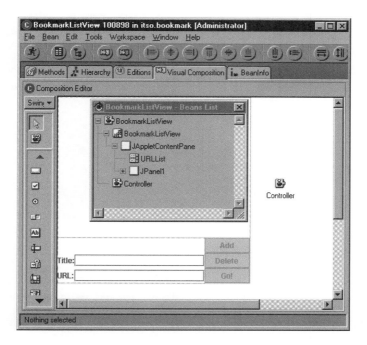

Figure 77. The BookmarkListView

Creating a Tear-off Property

Now you are going to tear off the appletContext property from the applet. The appletContext property is needed to surf to other URLs. You create a tear-off property to gain visual access to the encapsulated features of a bean. Creating a tear-off property can be necessary when a property is itself a bean and you want to connect to one of its features. The torn-off property is a variable that represents the property itself. Follow these steps to tear off a property from the primary bean (or applet in this case):

1. Place the cursor in an empty area over the free-form surface.

2. Click mouse button 2.

3. Select **Tear-Off Property**.

4. Select **appletContext** (Figure 78 on page 134).

5. Click **OK**.

Notice how variables are rendered differently from beans on the free-form surface. The variable is enclosed in square brackets (Figure 79 on page 135).

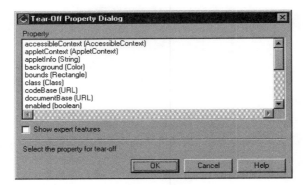

Figure 78. Tear-off Property

Adding a Variable

To access the title and URL of the bookmark selected in the list, you need a bookmark variable. Select the **Choose Bean** tool, type Bookmark in the *Interface / Class name* field and click **Browse**. Select Bookmark from the list and click **OK**. Enter SelectedBookmark in the **Name** field, select the **Variable** radio button, and click **OK** again.

The cursor now becomes a cross-hair. Move the cursor over an empty area of the free-form surface and click the left mouse button to drop the variable.

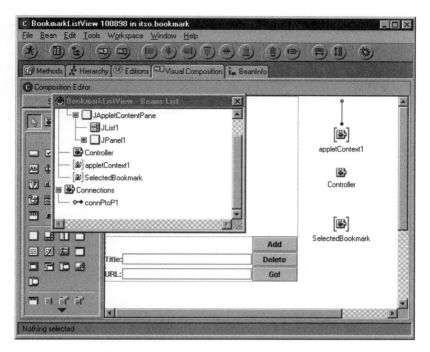

Figure 79. BookmarkListView with Variables

Saving and Generating the Bean

It is a good idea to save your work frequently while visually programming, so select **Save Bean** from the Bean menu bar item. This action generates the Java code to correspond to the interface and connections you have constructed in the Visual Composition Editor. To work with the code of the beans and connections you add in the Visual Composition Editor, you must save the bean first. You cannot just switch to another view and edit code.

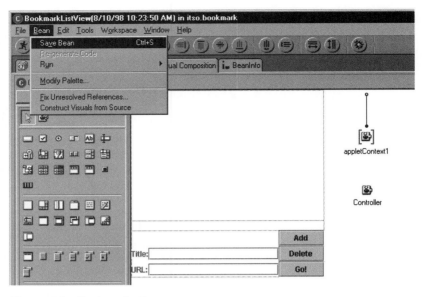

Figure 80. Saving the Bean

Connections

The Visual Composition Editor provides you with four connection types:

❑ Property-to-Property connections

❑ Event-to-Method connections

❑ Code (script) connections

❑ Parameter connections

Property-to-Property Connections

A *property-to-property* connection links two JavaBean properties together. This connection causes the value of one property to reflect the other. A property-to-property connection appears as a dark blue line with dots at either end. The solid dot indicates the target, and the hollow dot indicates the source. When your bean is constructed at runtime, the target property is set to the value of the source property. These connections never take parameters.

After the initial setting of the target property, property-to-property connections require events to fire the connection. Both the source and the target can have events to fire them. If one end of the connection does not have an event, the connection is unidirectional. If neither end has an event, the connection only fires once to initialize the target. If both ends have events, the connection is bidirectional.

Property-to-property connections have a Properties dialog where you can choose the source and target properties and events and reverse the connection.

For indexed properties, VisualAge for Java generates two get-set method pairs, one for the array and one for accessing elements within the array. When you connect indexed properties, VisualAge for Java uses the accessors for the entire array. If you want to access an individual element, you must create an event-to-method or event-to-code connection to the specific accessor.

Event-to-Method Connection

An *event-to-method* connection calls the specified method of the target object whenever the source event occurs. Often a good deal of the behavior of an application can be specified visually by causing a method of one bean to be invoked whenever an event is signaled by another bean.

If the method connected to takes parameters, you can specify them through the Connection Properties dialog box or with parameter connections. In the Connection Properties dialog box, you can also specify whether the parameter passed to the method will be the event object generated by the event.

An event-to-method connection appears as a unidirectional dark green arrow with the arrowhead pointing to the target.

New in V2!

Code (Script) Connections

Event-to-code connections were known as script connections in VisualAge for Java Version 1. It often happens that you want some processing to occur when an event is signaled, but none of the beans on the free-form surface exposes a method that does exactly what you want. In this case, VisualAge for Java enables you to connect to nonpublic methods in the class you are editing. These methods of the class are called code, to distinguish them from the public methods that you may have created for your primary class and exposed as bean methods.

A code connection appears as a unidirectional dark green arrow starting from the side of the free-form surface (representing the primary class) with the arrowhead pointing to a grey box containing the name of the method.

Code connections can simplify the number of connections you need to make in your application.

Parameter Connections

A parameter connection supplies an input value to the target of a connection by passing either a property's value or the return value from a method. In a *parameter-from-method* connection, the connection appears as a unidirectional violet arrow with the arrowhead pointing from the parameter of the original connection to the bean containing the method providing the value. In a *parameter-from-property* connection, the connection appears as a violet line with the dots at either end. The solid dot indicates the target, and the hollow dot indicates the source. The original connection is always the source of a parameter connection; the source feature is the parameter itself.

You can also make parameter connections from other connections. Some connections have return values, and all connections can throw exceptions. You can connect these return values (normalResult) and exceptions (exceptionOccurred) as parameters on other connections.

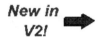

VisualAge for Java represents connections as private methods on the primary bean and names the connections on the basis of the type and number of connections using P (property/parameter), E (event), M (method), or C (code). For example, the first event-to-method connection in a bean would be named connEtoM1. You can change the connection names to make the code more readable.

Connection Properties

Each connection type in VisualAge for Java has a different set of properties that can be accessed through the Properties dialog box. To get to the Properties Dialog box, double-click on the connection or select the connection on the free-form surface or in the Beans List and select **Properties** from the pop-up menu.

The different property combinations for the connection types are:

Property-to-Property Connections

Source property
> The source bean for the connection

Target property
> The target bean for the connection

Source event
> The source bean event that fires the connection to set the target bean property

Target event

>The target bean event that fires the connection to set the source bean property

Event-to-Method Connections

Event

The source object event that fires the connection

Method

The target object method that is invoked when the connection fires

Pass event data

If true (or checked), and if the method takes parameters, the event object associated with the event is passed as a parameter

Code Connections

Code connections are essentially event-to-method connections, so you can specify the same properties.

Parameter Connections

Parameter connection properties are the same as property-to-property connection properties.

Creating Connections

Now that you have been deluged with connection information, you can make some connections in your BookmarkList applet. The first time you develop a program, using visual connections can be quite a change so make sure you read and understand the connection while you are making it. This will also help you avoid errors as you work through the examples. Once you understand why you are creating the connections in the example, you will be able to decide which connections you need in your own programs.

Keep in mind that almost all of the logic of the BookmarkListView is event driven. Unlike procedural programming where statements are simply executed one after another, in event driven programming events drive the execution of the program, and the order is governed by when events occur.

To understand the connections of the BookmarkListView, consider Table 5, which shows the functions of the BookmarkListView and the corresponding connections. Once you have read and understood the table, follow the example and create the specific connections.

Table 5. BookmarkListView Connection Overview

Function	Source of Connection	Target of Connection	Connection Type
Initialization: On startup the controller bean must be initialized.	Applet init event	Controller init method	Event-to-method
Selecting an element in the list: When an element is selected in the list of URLs, the URL and description should appear in the text fields.	URLList valueChanged event	Set URL and Title text fields with selected list element	Parameter-from-property
When the Add button is clicked, the URL and description in the textfields should be added to the list.	AddButton actionPerformed event	Controller addEntry method	Event-to-method
When the Delete button is clicked the selected URL should be deleted from the list.	DeleteButton actionPerformed event	Controller deleteEntry method	Event-to-method
When the Go! button is clicked, the browser should display the selected URL.	GoButton actionPerformed event	AppletContext showDocument method	Event-to-method

Pseudo Events

In some cases, such as init() for an applet, you may want to signal actions that are not actually JavaBean events. Initialization is one of these times. VisualAge for Java creates pseudo events that you can connect to when any component initializes. For applets, this pseudo event is the init() event; for all other beans it is the initialize() event. Connections that originate from these events are placed in the init() or initialize() method as appropriate and are called when the component is initialized.

VisualAge for Java also creates start(), stop() and destroy() pseudo events for applets. In Version 2.0 of VisualAge for Java you must connect these pseudo events from the visual representation of the applet, not from the free-form surface.

Event-to-Method Connection

When the BookmarkListView applet initializes, it should read the parameters with which it was supplied to build the URL list. The event that triggers this is the init() event. Follow these steps to connect the init() event to the init(JApplet) method on the Controller:

1. Click with the right mouse button on an empty area of the free-form surface (representing the primary class or applet). Select **Connect** from the pop-up menu. Select **Connectable Features**.

2. In the Start Connection from (BookmarkListView) dialog select the **Event** radio button. Then select **init()** and click **OK**.

3. The cursor is now a spider connected to the source of the connection. Click the left mouse button over the Controller bean and select **Connectable Features**. Select **init(com.sun.java.swing.JApplet)** from the list and click **OK**.

Now the connection is shown as a dotted line from the side of the free-form surface to the Controller. The dotted line indicates that the connection (or more accurately, the method called by the connection) requires a parameter, in this case the applet itself.

Parameter-from-Property Connection

To pass the applet as a parameter, you create a parameter-from-property connection from the applet itself to the connection.

The this Property and Event

As you probably know, in Java code, this refers to the current object, that is, the object in the context of which the code is currently executing.

Although this is not a true JavaBean property, VisualAge for Java exposes it as a read-only property on all beans on the free-from surface. You use this to connect to the bean as a whole, as opposed to one of its properties. The this entry on the preferred connection list refers to the this property not the event.

Variables on the free-form surface expose the this property as a bound readable and writable property because you set variables to the value of an instantiated bean. When the setter method is called on a variable, the this event fires.

Follow these steps to connect the applet's this property to the event-to-method connection you created in "Event-to-Method Connection" on page 141.

1. Click with the right mouse button on an empty area of the free-form surface (representing the primary class or applet). Select **Connect** from the pop-up menu. Select this from the Preferred List of features.

2. Move the cursor over the connection from init() until a small rectangle is displayed over the connection. Click with the left mouse button and then click on **applet** to supply the parameter.

The Applet Properties

To supply data to the applet, you must set the properties in the APPLET tag. Go to the Workbench window and select the BookmarkListView class. Select **Selected→Properties** and make sure that the **Applet** tab is selected. First set the *Width* and *Height* under Attributes, to 300 and 300, respectively, to match your applet size. Now add the parameters from your URL list. On one line in the Parameters text area enter:

```
<param name=Data value="IBM;http://www.ibm.com;IBM
Software;http://www.software.ibm.com;Javasoft;http://www.javasoft.com">
```

When you run your applet, the data will show up in the list.

Property-to-Property Connections

Follow these steps to create the property-to-property connections for the applet:

1. To connect the model to the view:

   Connect the bookmarkList property of the Controller to the model property of the URLList. Select the **Controller** and select **Connect** from the pop-up menu. Select **Connectable Features...** and then select **bookmarkList** from the dialog. Click over the URLList and select **model**(Figure 81).

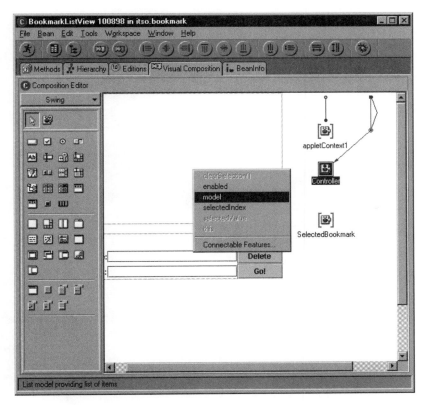

Figure 81. Connecting to the List Model

2. To connect the SelectedBookmark variable to the selected item in the list:

Connect the selectedValue property of the URLList to the this property of SelectedBookmark. For this connection to fire you must select an event to fire it. Double click the connection to open the Connection Properties dialog box (Figure 82 on page 144). Scroll down the Source event list and select **valueChanged**. This selection causes the connection to fire whenever the selected list value changes. Each connection has a different set of events in the source and target lists. The set of events each connection has depends on the types of beans involved in the connection.

3. To connect the features of the selectedBookmark to the text fields:

Click with the right mouse button over the SelectedBookmark and then select **title** from the Connectable Features dialog. Click over the TitleTextField and select **text** from the list. Repeat the connection from the url property to the URLTextField. For both connections open the Connection Properties dialog and select **this** as the *Source event*.

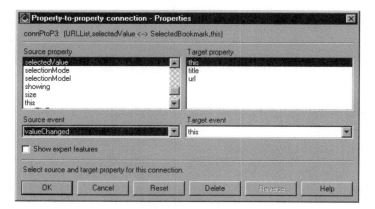

Figure 82. Connection Properties Dialog Box

Connecting the Button Events

Follow these steps to connect the button events to the appropriate methods on the applet context and the controller:

1. When the user clicks the Add button, the string in the title and URL text fields is added to URLList. From AddButton connect the actionPerformed event (Figure 83) to the addEntry(java.lang.String, java.lang.String) method of the Controller. Connect the title and URL parameters from the connection to the text properties of the TitleTextField and URLTextField. The connection becomes a solid line.

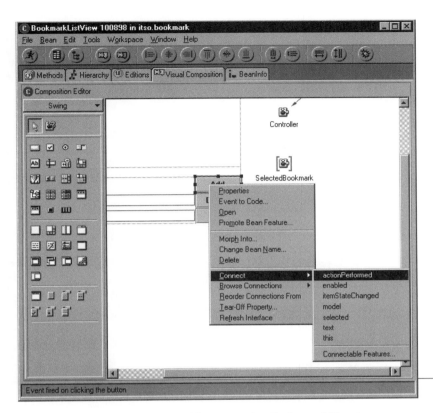

Figure 83. Connecting the AddButton actionPerformed Event

2. To delete an entry from the list, connect the Delete button to the deleteEntry method. From DeleteButton connect the actionPerformed event to the deleteEntry(java.lang.String) method of the Controller. Connect the title parameter from the connection to the title property of SelectedBookmark. The Delete button should clear the text in the text fields. Connect DeleteButton actionPerformed to the text property of TitleTextField. Although the connection is dotted, you can leave it as is because you only want to clear the field. Repeat the connection from DeleteButton actionPerformed to the text property of URLTextField.

3. To surf to a new URL, connect the Go! button to the showDocument method of the applet context (the connection will not function until you run the applet in a Web browser; see Chapter 10, "Deploying Your Java Programs" on page 327). From GoToButton, connect the actionPerformed event to the showDocument(java.netURL) method of appletContext1. Once again the connection is dotted, so connect this connection's url parameter to the SelectedBookmark url property.

Connecting Different Property Types

When you make a connection to a property or parameter, the two ends of the connection may not be the same type. For example, the showDocument method expects a java.net.URL type, and the TitleTextField text property is a String. If VisualAge for Java can convert the field, it will. For example, there is a constructor for a URL that takes a String. VisualAge for Java uses this constructor in the connection.

4. If a URL is not valid, you will want to see the status when you click the Go! button. To display the status of the link, follow these steps to connect exceptionOccurred from the previous connection to the showStatus method of AppletContext1:

Select the connection from the Go! button to AppletContext1→showDocument. Press the right mouse button and select **Connect**, then **exceptionOccurred**. Move the mouse over AppletContext1 and click with the left mouse button, select the **Method** radio button, and then select showStatus(java.lang.String). This connection appears as a dashed line. Open the property sheet for the connection and check the **Pass Event Data** checkbox to make the exception text appear in the browser status area. This will pass the exception to the showStatus method.

5. One final connection and you are done! In JFC Release 1.02 there is a bug in the JList code. When the first element in the list is deleted, an event is not fired to update the list. To work around this, you can cause a list repaint each time you delete an item. Connect actionPerformed on the DeleteButton to the repaint method on URLList.

Manipulating Connections

When you select a connection, small black squares appear on it. Each square is used to manipulate a part of the line representing the connection. When the cursor is over these squares, it changes to a drag icon and can be used only to drag the connection itself. If you make a mess of the connection, you can restore it through the **Restore Shape** item on the pop-up menu of the connection.

Figure 84 shows your applet with the connections. Now you can set your class path and test your applet. To set the class path, select the **BookmarkListView** class in the Workbench and then select **Selected→Properties**. Click the **Class Path** tab and then the **Edit** button to the right of the *Project Path* field. Make sure the checkbox next to *JFC Class Libraries* is selected and click **OK**. The class path will be discussed further in "The Class Path" on page 150.

Click the **Run** button on the menu bar to test your applet.

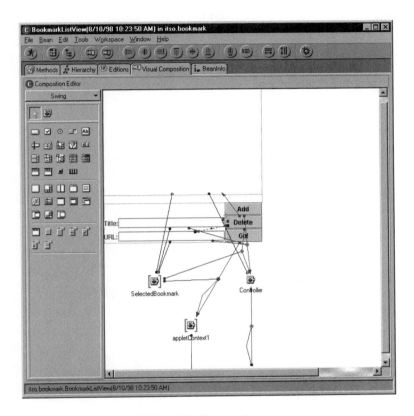

Figure 84. BookmarkList with Connections

Enhancing the BookmarkListView Applet

The usability of the applet would be enhanced if the user could only click those buttons that should be enabled. Specifically the applet should:

1. Start with all buttons disabled.

2. Only enable the Add button if there is text in both text fields.

3. Enable the Delete and Go! buttons when an element is selected.

4. Disable all buttons when no item in the list is selected.

Event-to-Code Connections

You will use additional connections and a setState method to enable or disable AddButton, DeleteButton, and GoToButton as appropriate on the basis of the state of the URLList. Follow these steps to enhance the applet:

1. From TitleTextField tear off the document(Document) property creating the document1 variable. Start the connection from the document event on the Document1 variable and click mouse button 2 over the free-form surface. Select **Event to Code** from the list. In the Event-to-Code dialog box, leave document as the event and **<new method>** selected as the *Method name*. Make sure the **Pass event data** checkbox is not selected.

2. Replace the code in the dialog box with the following code:

```
public void setState(){
    String titleText = getTitleTextField().getText();
    String urlText = getURLTextField().getText();

    if (titleText.equals("") || urlText.equals("")){
        getAddButton().setEnabled(false);
    }
    else{
        getAddButton().setEnabled(true);
    }
    if ( getURLList().getSelectedIndex() < 0){
        getDeleteButton().setEnabled(false);
        getGoToButton().setEnabled(false);
    }
    else{
        getDeleteButton().setEnabled(true);
        getGoToButton().setEnabled(true);
    }
    getappletContext1().showStatus("");
}
```

3. Click **OK** on the dialog box.

4. Tear off the document(Document) property from the URLTextField. Connect the document event from the torn-off document variable to the free-form surface and select **Event-to-Code**. In the Event-to-Code window leave document as the event, select setState as the *Method* name, and click **OK** to finish.

5. From the URLList valueChanged event, connect to the free-form surface and select **Event-to-Code**. In the Event-to-Code window leave valueChanged as the event, select setState as the *Method* name, and click **OK** to finish.

Figure 85 shows the connections of your applet at this point.

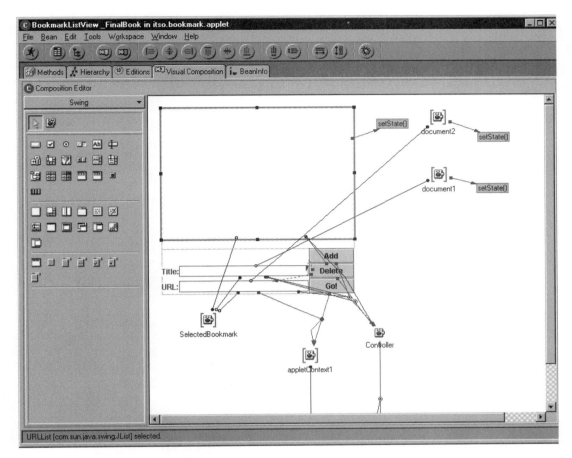

Figure 85. BookmarkListView Connection View

Now run the applet and ensure that it works as designed. Figure 86 shows the final applet.

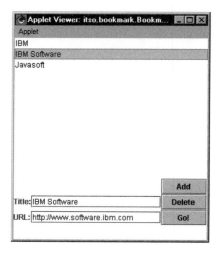

Figure 86. The BookmarkListView Applet

The Class Path

**New in
V2!**

As you know, Java uses the concept of a class path to locate classes that can
be loaded. In VisualAge for Java Version 1 the class path is only used to find
resources at runtime. In Version 2, there are several uses of and several ways
of setting the class path.

Runtime

In VisualAge for Java Version 2, the class path is used at runtime to locate
classes that are loaded dynamically and to locate resources used by the
program. Note that this also applies to design time for tools running in the
environment.

Classes are loaded dynamically (or referenced indirectly) through the
Class.forName() method. For example, Class c = Class.forName("myclass"); would
return an instance of the Class object representing the class myclass. You
then instantiate an instance of myclass, using c.newInstance(). The forName
method is commonly used with JDBC drivers.

You still have to import code into VisualAge for Java to use it in development.
That is, any class that you reference or any interface that you implement
must be in the workspace.

Resources are still located through the class path so, for example, any
property files that you open or images that you load would be searched for in
the class path.

Setting the Runtime Class Path

You can set the Runtime Class Path in several ways:

Workbench Options

Using the Workbench **Window→Options** dialog in the Resources section, you can set the class path for all classes in the workspace. You specify a directory, JAR, or Zip file, and any running class will look there for resources and dynamically loaded classes. For example, if you are using the JFC in a lot of programs, you could specify the JFC resources directory here rather than for each program.

Class Properties

You can also set the class path for each class separately. In the Workbench **Selected→Properties** dialog, select the **Class Path** tab (Figure 87 on page 152). Here you specify whether you want the current directory (the default project resources directory) in the class path. You can select the resource directories of other projects through the *Project path:* option and you can specify other directories or JAR or Zip files in the *Extra directories path:* field.

The current Workspace class path is shown as well as the complete class path in effect.

Compute Now

Click the **Compute Now** button to automatically add the project resources directory associated with any other packages your program uses.

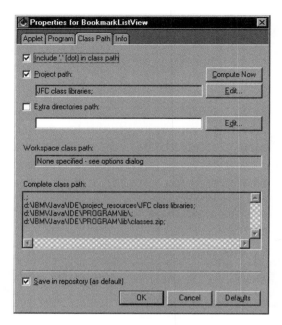

Figure 87. The Class Path Page

There are separate class paths to find external source code for debugging and BeanInfo classes. These class paths are set in the Options window.

5 Managing and Fixing Your Code

Before you finish building the ATM application and exploring other VisualAge for Java features, you should know a little more about managing and fixing your code in VisualAge for Java. VisualAge for Java comes with a powerful set of tools to store and manage updates in your programs as well as debug and fix problems in your code.

In this chapter you will learn about the workspace and the repository and how to work with multiple editions of program elements to facilitate code management. You will be introduced to the Repository Explorer and search capabilities that you can use to find workspace program elements, such as classes, interfaces, fields, or methods. You will also learn about the debugger and Inspectors, which you use to diagnose problem code.

Storing Your Code

When you start VisualAge for Java, a persistent working environment, called a *workspace,* is automatically loaded to store the program elements (projects, packages, classes, interfaces, and methods) you are working with as well as your current option settings and open windows.

Your code is also stored in a larger database, called the *repository*, which contains other program elements in a defined state, or *edition*. You can add these program elements to the workspace if you need to use them.

The workspace stores the bytecodes of the programs you are working with, and the repository stores the source for the program elements in the workspace as well as all other elements not currently in the workspace.

By integrating the IDE closely with code management, VisualAge for Java can support powerful features such as code clue, error detection, and searches.

VisualAge for Java Example Code
VisualAge for Java has a wealth of examples that are not shown in your workspace the first time you start the product. These examples include IBM Java Examples, Sun BDK Examples, Sun JDK Examples, Sun JFC Examples, and IBM Domino Examples. The examples are stored in the repository and you have load them into the workspace to use them.
In addition you have to explicitly load the following projects into the workspace to use them: IBM Data Access Beans, Domino Java Class Library, IBM IDE Utility Class Libraries, and Sun Class Libraries Unix.

As shown in Figure 88, Java code is *loaded* from the repository into the workspace and automatically *saved* from the workspace to the repository. The Workbench and other browsers are used to manage code in the workspace; the Repository Explorer is used to browse code in the repository.

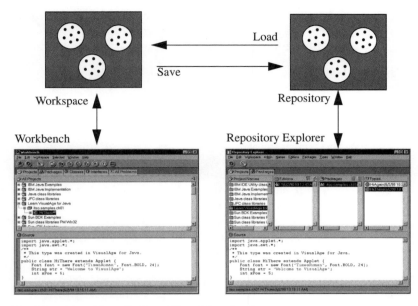

Figure 88. Managing Your Code in VisualAge for Java

Team Development

This book describes the single-user environment of the Professional version of VisualAge for Java. The Enterprise version of VisualAge for Java has a more powerful team programming environment that allows several programmers to share the same repository.

Although it is possible to use VisualAge for Java Professional to share code, using VisualAge for Java Enterprise will make your team more productive.

It is also possible to use external code management products with VisualAge for Java. See "Interface to External SCM Tools" on page 345.

The Workspace

The workspace is stored as a single file (IDE.icx) and contains the program elements that you are currently working with as well as your preferences and working environment. You use the IDE (Workbench and Class Browser) to manage the workspace.

Whenever you close the last window of a VisualAge for Java session or select **File→Exit VisualAge** from the Workbench menu bar, VisualAge for Java displays a dialog that prompts you to confirm the save of your workspace. If you click the **Cancel** button, VisualAge for Java does not exit and you stay in the Workbench.

You can also explicitly save the workspace during a long session by selecting **File→Save Workspace**.

The Repository

The repository is the database of your program elements. Each time you create or save a program element, it is stored in the repository as well as in the workspace. The repository contains all editions of all program elements, so it is usually quite a bit larger than your workspace. In addition, your workspace does not usually contain all of the program elements that are available in the repository, because you do not necessarily need them for your current project. You can load program elements from the repository into your workspace, and you can delete program elements from your workspace.

Resource Files

Java programs often use resource files, such as images, sound clips and property files. VisualAge for Java does not provide version control or management for resource files. VisualAge for Java creates a resources directory for each project that you create or import or that is installed with VisualAge for Java.

The directory hierarchy of resources directories under the main VisualAge for Java directory is:

\IBMVJava\ide\project_resources
    <project name 1>
    <project name 2>
    ...
    <project name n>

Because each project resources directory has the same name as the project, you must name a project with a valid directory name (the directory will be created for you). You may add resources to your project through the resources directory or modify your class path to point to another location for resource files.

Features

New in *V2!*

The Features item is in the **Available** palette category and the QuickStart dialog box. Features are Java class libraries and beans that have been added to the repository and can be added to the workspace. The Features dialog is a shortcut to the usual Add from Repository function.

If you want to provide beans or libraries to VisualAge for Java users, use the Feature Integrator. When the IDE starts, new features are automatically imported into the repository, and the user can then load them into the workspace. See the VisualAge for Java product documentation for instructions on using the Feature Integrator.

Version Control

VisualAge for Java supports a repository-based source control mechanism that enables you to keep track of all source code changes made over time. The VisualAge for Java source code repository is automatically updated each time you make a change to the source code. A history of all changes made to the source is kept in the repository, so you can back out of any or all source code changes.

As you will see in "Interface to External SCM Tools" on page 345, you can also integrate VisualAge for Java repository management with existing software configuration management systems. Thus you can use VisualAge for Java within your existing development processes.

Editions

All program elements (remember, a program element is a project, package, class, interface or method) in VisualAge for Java are stored as editions. There can be many editions of each program element.

You can have more than one edition of a program element in the repository, but you can only load one edition in workspace at any given time. Thus you have the flexibility to try several different approaches with the same program element.

Open Edition

An open edition is a program element that you can change. It is indicated by a time stamp containing the date and time of its creation. You cannot change this unique identifier. To see the edition names, click on the **Show Edition Names** button in the Workbench Toolbar.

VisualAge for Java automatically creates an open edition, if you modify an existing edition of a program element or create a new program element. You can think of an open edition as the default state of a program element before it is versioned.

Versions

A *version* is a read-only edition of a program element that is assigned a version number (such as 1.0). Whenever you version a program element, it is stored in the repository. You may want to version your program elements to:

❑ Take a snapshot of the state of your program elements to which you can revert if you want to abandon subsequent modifications

❑ Have a baseline for code that you import from the file system and plan to modify

❑ Freeze a finished program that you are ready to release

❑ Compact the repository

❑ Export an interchange file

In Figure 89 the current workspace is loaded with the 6/3/98 10:23:45 AM edition of a program element. This edition is also stored in the repository along with two different versions of the same program element.

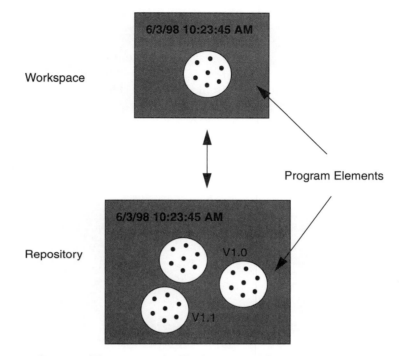

Workspace

6/3/98 10:23:45 AM

Program Elements

Repository

6/3/98 10:23:45 AM

V1.0

V1.1

Figure 89. Program Elements in the Workspace and Repository

Backups

Back up the repository and workspace files as well as the project resources directory frequently. Also, you may want to save the original versions of these files when you install VisualAge for Java, so that you can return to the original state of the repository if required.

The workspace file (IDE.icx) is in the program directory with the VisualAge for Java programs (IBMVJava\Ide\Program). The repository (ivj.dat) is in the repository directory under the main VisualAge for Java IDE directory (IBMVJava\Ide\repository).

Versioning Program Elements

When you version a program element, you create a read-only edition of the element. Versions are also created of each open edition program element contained within the element you are versioning. Already versioned program elements contained within the program element you are versioning are not changed. For example, assume you have the following package and classes:

ch01 (5/24/98 1:57:43 PM)
    HiThere 1.0
    AnotherApplet (5/24/98 1:57:43 PM)

The editions of ch01 and AnotherApplet are indicated in parentheses. The version of HiThere is 1.0. When you version ch01, the AnotherApplet class is also versioned, but HiThere is not versioned because it already is at version 1.0.

To version an edition of a program element, select it and then click **Selected→Manage→Version** in the menu bar. The Versioning Selected Items dialog box appears (Figure 90).

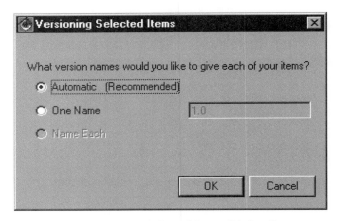

Figure 90. Versioning Selected Items Dialog Box

You have three options for naming your versioned elements:

❏ **Automatic:** Each program element to be versioned (that is, each open edition program element) is given a version name, which is an increment of its current version name.

❏ **One Name:** All program elements to be versioned are given the same name.

❏ **Name Each:** You are prompted to name each program element to be versioned.

VisualAge for Java versions the selected program element and its contained open edition elements and replaces the time stamps with the version names.

Editions of Methods

All program elements are managed by the VisualAge for Java code management system. However, methods are considered part of a class or interface for versioning purposes. That is, new editions of a method are created each time you save the method, but you cannot version a method.

Attributes of a class are not under separate code management, and a change to an attribute is considered a change to the class.

Managing Editions

Now that you are familiar with editions and versions, you are ready to manage editions of your program elements.

Creating New Editions

When you add new program elements to the workspace or import Java code from the file system, VisualAge for Java creates an open edition of each program element. The open edition is identified by a time stamp that indicates when VisualAge for Java created the edition. You can click the **Show Edition Names** Workbench toolbar button (the last button on the right) to show or hide the edition names with which you are currently working.

When you subsequently modify a program element that you have versioned, VisualAge for Java automatically creates a new edition of the element (marked with a time stamp). VisualAge for Java then stores the new edition in the repository and replaces the versioned workspace edition with the new edition. The previous edition is still available from the repository.

Any versioned program elements that contain the element that was modified also become new editions. For example, if you modify a TestClass class that is at version 1.0, in a testpkg package at version 1.1:

❑ A new edition of TestClass is created with a time stamp.

❑ A new edition of testpkg is created with a time stamp.

Deleting a Program Element from the Workspace

When you delete a program element from the workspace, the edition is still in the repository, so you can reload it later. To delete a program element, select the element and choose **Selected→Delete** from the Workbench.

Replacing One Edition with Another

The workspace contains, at any one time, only one edition of a given program element, whereas the repository holds all editions of all program elements. You may want to replace the edition of a program element in the workspace with another edition so that you can abandon the modifications that you made and revert to another edition that resides in the repository.

To replace an edition of a program element with another edition, select the edition in the Workbench, select **Selected→Replace With→Another Edition**, and choose from the list that is displayed (Figure 91). The edition that is currently in the workspace is marked, by default, with an asterisk (*).

Figure 91. Replacing Editions

To replace an edition with the edition from which it is derived, select the program element, and select **Selected→Replace With→Previous Edition**. When you replace an edition of a program element in the workspace, VisualAge also replaces the editions of the program elements that it contains, as required.

Loading Available Editions

To load an edition of a program element that is not currently loaded in the workspace, use the **Selected→Add** menu in the Workbench. The menu contains some of the following items, depending on the selected item:

- ❏ Project
- ❏ Package
- ❏ Class
- ❏ Interface
- ❏ Applet
- ❏ Method
- ❏ Field

You cannot use the Applet and Field selections to load an edition from the repository. You cannot load a field from the repository because fields are not under code management. The Applet selection only displays the Create Applet SmartGuide to create a new applet. To load an applet from the repository, use the Class selection.

If you want to add a project from the repository to the workspace, select the project in which you want to add the package. Then, select **Selected→Add→Project** to open the SmartGuide (Figure 92).

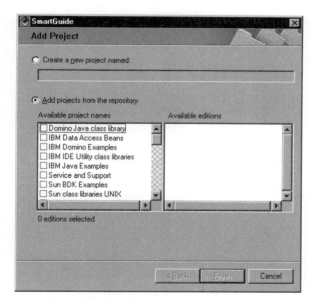

Figure 92.   SmartGuide to Load an Edition

Select **Add projects from the repository,** and VisualAge for Java shows you the available projects in the repository. Only the projects not currently in the workspace are displayed.

To load projects, select the projects that you want to load. If there is more than one edition of a project, select the edition to load. Once you have selected all projects and editions, click **Finish**.

Using the Repository Explorer

Use the Repository Explorer to browse the contents of the repository. You open the Repository Explorer (Figure 93) by selecting **Window→Repository Explorer**.

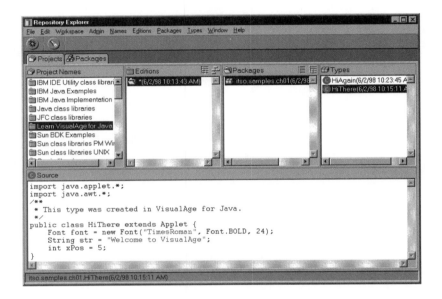

Figure 93. The Repository Explorer

To switch between the Projects and Packages views, click the Projects and Packages tabs. The Projects view shows all projects (Figure 93). To show the editions in the repository, just click the project, and the editions are listed in the list to the right of the project. Selecting an edition shows the packages in the selected edition, and selecting a package lists the types (classes and interfaces) in that package.

The Packages view shows you all packages in the repository. Selecting a package lists all editions of the selected package, and selecting an edition shows you the types in that edition.

To see all editions of a type (interface or class), select the type, then select **Open** from the **Types** menu bar and click the **Editions** tab.

To compare two editions in the Projects or Packages view, select two editions (if there is more than one) and then select **Editions→Compare** in the menu bar. A window (Figure 94) appears where you can analyze the differences. You can also compare editions in the Workbench, using **Selected→Compare With**.

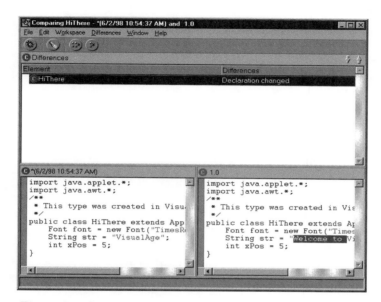

Figure 94. Comparing Two Editions

Compacting the Repository

During development you are bound to create program elements that you will not want to keep in the repository. These may be classes you created to explore possibilities or classes that just did not work out. In addition, at some point in the life of your projects, things will probably be stable enough so that you will not want to keep open editions or particular versions of code in the repository.

By periodically purging program elements and compacting the repository, you will increase the performance of VisualAge for Java.

In VisualAge for Java you can purge editions of program elements from the repository. Purging marks a program element for later removal from the repository. Until you compact the repository, these program elements can still be restored. The **Purge** and **Restore** functions are found on the **Names**

menu or the pop-up menu in the Repository Explorer. Before you compact the repository you must version all elements in the workspace.

To compact the repository, click the **Compact Repository** item on the **Admin** menu of the Repository Explorer. Compacting the repository:

❑ Creates a backup repository with a .bak extension

❑ Removes all open editions in the repository

❑ Removes all purged elements from the repository

❑ Removes all versioned editions of classes that are contained only in open editions of packages

Searching for Program Elements

Another aspect of code management is finding all places where a particular class, field, or method is used or declared. The following VisualAge for Java search capabilities make this task easy:

The Search dialog
> The Search dialog (accessed by selecting the **Workspace→Search** menu item) searches for references to, or declarations of, classes, methods, and fields in the workspace.

The Go To dialog
> The Go To dialog (accessed through **Selected→Go To**) finds classes and interfaces in the workspace or the repository.

The References To and Declarations Of functions

Improved in V2!
> The References To and Declarations Of functions are extremely powerful navigation tools that enable you to find methods, fields, and types referenced or accessed by a method or type.

If you are looking only for the declaration of a class, use the faster **Go To** dialog box. If you want to find out where a class was referenced or you are looking for methods or fields, use the Search dialog box.

The Search Dialog Box

The Search dialog box enables you to search for references to, or declarations of, classes, methods, and fields. You access the Search dialog box (Figure 95) by selecting **Workspace→Search**.

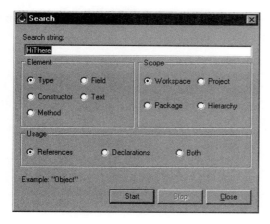

Figure 95. The Search Dialog Box

In addition to entering a search string (using the * and # wildcards), you can constrain the search by element type (type, field, constructor, text, and method), scope (workspace, project, package, hierarchy), and usage (references, declarations, or both).

A Search Results window (Figure 96) lists any items that were found.

Improved in V2!

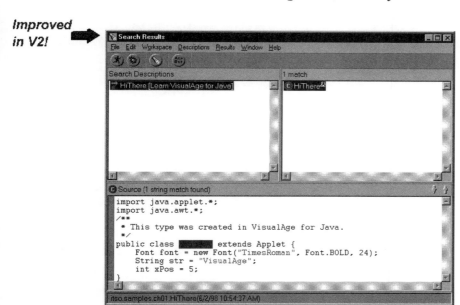

Figure 96. Search Results Window

While the Search Results window is open, you can switch to previous searches, and you can always restart any previous search. You can also sort the results by method or type name.

References To and Declarations Of Functions

Figure 97 shows the **References To** item in the Classes menu in the Class Browser. You can find references to:

This Type
> Find references to this type anywhere in the workspace.

Field
> Find any references of this field in the type. You are prompted with a list of all fields declared in the type or inherited.

Static Field
> Find any references of this static field in the type. You are prompted with a list of all static fields declared in the type or inherited.

Final Field
> Find any references of this final field in the type. You are prompted with a list of all final fields declared in the type or inherited.

Figure 98 on page 170 shows the **References To** and the **Declarations of** items in the Methods menu in the Class Browser and debugger. You can find references to, or declarations of:

This Method
> Find all references to or declarations of this method in the class.

Sent Methods
> Find all references to or declarations of methods called from this method.

Accessed Fields
> Find all references to or declarations of fields accessed within this method. You can define the scope of the search as workspace, project, package, or hierarchy in the Accessed Fields dialog box.

Referenced Types
> Find all references to or declarations of types referenced in this method. You can define the scope of the search as workspace, project, package, or hierarchy in the Referenced Types dialog box.

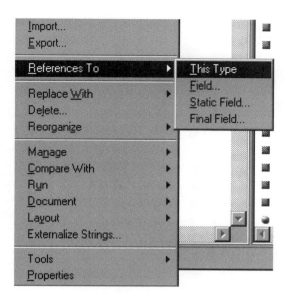

Figure 97. References To Type

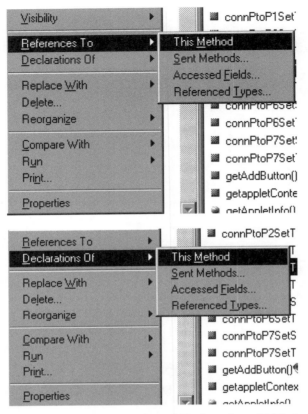

Figure 98. References To and Declarations Of Methods

Versioning Your Code

Now that you know how to use the VisualAge for Java versioning capabilities, you can use them to manage your code.

Version the itso.atm.model package to create a baseline for the work you do in the rest of the book:

1. In the Workbench, select the itso.atm.model package and **Selected→Manage→Version**. The SmartGuide prompts you for the names for the editions. The **Automatic (Recommended)** radio button should be selected, and the entry in the field next to the **One Name** radio button should be 1.0 (although it is greyed out).

2. Click **OK**. The Workbench window now displays your versioned package (Figure 99).

If you do not see the edition names, click the **Show Edition Names** button in the toolbar.

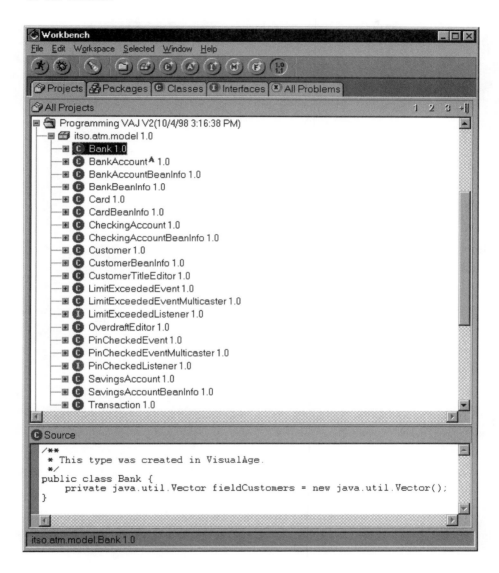

Figure 99. The Versioned itso.atm.model Package

Now you have a package version to which you can always revert. To illustrate switching editions: Modify the Bank class by simply adding a comment in the class declaration and saving the Bank class. VisualAge for Java creates a new edition of the Bank class and the itso.atm.model package.

You now have a new edition of the Bank class. The new edition name is displayed in the Workbench (Figure 100). Click the **Show Edition Names** toolbar button if you do not see the name.

Figure 100. The New Edition of the Bank Class

You can load the previously versioned editions of the project, package, and class back into your workspace. Now replace the Bank class. In the Workbench, select the Bank class and select **Selected→Replace With→Another Edition**. VisualAge for Java displays a list of the available editions in the repository. Select the 1.0 version you created previously and click the **OK** button. The selected edition is loaded, and the Workbench shows your package restored to the version shown in Figure 99.

Versioning the Bookmark List Packages

As you progress through this book, you will improve on and modify the Bookmark List. Even though you will use different packages for most of the examples, you should version the packages after each chapter. Create a version of itso.bookmark and itso.bookmark.applet called _FinishedApplet:

1. In the Workbench, select the **itso.bookmark** and **itso.bookmark.applet** packages and **Selected→Manage→Version**. The SmartGuide prompts you for the names for the editions. Select the **One Name** radio button and enter _FinishedApplet in the text field. The underscore is used simply to make the version more readable when displayed in the browser.

2. Click **OK**. The Workbench window now displays your versioned package (Figure 101).

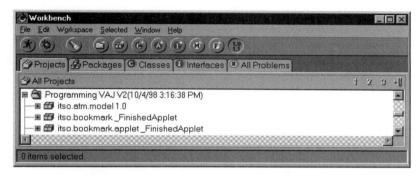

Figure 101. _FinishedApplet Version of Bookmark List

Debugging a VisualAge for Java Program

Now you will learn more about analyzing and fixing errors during development. VisualAge for Java provides several tools, including the Scrapbook, Inspectors, and the debugger, to find problems in your programs.

Inspectors

You can use Inspectors to view and change the state of objects in your programs. For example, if you are working in the Scrapbook, you can open an Inspector by following these steps.

1. Open the Scrapbook and type the following code:

```
new java.awt.Point(1,2);
```

2. Highlight the code and from the menu bar select **Edit→Inspect**. An Inspector window similar to that in Figure 102 on page 174 opens.

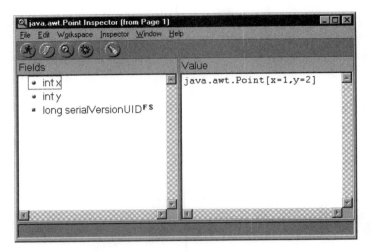

Figure 102. An Inspector Window

Opening an Inspector Window
An alternative way of opening an Inspector is to insert an instruction in your Java code to inspect a specific object. This is a useful method if you have a difficult-to-debug program that should not be interrupted with breakpoints. In the Scrapbook type the following code:
String[] numbers = {"one", "two", "three"};
com.ibm.uvm.tools.DebugSupport.inspect(numbers);
Highlight the code and from the menu bar select **Edit→Run** (or press **Ctrl-E** or click the **Run** navigation button). The com.ibm.uvm.tools.DebugSupport.inspect(anObject) instruction advises the JVM to open an Inspector on the specified object.

You can also open an Inspector by highlighting the code and then pressing the accelerator key, **Ctrl-Q**, choosing **Inspect** from the pop-up menu, or clicking the **Inspect** navigation button (the magnifying glass).

Inspectors are most useful when you are using the debugger. You can open an Inspector on each object in which you are interested. As you step through the program, you can see the state of all inspected objects at once.

The Inspector Window

The title bar of an Inspector window displays the type of the displayed class and the context in which you have opened the Inspector. In the example in Figure 102 on page 174, the class is *java.awt.Point*, and the context is *Page 1*. There are two panes in the Inspector window:

Fields

> Shows the fields of the object

Value

> Displays the values of the fields of an object

The Fields pane displays items in hierarchical order with the inherited fields first. Therefore, when you inspect a more complex object, the fields that you have declared in your object are at the bottom of the Fields pane.

Changing the Value of a Field

In the Value pane of the Inspector window you can manipulate the values of the object's fields (Figure 103 on page 175). Select the int x field and change 1 to 100, then select **Edit→Save** (or use the accelerator key, **Ctrl-S**, or **Save** from the Value pane's pop-up menu). VisualAge for Java also prompts you to save the field when you access another field.

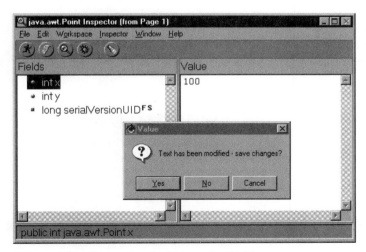

Figure 103. Changing the Value of a Field

When stepping through your code with the debugger, you also can change a field value on the fly and resume the execution of your program with the changed field value.

Navigating to Other Fields or Objects

If you have a more complex object, say, an aggregation of several objects, it is easy to open an Inspector on the other objects. Just select the other object in the Fields pane and choose **Inspector→Inspect**. In this way you can inspect very complex data structures by accessing their different layers, just like peeling an onion.

The String Class
Because the String class represents immutable strings, you cannot change the characters of a String object in an Inspector window. However, you can change the characters of a StringBuffer. In this case, you must enclose the new character in single quotes.

Controlling the Display of Fields

When an Inspector first appears, all public, protected, and private fields of the inspected class and the inherited classes are displayed. You can modify the fields that are displayed, using any of these Inspector menu bar items:

❑ Field Names Only

❑ Public Fields Only

❑ Hide Static Fields

❑ Show Fields In

• Actual Type

• Declared Type

Evaluating Code in the Context of an Object

If you open an Inspector on a particular object, you can apply methods to that object and inspect the results. In Figure 104 on page 177, for example, the getLocation method is invoked on a Point object.

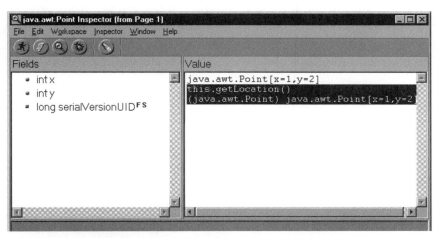

Figure 104. Evaluating Code in the Context of an Object

To evaluate an expression and display its result, type in the expression in the Value pane, highlight it, and select **Display** from the menu bar or from the Value pane pop-up menu.

The Debugger

You use the debugger to step through and fix your Java code. As with the Inspectors, you can also inspect and change the state of objects. Because the debugger is tightly integrated with the VisualAge for Java IDE, you can make changes to code in the debugger, and these changes are reflected in your workspace.

The debugger display consists of two pages: Debug and Breakpoints.

The Debug Page

The Debug Page toolbar (Figure 105) provides easy access to common debug functions.

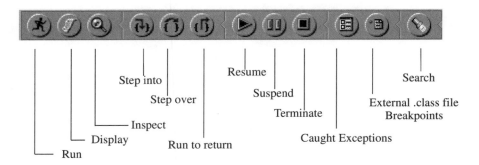

Figure 105. Debug Page Toolbar

The Debug page shows all currently running threads, grouped by program in the All Programs/Threads pane. The running programs can be of three types (Figure 106 on page 179):

System programs
If you have selected the **Show system programs in debugger and console** option, system programs, including any open Visual Composition Editor sessions will be displayed. A Visual Composition Editor session can be identified in the list of running programs by the format of the program name:
classname (VCE) (System) time.
For example:
BookmarkListView (VCE) (System) (8/17/98 1:46:34 PM)
Visual Composition Editor programs have two threads: the common AWT event queue and a timer queue. Displaying these programs in the debugger is useful for debugging code, such as property editors or customizers, that is invoked by the Visual Composition Editor.

Scrapbook sessions
Scrapbook sessions are shown in the All Programs/Threads pane with the name of the Scrapbook page as the title in the form:
page (time).
For example:
Page 1(8/17/98 1:56:51 PM)
Simple Scrapbook programs have one thread named main.

Applets and applications
Applets and applications are shown in the All Programs/Threads pane in the form:
Applet classname (time) for applets
classname.main() (time) for applications.
For example:

Applet itso.bookmark.BookmarkListView (8/17/98 1:57:42 PM)
itso.bookmark.BookmarkListView.main() (8/17/98 1:57:53 PM)
Applets and applications have at least three threads: the AWT event queue, a timer queue, and the other threads of the applet or application. When a program is suspended because of a breakpoint, the AWT event queue thread shows the call stack of your applet or application. If the program is suspended because of an exception, the call stack shows up in the thread that threw the exception.

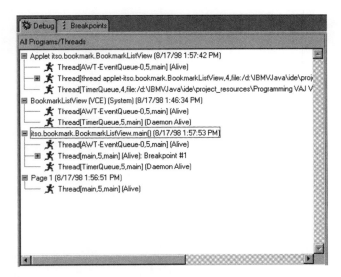

Figure 106. Running Programs in the Debugger

When a program is expanded, the threads in the program are shown. When a suspended thread is expanded, the execution or call stack is shown. The execution stack shows the methods entered leading up to the method that was executing when the thread was suspended.

The other panes on the Debug page show code relating to a selected suspended thread:

Visible Variables
Show the visible variables in the thread.

Value
Show the value of the selected variable.

Source
Show the source of the method that is suspended.

The Breakpoints Page

The Breakpoints page shows:

❑ All methods in the workspace that have breakpoints set in them

❑ The source code for the methods

The Breakpoints page toolbar (Figure 107) provides buttons for manipulating breakpoints.

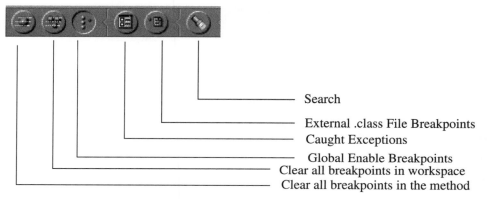

                       — Search

                       — External .class File Breakpoints

                       — Caught Exceptions

                       — Global Enable Breakpoints

                       Clear all breakpoints in workspace

                       Clear all breakpoints in the method

Figure 107. Breakpoints Page Toolbar

Adding Breakpoints

Breakpoints can be set on any instruction in source code in the workspace. The code must be saved and error free. You can set breakpoints only on instructions, not on all statements in your code. For example, you cannot set breakpoints:

❑ In class declarations
❑ In inner classes
❑ On try or catch statements
❑ On else or case statements
❑ On comments

VisualAge for Java does not let you set a breakpoint in a class declaration. If you try and set a breakpoint on an invalid statement in a method, the breakpoint will be set on the next valid statement.

Breakpoints can be set at any time, including while code is being debugged; that is, you can add a breakpoint to a method in a suspended thread's stack without the execution of the program being reset to the beginning of the method.

Follow these steps to set a breakpoint in the paint method of the HiThere applet (see "Building Your First Applet" on page 5):

1. Go to the Workbench and select the itso.samples.ch01 package and then the paint method of the HiThere applet.

2. Double-click the left margin of the line containing g.drawString(str, xPos, 50).

   You can also place the cursor in the line of code and set a breakpoint by selecting **Breakpoint** from the **Edit** menu, typing Ctrl-B, or selecting **Breakpoint** from the pop-up menu.

A breakpoint symbol appears in the margin of the Source pane next to the line in which you set the breakpoint (Figure 108 on page 181).

Figure 108. Breakpoint in the Paint Method

Opening the Debugger
An alternative way of halting your program and opening the debugger is to insert the halt method in your Java code. Like the inspect method, the halt method is useful if you have a difficult-to-debug program that should not be interrupted with breakpoints. However, it is most useful in debugging inner classes where you cannot set breakpoints. To halt your program and open the debugger insert the following code in your program:
com.ibm.uvm.tools.DebugSupport.halt();

Removing Breakpoints

Once a breakpoint is set, you can remove it at any time, including while you are debugging the code that contains the breakpoint. If you remove a breakpoint from a method while the thread it is in is suspended, the debugger does not drop to the top of the method.

To remove a breakpoint in source code, double-click its symbol in the margin of the pane. You can remove breakpoints from any Source pane (not just the Source pane in the Breakpoints page in the debugger).

If you are in the Breakpoints page, you can also use the clear toolbar buttons to clear breakpoints.

Disabling Breakpoints

Suppose you want to run a program that has breakpoints set throughout its code, but you do not want the debugger to open during this execution of the program. You can disable the breakpoints by clicking the **Enable Breakpoints** toolbar button so that it is in the "up" position. The IDE ignores all breakpoints it encounters (although the debugger may still launch for other reasons, such as an uncaught exception). All debugger symbols in the margin of Source panes change color from blue to grey.

To reenable all breakpoints in the workspace, click the **Enable Breakpoints** button so that it is in the "down" position.

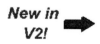
New in V2!

Conditional Breakpoints

Conditional breakpoints are breakpoints that suspend code and open the debugger only when certain conditions are met. For example, you can set a breakpoint to suspend code only if a variable's value falls within a particular range of values.

To set conditions on the breakpoint in the paint method, click mouse button 2 on the breakpoint symbol, and select **Modify** from the pop-up menu. Enter xPos == 50 and click **OK** (Figure 109). The debugger opens on this breakpoint only if the xPos variable is equal to 50.

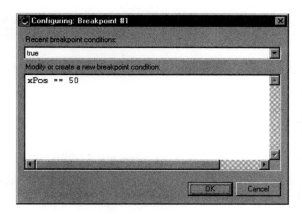

Figure 109. Conditional Breakpoint Configuring Dialog Box

In the Configuring dialog box (Figure 109), you can select a condition, or you can type in your own condition. The dialog box contains up to 10 conditions you have previously set on breakpoints. If the condition is evaluated to a boolean value of true, VisualAge for Java suspends the code and opens the debugger.

You can also configure a breakpoint to run a Java statement and then return true or false. For example, when the IDE encounters the breakpoint, you can have it output a message and then evaluate to false and not suspend the code (Figure 110 on page 184).

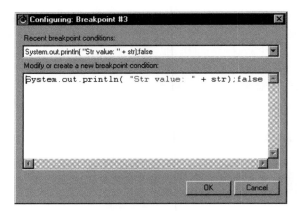

Figure 110. Conditional Breakpoint Configuring Dialog Box: Printing Diagnostics

Code Assist
The text entry field in the Conditional Breakpoint dialog has Code Assist. If you type in the start of a package or class name, you can press **Ctrl+Spacebar** to get a pop-up list of available classes, methods, and fields. Select the desired class, method, or field by continuing to type or by using the arrow keys, and press Enter.

New in
V2!

Caught Exceptions

If an exception is thrown while a program is running in the IDE, and the program does not catch it, usually the IDE debugger opens and the offending thread is suspended. However, if the program catches the exception, the debugger will not open, and the program will continue. Even if the program outputs the stack trace when it catches the exception, you might not be able to determine the exception's origin.

To facilitate debugging, the IDE debugger lets you effectively set breakpoints on types of exceptions. Therefore any time an exception of a certain type or a subtype of that exception is thrown, the JVM suspends the thread that threw the exception and opens the debugger. The suspended thread will be of the form className (Exception Caught) exceptionclassname.

Follow these steps to select a type of exception to be caught by the debugger:

1. Select **Debug→Caught Exceptions** from the **Window** menu or click the **Caught Exceptions** toolbar button in the debugger.

2. From the list of available exception types (Figure 111), enable the checkboxes of the types of exceptions on which you want to set breakpoints. Remember that all subtypes of an exception are caught, so if you select **java.lang.Exception**, all exceptions thrown will cause the program to suspend.

3. Click **OK**.

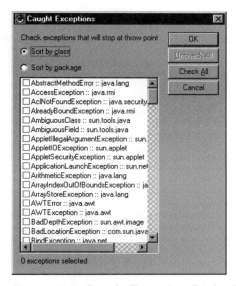

Figure 111. Caught Exceptions Dialog Box

Now when you run a program that throws an exception (of the types you selected), the thread is suspended and the debugger browser opens, regardless of whether the program catches the exception.

The handleException Method

When VisualAge generates the code in the Visual Composition Editor, it generates a handleException method for each class. This method is called when any generated code throws an exception. By default the body of this method is commented out, and you will not see exceptions being thrown.

By removing the comment symbols from the lines in handleException, you can see the message and stack trace for each exception that causes handleException to be run. Thus it is easy to spot problems during development, although many exceptions may be displayed, especially if you have many property-to-property connections where one side of the connection is not initialized when the program starts. It is possible to catch these exceptions within the user code section of the connection itself.

External Debug

New in V2!

VisualAge for Java Version 2 can run programs that dynamically load and run external classes. External classes are classes that have not been imported into the workspace, but rather reside in a class, Zip, or JAR file on the file system. The path to the file must be part of the class path for the program or the workspace.

If you want to debug such a program, you have the option of setting breakpoints on methods in the external classes. Follow these steps to set a breakpoint on a method in an external class:

1. Select **Debug→External .class file breakpoints** from the **Window** menu, or click the **External Breakpoints** toolbar button in the debugger browser.

2. The External Method Breakpoints dialog box shows a list of methods available for setting breakpoints. Add methods to the list by clicking **Add**.

3. The Add External Methods dialog looks into class, Zip, and JAR files and lets you select methods of classes within those files to add to the list of methods available for setting breakpoints. To access methods in a .class file:

   a. Click **Directory**.

   b. Browse through the file system to the directory that contains the .class files in which you want to set breakpoints.

To access methods in a .class file that has been archived:

a. Click **Archive.**

b. Select **Zip Files** (*.zip) or **Jar Files** (*.jar) in the Files of Type drop-down list.

c. Browse to the archive file that contains the .class files in which you want to set breakpoints.

The dialog lists all of the class files in the selected directory or archive. Select a file to see the list of methods available for setting breakpoints.

4. If you want to add one of the listed methods to the list of methods available for setting breakpoints, enable its checkbox.

5. When you have selected all of the methods you want, click **OK**. The list of methods in the External Method Breakpoints dialog box now shows the methods you selected.

6. To set a breakpoint on one of these methods, enable its checkbox.

7. Click **OK** to exit the dialog.

Figure 112 on page 188 shows the dialogs used to set external breakpoints. As you can see, the breakpoints are set at the method level, not on individual statements. To see the source for the external file in the debugger, the Java code must be available and included in the *Source path for dynamically loaded classes* setting in the Debugging section of the Options dialog. Once the breakpoint is set, any thread that calls it will be suspended when the method is entered. External breakpoints cannot be conditional and do not display the breakpoint symbol in the Source pane margin.

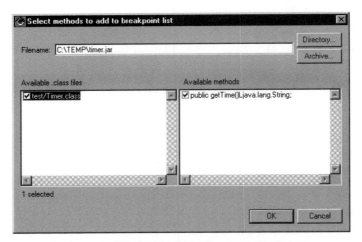

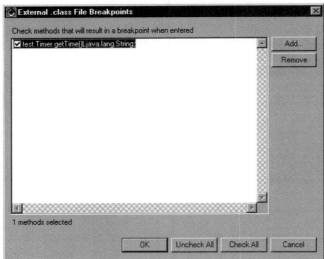

Figure 112. External Method Breakpoint Dialogs

Removing External Debug Breakpoints

To remove a breakpoint from an external method, clear its checkbox in the External Method Breakpoints dialog. You can leave the method on the list so that it is easily accessible if you want to set the breakpoint again later. If you want to remove the method from the list, however, select it and click **Remove**.

Generating a Class Trace

New in
V2! The debugger generates a trace of class loading and initialization if you enable the Class Trace option. The class trace is useful for determining which classes your program uses and can help in debugging.

The trace is enabled through the **Trace class initialization for running programs** option in the Debugging section of the Options dialog.

> **Performance and the Class Trace Option**
> When the Class Trace option is enabled, some processing time is required to compute and store the trace. As a result, the program may run significantly more slowly.

To see the trace, select the program (not a thread) in the All Programs/Threads pane of the debugger. The trace is shown in the Source pane.

6 Finishing the ATM Application

You can promote code reuse and make your applications easy to maintain and change by creating applications that are made up of distinct pieces or components. This is true for both nonvisual beans and the GUI of your applications.

In this chapter you will finish constructing the ATM application. You use the model that you built in "Building the ATM Model" on page 68 as well as the knowledge you gained using the Visual Composition Editor and Swing classes in Chapter 4, "Building User Interfaces".

You finish the ATM application by building separate panels and then composing them together to create the final application.

ATM Application

You are now ready to construct and combine the panels for the ATM application following the design in "ATM Application" on page 49. This chapter is all about creating and then combining user interface components and subpanels to produce a final application.

The ATM is a fairly complex application consisting of several different panels. First you need the infrastructure that will provide the data transfer and reusable beans for your application. The first bean you build is the AtmController, that manages the application flow and provides the mechanism for data transfer between the different panels. After you have constructed the AtmController, you will build the main window, AtmView; some reusable beans (Keypad, AtmButtonPanel, and AtmNamePanel); and the panels that make up the ATM application.

Finally you will combine the panels on a panel, using CardLayout in the AtmView. Figure 113 shows the relationships among the Controller on the AtmView and the ControllerVariable on each panel as well as the addition of each panel to the MainPanel.

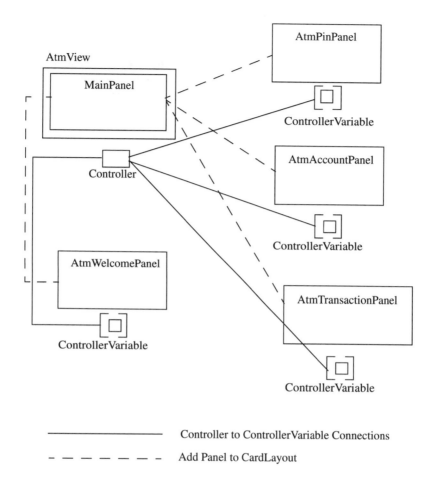

AtmView

MainPanel

Controller

AtmWelcomePanel

AtmPinPanel

ControllerVariable

AtmAccountPanel

ControllerVariable

AtmTransactionPanel

ControllerVariable

ControllerVariable

——————————— Controller to ControllerVariable Connections

— — — — — — — Add Panel to CardLayout

Figure 113. Relationships among Panels in the ATM Application

AtmController

The AtmController manages the flow of the ATM application, using a CardLayout variable, and provides the data transfer between the different panels, using Bank, Card, Customer, and Account beans or variables. In addition the AtmController exposes several methods (next, previous, and exit) to navigate through the application.

To create the AtmController, create a new class, AtmController, that extends Object in the package, itso.atm.view. If you did not create the itso.atm.view package in "Creating Packages" on page 35, create it now. Type itso.atm.view in the *Package* field in the Create Class SmartGuide to create the package.

Open the AtmController in the Visual Composition Editor and add the Beans Listed in Table 6 to the free-form surface. The bean type is selected in the Choose Bean dialog when you are adding the beans to the free-form surface. Make sure you check that you are adding a variable or a bean as directed in the instructions as you work through the examples.

Note that there is no visual representation of the bean on the free-form surface: this is not a visual bean.

Table 6. AtmController Beans

Bean Name	Class Name	Bean Type
LayoutVariable	java.awt.CardLayout	Variable
Bank	itso.atm.model.Bank	Class
CustomerVariable	itso.atm.model.Customer	Variable
CardVariable	itso.atm.model.Card	Variable
AccountVariable	itso.atm.model.BankAccount	Variable

Adding Classes and Variables
Make sure you check the Bean Type setting when adding classes and variables or serialized beans. The setting remembers the previous type. For example, if you are dropping a class after a variable, you have to explicitly set the Bean Type to Class.
You can drop a class or an interface as a variable and then initialize it or call static methods on it. You cannot drop a variable on the visual portion of the bean on the free-form surface.
You can also drop instances of serialized beans that read their state from a file.

After you add the beans, the free-form surface should look like that in Figure 114. Note the angle brackets around the variables on the free-form surface. Now save the bean, using **Bean→Save Bean**.

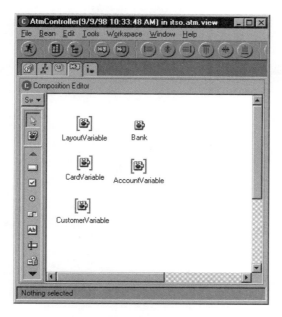

Figure 114. AtmController Free-Form Surface

Promotion

The VisualAge for Java promotion function takes a feature on a bean on the free-form surface and promotes it to the BeanInfo interface of the container bean that holds it.

In this example, all of the beans you added to the AtmController free-form surface will have their this property promoted. Therefore other beans can access the promoted beans directly. In the application you will tear off the promoted beans that you need in each panel.

Previously Promoted Features
When you are working with the Promote Feature dialog, you do not see any of the previously promoted features. These features are accessed through the BeanInfo page of the container bean. This is a change from Version 1 where promotion information is maintained in the Visual Composition Editor.

Select each of the beans you just added to the free-form surface and promote the this property. Select the bean, press mouse button 2, and select **Promote Bean Feature** (Figure 115).

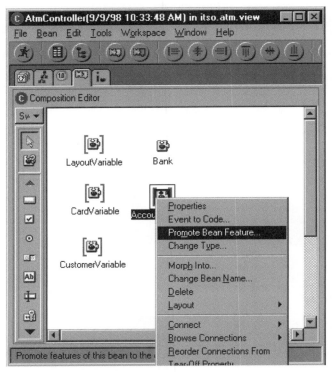

Figure 115. Promoting the AccountVariable this Property

Make sure that the **Properties** radio button is selected, select the this property, click on the **>>** button, and then click **OK** (Figure 116).

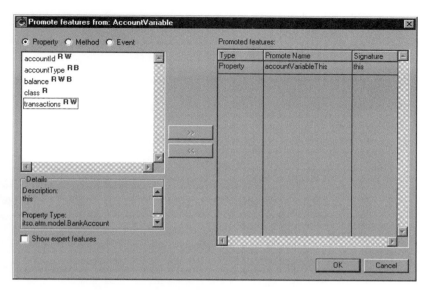

Figure 116. The Promotion Dialog for the AccountVariable this Property

On the BeanInfo page add two new readable and writeable property features to the AtmController bean:

Name	Type	Bound
container	java.awt.Container	false
frame	com.sun.java.swing.JFrame	false

Add three new method features to the AtmController bean:

Name	Return Type	Parameters
exit	void	0
next	void	0
previous	void	0

The method bodies for the three method features are:

```
public void exit()
{
    getFrame().dispose();
    System.exit(0);
```

```
}
public void next()
{
    getLayoutVariable().next( getContainer());
}
public void previous()
{
    getLayoutVariable().previous( getContainer());
}
```

 Create Method and Method Feature Shortcuts
A quick way of creating method features is to go to the Source
pane in the Methods, BeanInfo, or Hierarchy page and type the
new method over existing methods. Then go back to the BeanInfo
page and add the method features, using **Add Available
Features**.
To create a method you can type over an existing method or enter
the complete method in the class declaration. To replace a method,
use **Shift-Control-S** to save and replace (as long as you have not
changed the *Accelerator keys for saving methods* option in the
Options dialog box).

The AtmController is now ready to be used in the ATM application!

AtmView

The AtmView is the main window of the ATM application (Figure 117). It is a
subtype of JFrame and holds the AtmController as well as the MainPanel, that
uses CardLayout and holds the subpanels. The AtmView also provides a
scrolling marquee, at the bottom of the window, that can show
advertisements or instructions. Before creating the AtmView you have to
create the scrolling marquee or Ticker.

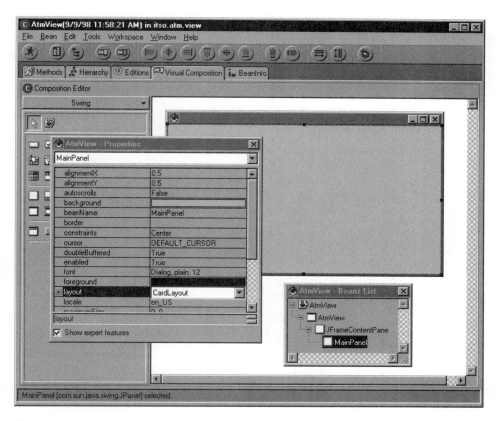

Figure 117. The AtmView

Creating the Ticker Bean

The Ticker is a generic marquee that scrolls text from right to left. It extends the JPanel class and holds the message property feature.

To create the Ticker, create a new class, itso.atm.view.Ticker, that inherits from com.sun.java.swing.JPanel. Deselect the **Compose the class visually** checkbox. Click **Next** and deselect the **Copy constructors from superclass** checkbox. Click the **Add** button to the right of the *Which interfaces should this class implement* area. Enter or select **Runnable** and then click **Add** then **Close**. Click on **Finish** to create the class. By selecting Runnable you have instructed VisualAge for Java to create a stub for the method defined in the Runnable interface, run.

Open the class in the Class Browser and add the following attribute to the class declaration:

```
private int xOffset = getSize().width;
```

Switch to the BeanInfo page. Add a read-write property feature with message as the *Property name* and java.lang.String as the *Property type*. Because the bean does not need to send an event when this property is changed, you can uncheck the **bound** checkbox. Click **Finish** to create the property.

Switch to the Methods page. Create a paint method with the following signature and body:

```
public void paint(java.awt.Graphics g)
{
    int fSize = getFont().getSize();
    java.awt.FontMetrics fm = getFontMetrics(getFont());
    int xMin = -fm.stringWidth(getMessage());
    int yOffset = (getSize().height - fSize) / 2 + fSize;
    g.clearRect( 0, 0, getSize().width, getSize().height);
    g.drawString(getMessage(), xOffset, yOffset);
    xOffset -= 1;
    if (xOffset < xMin) {
        xOffset = getSize().width;
    }
}
```

Create a default constructor for the Ticker, using the following code:

```
public Ticker() {
    super();
    if( !java.beans.Beans.isDesignTime()){
        setMessage("");
        Thread paintThread = new Thread(this);
        paintThread.start();
    }
}
```

The java.beans.Beans.isDesignTime() method queries the current environment. If it is a runtime environment, the Ticker will run. If you are using the bean in a builder such as VisualAge for Java, there is no point in having the text scroll.

Fill in the run method body:

```
public void run() {
    while (true) {
    repaint();
    try {
        Thread.sleep(10);
    }
    catch (InterruptedException e)
        { } // if the thread is interrupted (woken early) it does not matter
    }
```

}

Testing the Ticker

To test the Ticker (Figure 118), open the Scrapbook and enter the following code:

```
com.sun.java.swing.JFrame f = new com.sun.java.swing.JFrame();
itso.atm.view.Ticker t = new itso.atm.view.Ticker();
t.setMessage("This is a message");
f.getContentPane().add("Center", t);
f.setSize( new java.awt.Dimension(300, 100));
f.show();
```

Figure 118. Testing the Ticker

 **Test Code in the main() Method**
You can place the code for testing the Ticker in the main() method of the class, so to test the class you simply run it.
This is a good strategy for visual beans; the simple test case stays with the class, and the class is easily tested.

How the Ticker Works

In order for the Ticker to work, you must separate the process of repainting the message from the rest of the program by using a thread. The *thread* executes in the same memory space as the rest of the program.

Java supports multithreading through the Thread class. Thus, you can separate your program into independently running sections, or threads. Multiple threads make your program more responsive to user interaction or able to perform actions (such as the scrolling text) that require processing in real time. To create a thread in your program, you create an object of the Thread class.

Objects that can run as threads implement the Runnable interface that provides the run method — the method called when you invoke start on a thread.

Creating and Adding Beans to the AtmView

Create a new class, AtmView, that extends com.sun.java.swing.JFrame. Open AtmView in the Visual Composition Editor and select **JFrameContentPane** (the panel on the frame). Open the Property sheet for JFrameContentPane and set *layout* to BorderLayout.

Drop an instance of the Ticker bean (make sure to select the **Class** Bean Type) into the South portion of the JFrameContentPane. Once the cursor is loaded with the Ticker, hold down mouse button 1 as you move the cursor over the JFrameContentPane. You should see bounding boxes for each of the portions of the BorderLayout. Drop the bean when the rectangle is in the South portion of the MainPanel. If you do not get it right, you can always change the *constraint* property in the Property sheet for the Ticker. In the Ticker Property sheet set the *preferredSize* to 10,20 and the *message* to: "Welcome to the ATM, this week get a 5% mortgage rate! Apply Now!". You will not see *preferredSize*, which is an expert feature, unless you select the **Show expert features** checkbox on the Property sheet.

Add a JPanel to the Center portion of the JFrameContentPane. Set the new panel's *beanName* to MainPanel and *layout* to CardLayout.

Adding Beans or Variables to the Free-Form Surface
It is extremely important that you add the correct form of a class throughout the examples in the book. If the text says add a bean or an instance, you are adding an instance of a bean, and you select **Class** for the *Bean Type*. If the text says add a variable, you are adding an attribute that will reference another instance, and you select **Variable** for the *Bean Type*.
Whenever you add something from the palette, except the variable "bean" itself, it is always a bean, not a variable.
When you are creating your own programs, your design and understanding of the program should make clear what you should add.

Drop an instance of AtmController anywhere on the free-form surface of the AtmView bean and name it Controller. Connect the *layout* property of the MainPanel to the *layoutVariableThis* property of AtmController. Open the Connection Property dialog and set the **Target event** to <none>. Connect the this property of MainPanel to the container property of the AtmController and the this property of the AtmView to the frame property of the AtmController. Figure 119 shows the Visual Composition Editor with the Controller bean and connections.

The AtmView bean (Figure 119) is now ready for the subpanels that make up the flow of the application, but first you have to create some more of the infrastructure: the reusable beans used in the subpanels.

For now, select **Bean→Save Bean** and continue on to build the Keypad.

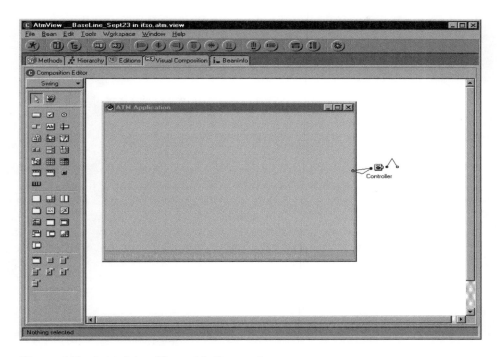

Figure 119. Initial AtmView with Connections

Keypad

The ATM application will use some beans several times. You build these now and then reuse them as you build the other panels.

The Keypad (Figure 120) is a generic keypad that can be used to enter a number. The Keypad consists of 12 buttons (the numbers 0–9, a decimal point, and C for clear). The purpose of the Keypad is to accept button clicks and key presses and build a number that other beans can access.

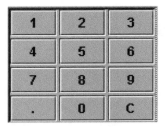

Figure 120. The Keypad

There are many ways to build a keypad. One efficient way is to use an inner class.

Inner Classes

In the JDK 1.0 only top-level classes can be defined, that is, classes cannot be defined within other classes. It turns out that classes defined within other classes, or inner classes, are very powerful tools. They are especially helpful in building the glue or adapter code needed to allow beans to exchange information, especially for callback functionality in event handling where a method is invoked on the listener object. Inner classes can be defined as members of other classes, within a block or (anonymously) within an expression. A complete introduction to inner classes is outside the scope of this book, but many of the newer Java language books and the JDK documentation describe inner classes.

For the ATM you define an inner class named Controller within the Keypad. This inner class can access all the instance information of the enclosing Keypad. The Controller listens for the actionPerformed event from the Keypad buttons and key presses. By using an inner class you keep all code that performs event handling with the rest of the Keypad code while still maintaining a logical separation from the code that implements the Keypad itself. Each Keypad controls access to a single instance of the Controller, using the getController method. Thus the Controller can be added as a listener for events outside the Keypad.

Using an inner class as an adapter, you can create classes that are not linked to a particular means of communicating their state. You can also use an inner class as an adapter to create the correct form for sending and receiving data. Inner classes are used extensively in the JFC.

New in V2! VisualAge for Java supports the import, creation, and use of inner classes. You define inner classes by entering the source code for the inner class within an existing class declaration, block, or expression. If you import a class that defines inner classes, the inner classes show up as classes in the package list.

If you define the inner class within VisualAge for Java or import Java source, the inner class is shown only in the source for the class declaration or in the method where the inner class is defined. The enclosing method or class definition is also returned in a search for an inner class.

Creating the Keypad

The Keypad has one nested inner class, Controller, that handles both button clicks or key presses and sets a string representing the number being entered.

To create the Keypad, follow these steps:

1. Create a Keypad class in the itso.atm.view package that inherits from com.sun.java.swing.JPanel. Make sure the **Compose the class visually** radio button is not selected.

2. Click **Next** and deselect the **Copy constructors from superclass** checkbox, so that VisualAge for Java will not generate all constructors that a JPanel implements. Click **Finish** to create the class and load it in the Class Browser (Figure 121).

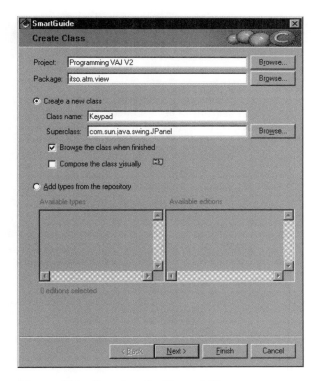

Figure 121. Creating the Keypad Class

3. Switch to the BeanInfo page and create a new property feature:

Name	Type	Bound	Readable	Writeable
valueAsString	java.lang.String	True	True	True

4. Select the setter method (setValueAsString) for the property in the Definitions pane and then change the declaration for the setter to private by typing over the public access modifier in the Source pane.

   When you change the setter to private, beans of other types cannot change the value of the Keypad — which is what you want. You could create the setter manually with the private access modifier, but when you use steps 3 and 4 above, VisualAge for Java generates the property change code for you.

Generating Getter and Setter Methods
You can use the Create Field SmartGuide to add attributes to a class. With this SmartGuide you can specify the modifiers for the field and an initial value and generate getters and setters. You can even specify code in the initial value and invoke a constructor.
You can also add the attribute as a property feature automatically through introspection or (if a BeanInfo class exists) through **Add Available Features**.
You cannot easily make the property bound or constrained, however. If you set *bound* or *constrained* to true in the Bean Information pane, the property will be marked as bound or constrained, but events will not be fired when the property is changed.

5. Select the new property, valueAsString, and in the Property Feature Information pane set *Preferred* to true, then select **Information→Save**. Now the valueAsString property will show up in the preferred list of the Keypad bean.

6. Switch to the Hierarchy page and change the class declaration of Keypad to (you can copy this code from KeypadDeclaration.txt in the sample code):

```
import com.sun.java.swing.*;
import java.awt.event.*;
import java.awt.*;
import java.math.BigDecimal;
```

```
public class Keypad extends JPanel {
    private String[] buttonText = {
        "1", "2", "3", "4", "5", "6", "7", "8", "9", ".", "0", "C"
    };
    private JButton[] button = new JButton[12];
    private String fieldValueAsString = new String();
    private Controller controller = null;
    protected class Controller implements ActionListener, KeyListener{
        public void actionPerformed(ActionEvent e){
            if( ((JButton)e.getSource()).getText().equals( "C")){
                setValueAsString(""); // empty string - no spaces
            }
            else{
                setValueAsString( getValueAsString() +        ((JButton)e.getSource()).getText());
            }
        }
        public void keyTyped(KeyEvent e){
            for( int i = 0; i < button.length; i++){
                if( button[i].getText().charAt(0) == e.getKeyChar()){
                    if( button[i].getText().equals( "C")){
                        setValueAsString( "");
                    }
                    else{
                        setValueAsString( getValueAsString() +
                            button[i].getText());
                    }
                }
            }
        }
        public void keyPressed(KeyEvent e){
        }
        public void keyReleased(KeyEvent e){
        }
    }
}
```

In the above code you defined the inner class, Controller. In VisualAge for Java you define inner classes in source code, not through SmartGuides.

Notice the stub methods for keyPressed and keyReleased. Whenever you implement an interface, in this case KeyListener and ActionListener, you must implement all methods of the interface.

7. Create an access method, getController, in the Keypad class that returns the controller. The Keypad$Controller specifies that the method returns an instance of Controller that is an inner class of Keypad.

```
public Keypad$Controller getController()
{
```

```
    if( controller == null){
        controller = new Controller();
    }
    return controller;
}
```

8. Switch to the BeanInfo page again and add the getController method as a Method Feature, using **Add Available Features** to make it possible for other beans to add the Controller as a KeyListener. You will add keyboard support for the ATM in "Adding Keyboard Input to the ATM Application" on page 246.

9. Add a new method feature, clear, that takes no parameters and has a return type of void with the following method body:

```
public void clear() {
    setValueAsString("");
}
```

10. Create a default constructor for the Keypad and fill in the body:

```
public Keypad()
{
    super();
    setBorder( new com.sun.java.swing.plaf.basic.BasicFieldBorder());
    GridLayout g = new java.awt.GridLayout(4, 3);
    g.setVgap(2);
    g.setHgap(2);
    setLayout(g);
    for( int i = 0; i < button.length; i++){
        button[i] = new JButton( buttonText[i]);
        add( button[i]);
        button[i].addActionListener( getController());
    }
}
```

Notice that the buttons are added to the Keypad through code instead of the Visual Composition Editor and that the event handling connections are also made in code. In some cases coding the user interface is more efficient and more understandable than using the Visual Composition Editor.

Now you have a self-contained Keypad that handles its own events and presents the complete number to other beans, whether the number was entered through the buttons or the keyboard (provided the Controller is added as a KeyListener).

AtmButtonPanel

All ATM panels use the same set of buttons to navigate through the application. This composite bean is made up of Next, Previous, and Exit buttons. The ability to listen for events from the buttons and enable and disable the buttons is provided through promotion.

Building the AtmButtonPanel

Create a new class, itso.atm.view.AtmButtonPanel, which extends com.sun.java.swing.JPanel. Open the class in the Visual Composition Editor, select the panel, set the *layout* to FlowLayout, and add three JButtons. Set the *beanName* and *text* properties as shown in Table 7.

Table 7. AtmButtonPanel Button Properties

beanName	text
PreviousButton	<Previous
NextButton	Next>
ExitButton	Exit

Resize the panel so that it holds the three buttons horizontally and save the bean. For each button, promote the enabled property and the actionPerformed event.

Follow these steps to promote the features for the PreviousButton:

1. Select the button, hold down mouse button 2, and select **Promote Bean feature.**
2. Select the **Property** radio button in the Promote features from dialog box.
3. Select enabled in the list below the Property radio button.
4. Click the **>>** button.
5. Select the **Event** radio button, then select actionPerformed from the list, and click **>>**, to promote the actionPerformed event.
6. Click **OK**.

Repeat steps 1 through 6 for the NextButton and ExitButton, then save the bean. Figure 122 shows the completed AtmButtonPanel.

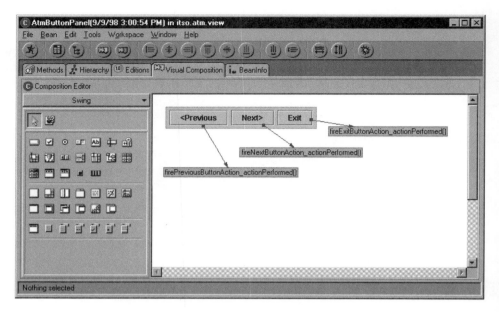

Figure 122. AtmButtonPanel with Promoted Features

AtmNamePanel

The customer name is required in several places in the ATM application. The name is stored as three separate properties in the Customer bean, but it would be nice to access the visual representation with one bean. You create the AtmNamePanel to accomplish this.

Create a new class, itso.atm.view.AtmNamePanel, that extends JPanel. Set the *layout* to FlowLayout and add four JLabels. (Remember that the Sticky function, invoked by holding down the Control key when you select a bean from the palette, allows you to drop more than one bean of a type.) Change the *text* of the first label to Customer Name:. Change the text of the second label to Title; of the third, to First Name; and of the fourth, to Last Name. Resize the panel so that it holds the four labels horizontally and there is a small amount of space around each label.

Drop an itso.atm.model.Customer variable on the free-form surface and name it CustomerVariable. Connect the title, firstName, and lastName properties to the text property of the appropriate JLabels. Select this for the source event to fire the connections and select <none> for the target event (Figure 123). You want this connection to fire as soon as the Customer1 variable is set (the this event fires), and you only want the connection to go one way — from the variable to the labels.

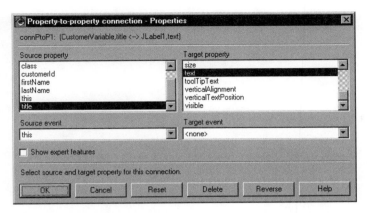

Figure 123. Setting the Source Event for a Property-to-Property Connection

Reversing a Connection
Property-to-property connections have an implied direction that affects which end of the connection is set at initialization. If you want to reverse the direction, click the **Reverse** button in the Connection Properties dialog.
The firing of the event after initialization depends on the source and target events selected.

Finally, save the bean and then promote the this property of the CustomerVariable. Figure 124 shows the finished AtmNamePanel.

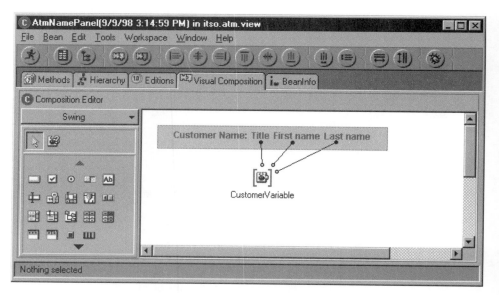

Figure 124. The AtmNamePanel

AtmWelcomePanel

Now you are ready to build your first complete subpanel for the application! The AtmWelcomePanel (Figure 125 on page 213) displays a query for an ATM card ID number.

Figure 125. ATM Application AtmWelcomePanel

Follow these steps to create the AtmWelcomePanel:

1. In the itso.atm.view package create an AtmWelcomePanel class that inherits from com.sun.java.swing.JPanel. Make sure the **Compose the class visually** checkbox is selected. Click **Finish** to create the class and load it in the Visual Composition Editor.

2. In the Visual Composition Editor, select the AtmWelcomePanel and set the *layout* to GridBagLayout. If you are not clear about using the GridBagLayout, see "GridBagLayout" on page 111 and "Adding the GUI Beans" on page 131.

3. Drop a JTextField onto the AtmWelcomePanel. Set the *beanName* to NumberTextField. Open the Property sheet and set *enabled* and *editable* to false, then check that the *background* to white. To set the background to white:

   a. Click in the field containing the current background color.

   b. Click the button that appears at the right end of the field.

   c. Click the **Basic** radio button.

   d. Select **white** from the list.

e. Click **OK**.

Set the *disabledTextColor* to Black.

Set the constraints for the bean as shown in Table 8 on page 214. It is easiest to set each bean's constraints when you are working with the bean. To set the individual constraints, expand the *constraints* property by clicking on the plus sign.

4. Drop a JLabel in the AtmWelcomePanel in the row below the NumberTextField. Set the *beanName* to MessageLabel and the *text* to Please enter your card number. Expand the AtmWelcomePanel as needed while you add beans. Set the constraints for the bean as shown in Table 8 on page 214.

5. Drop an itso.atm.view.Keypad bean below the MessageLabel. Again, set the constraints for the bean as shown in Table 8 on page 214.

6. Drop an itso.atm.view.AtmButtonPanel in the AtmWelcomePanel in the row below the Keypad. Open the Property sheet and set *previousButtonEnabled* to false. Set the constraints for the bean as shown in Table 8 on page 214.

7. If you were not able to position the beans visually, set the gridX and gridY properties of the beans as shown in Table 8.

Table 8. AtmWelcomePanel Bean Constraints

Bean Name	text	anchor	fill	grid X	grid Y
NumberTextField	N/A	WEST	HORIZONTAL	0	0
MessageLabel	Please enter your card number.	WEST	HORIZONTAL	0	1
Keypad1	N/A	WEST	BOTH	0	2
AtmButtonPanel1	N/A	WEST	HORIZONTAL	0	3

Leave all other constraints as the default values.

8. Drop an AtmController on the free-form surface with a Bean Type of **Variable** and name it ControllerVariable.

Now you have all the beans on the surface (Figure 126 on page 215). You have to connect them as well as add one method to the bean:

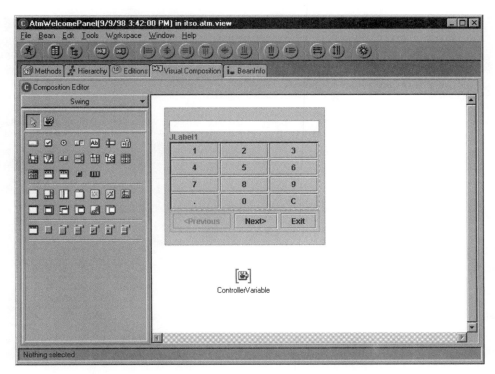

Figure 126. AtmWelcomePanel with Beans

1. Tear off the bank property, the cardVariableThis property and the customerVariableThis property from the ControllerVariable. Name them BankVariable, CardVariable, and CustomerVariable. Tearing off the properties will generate three property-to-property connections and three variables on the free-form surface. You can drag these connections and variables anywhere on the free-form surface to make the display more understandable.

2. Connect the valueAsString property of Keypad1 to the text property of the NumberTextField.

3. Connect the AtmButtonPanel1.exitButtonAction_actionPerformed(java.awt.event ActionEvent) event to the exit method on the ControllerVariable.

4. Connect the AtmButtonPanel1.nextButtonAction_actionPerformed(java.awt.event ActionEvent) event to the validCard method on the BankVariable.

5. Connect the valueAsString property of Keypad1 to the cardParam parameter on the connection in Step 4.

6. Save the bean, using **Bean→Save Bean**, so that you can use the generated code in an event-to-code connection in step 7.

7. Create an event-to-code connection from the normalResult (Figure 127 on page 216) of the event-to-method connection in Step 4 (nextButtonAction_actionPerformed event to the validCard method) by selecting the connection, selecting **Connect→normalResult** from the pop-up menu, clicking on any empty area on the free-form surface, and selecting **Event To Code**.

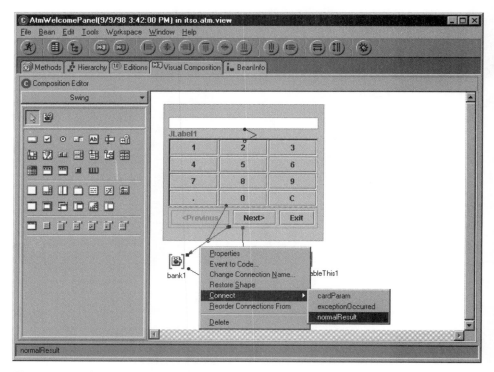

Figure 127. Connecting from the Normal Result of a Connection

8. Make sure the **Pass event data** checkbox is selected and replace the code in the Event-to-Code dialog (Figure 128 on page 217) with the following code:

```
public void checkCardResult(itso.atm.model.Card arg1) {
    if( arg1 != null){
        setCardVariable( arg1);
        getControllerVariable().next();
        setCustomerVariable( getBankVariable().getCustomer( arg1));
        getKeypad1().clear();
    }
    else{
        getMessageLabel().setText("Invalid Card Number, try again");
    }
```

}

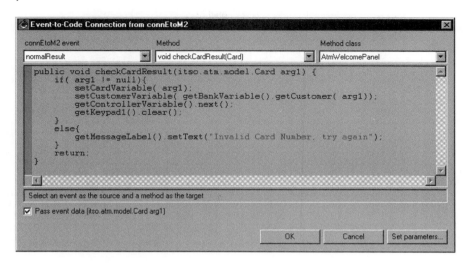

Figure 128. Event-to-Code Dialog Box

9. Save the bean and promote the ControllerVariable this property.

Note how the customer variable is set in code of the checkCardResult method.

Figure 129 shows the Visual Composition Editor with the completed AtmWelcomePanel. Save and test the appearance of the panel by clicking the **Run** button. Remember that this is your first panel, so the Next button is not going to do much yet. Test each panel as you complete it, using the **Run** button. Not only do you catch errors early, you see that you are actually completing something!

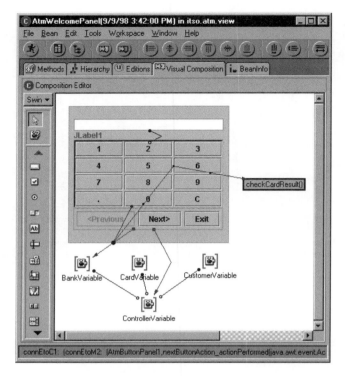

Figure 129. The AtmWelcomePanel

AtmPinPanel

The AtmPinPanel (Figure 130 on page 219) enables users to enter the PIN associated with their ATM card. The AtmPinPanel is very similar to the AtmWelcomePanel.

Adding Beans of the Same Type
You can use the drop-down list in the Interface/Class name field of the Choose Bean dialog to add recently used beans to the free-form surface.

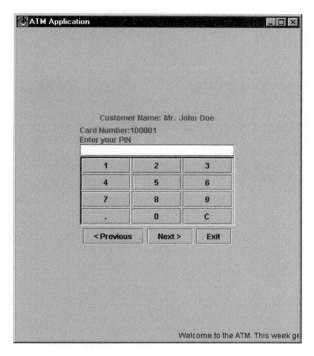

Figure 130. ATM Application AtmPinPanel

Create a new class, AtmPinPanel, that extends JPanel. Open the AtmPinPanel in the Visual Composition Editor and set the *layout* to GridBagLayout.

Now that you have progressed this far in the book, you do not need the same level of detail that you needed earlier in the book. The instructions in the rest of the book are less detailed and often in table form. You should also resize the panels as needed when you are adding beans.

Drop the visual beans listed in Table 9 on page 220 on the visual part of the panel and set their properties as shown. The N/A in some table cells indicates that you do not need to enter a value for cells in the column. For example, in the *beanName* column, N/A means you can accept the default name that VisualAge for Java assigns. Use the placement of the GUI beans on the accompanying figures to determine where to place a bean. Figure 131 on page 221 shows the GUI beans on the ATMPinPanel.

When you use the Choose Bean tool to add visual beans to the visual representation of the primary bean, the Bean Type is always Class. When you add a bean from the palette, the Bean Type is implicitly Class.

Table 9. Visual Beans in the AtmPinPanel

beanName	Interface/ Class Name	text	anchor	fill	gridX	gridy	gridWidth
N/A	AtmName Panel	N/A	WEST	HORIZONTAL	0	0	2
N/A	JLabel	Card Number:	WEST	HORIZONTAL	0	1	1
CardNumber Label	JLabel	N/A	CENTER	HORIZONTAL	1	1	1
MsgLabel	JLabel	Please enter Your PIN number	WEST	HORIZONTAL	0	2	2
PinTextField	JTextField	N/A	WEST	HORIZONTAL	0	3	2
N/A	Keypad	N/A	WEST	BOTH	0	4	2
N/A	AtmButton Panel	N/A	WEST	HORIZONTAL	0	5	2

Note: For a more realistic ATM you should make the PinTextField a JPasswordField once you have tested the application. This way the PIN is not echoed back to the screen.

The Morph Into Function
Although **Morph Into** was designed primarily to help migrate from AWT to Swing components, you can use it to change a class into a variable and vice versa. If you make a mistake and drop a variable instead of a class, use **Morph Into** from the pop-up menu to change the bean to the correct bean type.

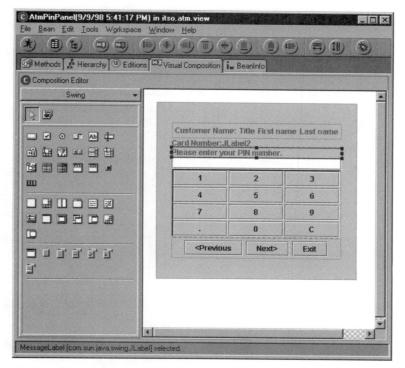

Figure 131. AtmPinPanel with Visual Beans

Open the Property sheet for the PinTextField and set *enabled* and *editable* to false, *background* to white, and *disabledTextColor* to Black.

Now you need to add a controller to the free-form surface. Drop a variable called ControllerVariable of type AtmController, tear off the cardVariableThis property, and rename it CardVariable.

Now make the connections shown in Table 10. In the table, the *Connection from* and *Connection to* columns show bean_name,feature or bean_name,feature.method, for example, CardVariable,pincheck.handleValidPin. This corresponds to the way connections are shown in the status area at the bottom of the Visual Composition Editor window. For clarity, the connections in the figures are arranged quite differently from the way they are drawn when you connect beans. If you use different naming conventions for beans or create an incorrect number of beans, the connection tables and descriptions will show names that differ from the names you see in your session. If this is a problem, you can load the sample code and follow it instead.

Table 10. AtmPinPanel Connections

Connection Number in Figure 133	Connection Type	Connection from	Connection to	Comments
1	EtoM	AtmButtonPanel1, exitButtonAction _actionPerformed	ControllerVariable, exit()	Exit the application.
2	EtoM	AtmButtonPanel1, nextButtonAction _actionPerformed	CardVariable, checkPin(String)	Check the Pin number (parameter from connection 3).
3	PfromP	Connection 2 parameter: apinEntered	Keypad1, valueAsString	Supply pin number to the checkPin method.
4	PtoP	KeyPad1, valueAsString	PinTextField,text	Connect current Keypad value to text field.
5	EtoM	AtmButtonPanel1, previousButtonAction _actionPerformed	ControllerVariable, previous()	Return to the previous application panel.
6	EtoM	CardVariable, pinchecked. handleValidPin	ControllerVariable, next()	Go to the next application panel.
7	EtoM	CardVariable, pinchecked. handleInValidPin	MsgLabel,text	Set the connection parameter to: Invalid Pin, please try again. The process is explained immediately following this table.
8	PtoP	ControllerVariable, CustomerVariableThis	AtmNamePanel1, customerVariableThis	Show the customer name in the panel. Use customerVariableT his as the source event and set the target event as none.
9	PtoP	CardVariable, cardNumber	CardNumberLabel, text	Source Event: this Target Event: None

Connection Number in Figure 133	Connection Type	Connection from	Connection to	Comments
10	*PtoP*	*ControllerVariable, CardVariableThis*	*CardVariable,this*	*Automatically generated by tear off*

Notes:
1. You can deduce the type of feature from the connection type, where P stands for property, E for Event, M for Method, and C for Code.
2. Connections automatically generated by VisualAge for Java are shown in *italic*.

To set the connections parameter in Connection 7, double-click the connection (not on one of the black squares used to move the connection) and click **Set Parameters** in the Connection Properties dialog. Enter the text for the parameter and then click **OK** in the Constant Parameter Value dialog and click **OK** in the Connection Properties dialog.

Now save the bean and promote the ControllerVariable this property.

Add the getKeypad1().clear() method to the connections that call previous() and next(), to clear the current value in the Keypad in case you return to it later. Select the connections (5 and 6 in Figure 133) and note their names in your session.

Switch to the Methods page, select the two methods representing the connections, and add the getKeypad1().clear(); statement in the user code section of the connection code as shown in Figure 132 for the previous() connection.

The completed AtmPinPanel with the connections in Table 10 is shown in Figure 133 on page 225.

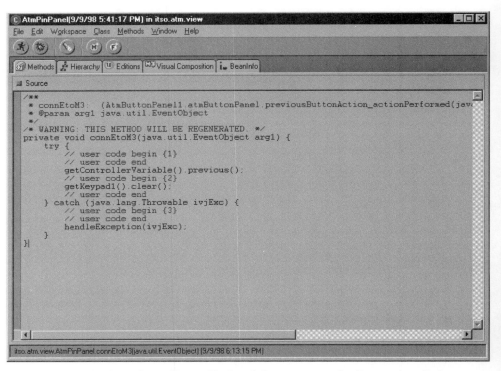

Figure 132. Adding the getKeypad().clear() Statement to the Connection Code

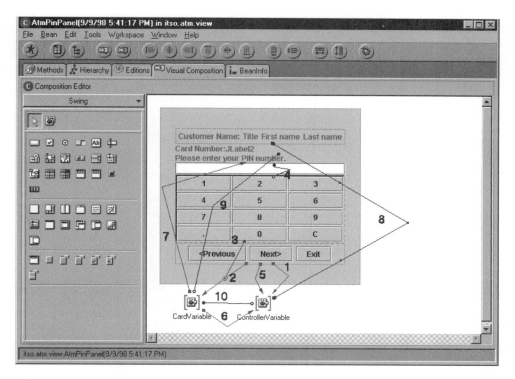

Figure 133. AtmPinPanel with Connections

AtmAccountPanel

The AtmAccountPanel (Figure 134) enables users to choose the account they want to perform transactions on once the PIN is validated.

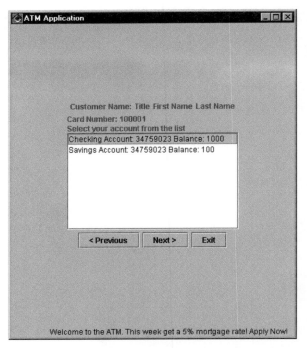

Figure 134. ATM Application AtmAccountPanel

Create a new class, AtmAccountPanel, that inherits from JPanel. Once again the panel uses GridBagLayout.

Working with Layouts, Lists, Panels, and Panes
To be able to scroll a JList, it must be embedded in a JScrollPane. If you drop a JScrollPane or a panel directly into a container that is using a layout manager, it is extremely difficult to manipulate it because its size is effectively zero. To work around this, drop panels and panes outside the container and add beans to them before moving them into the final container.

Drop a JScrollPane on the free-form surface and name it ScrollPane. Drop a JList inside the ScrollPane. In Table 11, ScrollPane refers to the ScrollPane you just constructed. Use the Beans List to move the ScrollPane into the AtmAccountPanel and set the properties once it is within the panel.

Add the visual beans in Table 11 to the AtmAccountPanel.

Table 11. Visual Beans in the AtmAccountPanel

Bean Name	Interface/ Class Name	text	anchor	fill	grid X	gridy	gridWidth
N/A	AtmName Panel	N/A	WEST	HORIZONTAL	0	0	2
N/A	JLabel	Card Number:	WEST	HORIZONTAL	0	1	1
CardNumber Label	JLabel	N/A	CENTER	HORIZONTAL	1	1	1
MsgLabel	JLabel	Please select your account.	WEST	HORIZONTAL	0	2	2
ScrollPane	Composite	N/A	WEST	BOTH	0	3	2
N/A	AtmButton Panel	N/A	WEST	HORIZONTAL	0	4	2

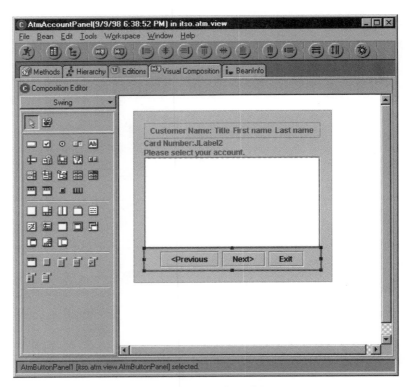

Figure 135. AtmAccountPanel with Visual Beans

You do not want users to be able to click **Next** until they select an account, so set the *nextButtonEnabled* property in the AtmButtonPanel to false.

Drop an AtmController variable on the free-form surface and name it ControllerVariable. Drop a com.sun.java.swing.DefaultListModel bean on the free-form surface and name it ListModel. Be careful that you create the ControllerVariable as a variable and the ListModel as a bean, that is, with a Bean Type of **Class**.

Tear off the cardVariableThis and the accountVariableThis properties from the ControllerVariable and name them, respectively, CardVariable and AccountVariable.

Now create the connections in Table 12 to complete the AtmAccountPanel (Figure 136 on page 231).

Table 12. AtmAccountPanel Connections

Connection Number in Figure 136	Connection Type	Connection from	Connection to	Comments
1	PtoP	CardVariable, cardNumber	CardNumberLabel, text	Source event: this Target event: None
2	EtoC	CardVariable,this	new fillList method	Described in the text that follows this table.
3	EtoM	AtmButtonPanel1, exitButtonAction _actionPerformed	AtmController, exit()	Exit the application.
4	EtoM	AtmButtonPanel1, previousButtonAction _actionPerformed	AtmController, previous()	Return to the previous application panel.
5	PtoP	ListModel,this	JList1,model	Set the model for the JList.
6	EtoM	JList1, valueChanged	AtmButtonPanel1, nextButtonEnabled	Set the parameter on this connection to true.
7	PtoP	ControllerVariable, customerVariableThis	AtmNamePanel1, customerVariableThis	Show the customer name in the panel.
8	EtoM	AtmButtonPanel1, nextButtonAction _actionPerformed	AccountVariable, this	Set the account object (parameter from Connection 9).
9	PfromP	connection 8 parameter	JList1, selectedValue	Account selected in list instantiates Account object.
10	EtoM	AtmButtonPanel1, nextButtonAction _actionPerformed	AtmController, next()	Go to the next application panel.
11	*PtoP*	*ControllerVariable, CardVariableThis*	*CardVariable, this*	*Automatically generated by tear off*

Connection Number in Figure 136	Connection Type	Connection from	Connection to	Comments
12	*PtoP*	*ControllerVariable, accountVariableThis*	*AccountVariable, this*	*Automatically generated by tear off*

Notes:
1. You can deduce the type of feature from the connection type, where P stands for property, E for Event, M for Method, and C for Code.
2. Connections automatically generated by VisualAge for Java are shown in *italic*.

Reordering Connections
Connections from a bean are fired in the order in which they were created. Quite often this is not what you want to happen. To reorder connections, select the bean and select **Reorder Connections** from the pop-up menu. The connections are listed in firing order, and you can reorder them by dragging them before or after other connections.

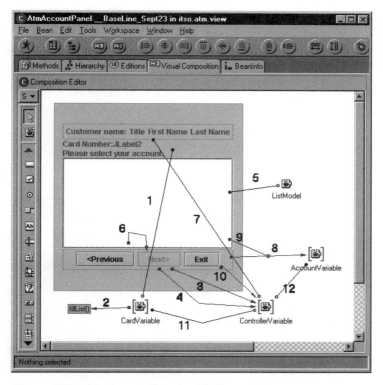

Figure 136. AtmAccountPanel with Connections

Save the bean and then enter the following code for the method created in the event-to-code (EtoC) connection (connection 2 in Table 12):

```
public void fillList(itso.atm.model.Card arg1) {
   getListModel().clear(); // clear the list first
   for( int i = 0; i < arg1.getAccounts().size(); i++){
      getListModel().addElement( arg1.getAccounts().elementAt(i));
   }
}
```

The valueChanged events from the JList indicate that a list element has been selected or deselected. You only want to respond to events that indicate that an item has been selected.

Find the method containing connection 6 (that enables the Next button) by saving the bean, selecting the connection on the free-form surface, and looking in the status line at the bottom of the Visual Composition Editor window. You will see a status line similar to this: connEtoM3: (JLIst1,valueChanged--> AtmButtonPanel1,nextButtonEnabled) selected. The that contains the selection shown in the status line is: void connEtoM3(com.sun.java.swing.event.ListSelectionEvent).

To locate the method, you can also select the connection, and the corresponding method is then highlighted in the Beans List.

Open the method in your environment that contains connection 6. In the first user code section (see Figure 137) enter the following code:

```
if(getJList1().isSelectionEmpty()){
    getAtmButtonPanel1().setNextButtonEnabled(false);
    return;
}
```

VisualAge for Java provides user code sections so that you can associate logic with the firing of the connection. Add only simple, connection-related logic (such as setting a wait cursor) in the user code sections.

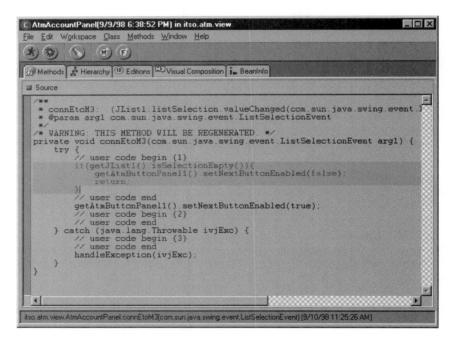

Figure 137. Checking for a Selected Item in JList1

Call the getJList1().clearSelection() method in the two connections that call getControllerVariable().next and getControllerVariable().previous. Figure 138 shows the clear statement in the connection to the next method. Make sure that the connection that calls getControllerVariable().next (connection 10) is invoked after the connection that calls setAccountVariableThis() (connection 9).

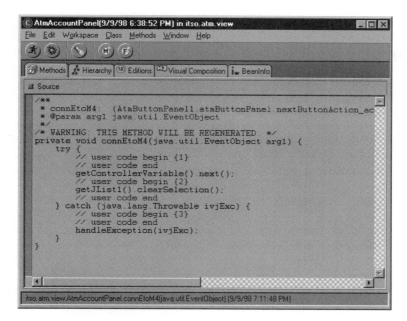

Figure 138. Clearing the List Selection in the AtmAccountPanel

Now save the bean and promote the ControllerVariable this property.

AtmTransactionPanel

The AtmTransactionPanel is where users deposit and withdraw amounts from their accounts (Figure 139 on page 234). The panel is similiar to those you have already created. It has buttons to select the type of transaction and lists the history of transactions that the user has already completed.

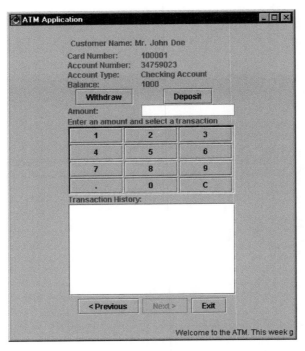

Figure 139. ATM Application AtmTransactionPanel

As usual, create the itso.atm.view.AtmTransactionPanel as a subtype of JPanel and use the GridBagLayout. Drop the visual beans in Table 13 onto the panel (see Figure 140), using the properties listed in the table. Resize the panel as needed to hold all of the beans.

To create the ScrollPane bean you will use in Table 13, drop a JScrollpane named ScrollPane onto the free-form surface, and add a JList to it (see "AtmAccountPanel" on page 225).

Table 13. Visual Beans in the AtmTransactionPanel

Bean Name	Interface/ Class Name	text	anchor	fill	grid X	gridy	gridWidth
N/A	AtmName Panel	N/A	WEST	HORIZONTAL	0	0	2
N/A	JLabel	Card Number:	WEST	NONE	0	1	1
CardNumberLabel	JLabel	N/A	CENTER	HORIZONTAL	1	1	1

Bean Name	Interface/ Class Name	text	anchor	fill	grid X	gridy	gridWidth
N/A	JLabel	Account Number:	WEST	NONE	0	2	1
AccountNumberLabel	JLabel	N/A	CENTER	HORIZONTAL	1	2	1
N/A	JLabel	Account Type:	WEST	NONE	0	3	1
AccountTypeLabel	JLabel	N/A	CENTER	HORIZONTAL	1	3	1
N/A	JLabel	Balance:	WEST	NONE	0	4	1
BalanceLabel	JLabel	N/A	CENTER	HORIZONTAL	1	4	1
WithdrawButton	JButton	Withdraw	CENTER	NONE	0	5	1
DepositButton	JButton	Deposit	CENTER	NONE	1	5	1
N/A	JLabel	Amount:	WEST	NONE	0	6	1
AmountTextField	JTextField	N/A	CENTER	HORIZONTAL	1	6	1
MsgLabel	JLabel	Enter an amount and select your transaction	WEST	HORIZONTAL	0	7	2
N/A	Keypad	N/A	CENTER	BOTH	0	8	2
N/A	JLabel	Transaction History:	WEST	NONE	0	9	1
ScrollPane	N/A	N/A	WEST	HORIZONTAL	0	10	2
N/A	AtmButton Panel	N/A	WEST	HORIZONTAL	0	11	2

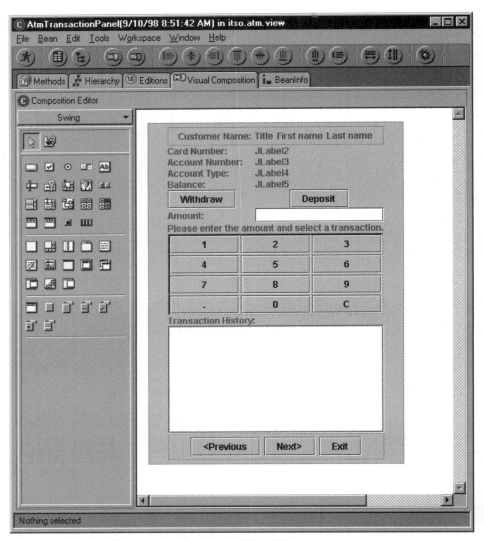

Figure 140. AtmTransactionPanel with Visual Beans

Open the Property sheet for the AmountTextField and set *enabled* and *editable* to false, *background* to white, and *disabledTextColor* to Black.

Open the Property sheet for the AtmButtonPanel1 and set *nextButtonEnabled* to false because this is the last panel in the application.

Now drop an AtmController variable on the free-form surface, name it ControllerVariable, and drop a DefaultListModel class and name it ListModel.

Again, be careful that you create the ControllerVariable as a variable and the ListModel as a bean, that is, with a Bean Type of Class.

Tear off the accountVariableThis and cardVariableThis properties from the ControllerVariable and name them AccountVariable and CardVariable, respectively. Create the connections listed in Table 14 to complete the AtmTransactionPanel (see Figure 141 on page 239).

Table 14. AtmTransactionPanel Connections

Connection Number in Figure 141	Connection Type	Connection from	Connection to	Comments
1	*PtoP*	*ControllerVariable, cardVariableThis*	*CardVariable, this*	*Automatically generated by tearoff.*
2	*PtoP*	*ControllerVariable, accountVariableThis*	*AccountVariable, this*	*Automatically generated by tearoff.*
3	PtoP	ListModel,this	JList1,model	Set the model for the JList.
4	PtoP	AccountVariable, balance	BalanceLabel, text	Source Event: balance Target Event: none
5	PtoP	AccountVariable, accountId	AccountNumberLabel, text	Source Event: this Target Event: none
6	PtoP	CardVariable, cardNumber	CardNumberLabel, text	Source Event: this Target Event: none
7	PtoP	AccountVariable, accountType	AccountTypeLabel, text	Source Event: this Target Event: none
8	EtoM	AtmButtonPanel1, exitButtonAction _actionPerformed	ControllerVariable, exit()	Exit the application.
9	EtoM	AtmButtonPanel1, previousButtonAction _actionPerformed	ControllerVariable, previous()	Return to the previous application panel.
10	EtoM	WithdrawButton, actionPerformed	AccountVariable, withdraw	Parameter is connection 11.
11	PfromP	Connection 10 parameter, amount	Keypad1, valueAsString	Pass amount to withdraw method.
12	EtoC	connection 10 normalResult	new method updateTransactions	updateTransactions is described in the text that follows this table.

Connection Number in Figure 141	Connection Type	Connection from	Connection to	Comments
13	EtoM	connection 10 normalResult	Keypad1,clear()	Clear the Keypad value.
14	EtoM	DepositButton, actionPerformed	AccountVariable, deposit	Parameter is connection 15.
15	PfromP	Connection 14 parameter	Keypad1, valueAsString	Pass amount to deposit method.
16	EtoC	connection 14 normalResult	updateTransactions method	
17	EtoM	connection 14 normalResult	Keypad1,clear()	Clear the Keypad value.
18	EtoM	AccountVariable, handleLimitExceeded	MsgLabel,text	Set parameter as "Insufficient funds for withdrawal."
19	EtoM	AccountVariable, balance	MsgLabel,text	Set parameter as "Enter an amount and select a transaction."
20	PtoP	ControllerVariable, customerVariableThis	AtmNamePanel1, customerVariableThis	Source Event: customerVariableThis Target Event: none
21	PtoP	Keypad1, valueAsString	AmountTextField, text	

Notes:
1. You can deduce the type of feature from the connection type, where P stands for property, E for Event, M for Method, and C for Code.
2. Connections automatically generated by VisualAge for Java are shown in *italic*.

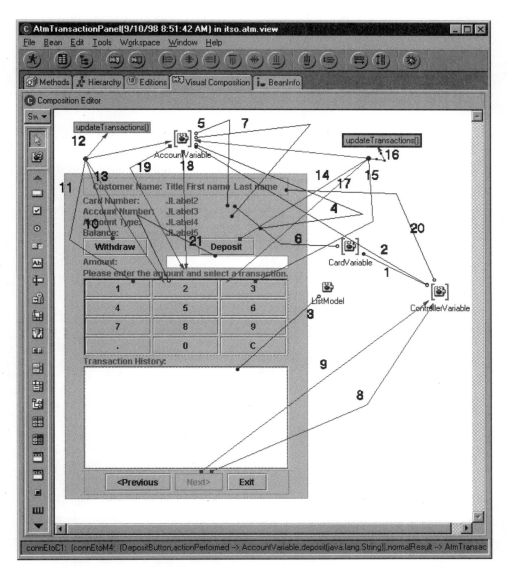

Figure 141. AtmTransactionPanel with Connections

Here is the code for the updateTransactions() method (save the bean before entering the code):

```
public void updateTransactions(){
    getListModel().clear();
    for( int i = 0; i < getAccountVariable().getTransactions().size(); i++){
        getListModel().addElement( getAccountVariable().getTransactions().
```

```
        elementAt(i));
    }
}
```

Now you add code to clear both the transaction list and the Keypad value when the user clicks the Previous button. Find the method representing connection 9, the event-to-method connection from the AtmButtonPanel1.previousButtonAction_actionPerformed event to the ControllerVariable.previous() method, and open the method in a Source pane. In user code section 2, enter the following lines as shown in (Figure 142):

```
getListModel().clear();
getKeypad1().clear();
```

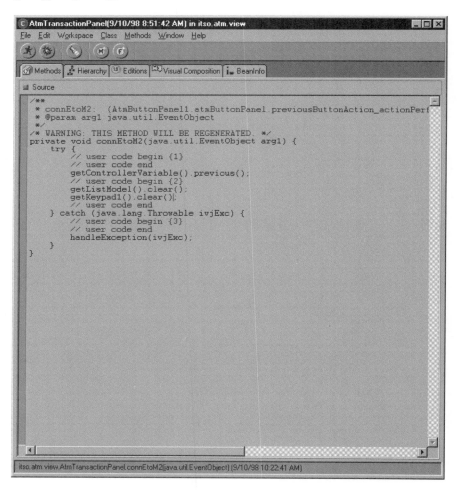

Figure 142. Clearing the Transaction List and Keypad in the AtmTransactionPanel

You will also want to list the transactions when the user presses the Previous button and returns to the `AtmTransactionPanel`. As with most code you create in VisualAge for Java, you can add the function through a visual connection or through code.

In this case, create an event-to-code connection from **componentShown** of the ATMTransactionPanel to the **updateTransactions**() method.

Finally, save the bean and promote the `ControllerVariable this` property.

Finishing the AtmView

Now that you have created the infrastructure, you have the relatively easy job of composing the final application.

Open the `AtmView` in the Visual Composition Editor. Add the subpanels to the `MainPanel` in the order in which they will be accessed:

1. AtmWelcomePanel
2. AtmPinPanel
3. AtmAccountPanel
4. AtmTransactionPanel

If you do not drop the beans in the correct order, you can use the Beans List to rearrange the order. Once you have dropped more than one panel in the card layout, you can use **Switch To** on the pop-up menu to display the different panels.

Resize the `AtmView` frame so that the `AtmTransactionPanel` has enough space and set the `AtmView` *title* property to `ATM Application`.

For each panel connect the `AtmController` bean in the `AtmView` to the promoted `controllerVariableThis` property in the panel. This is best done using the Beans List.

Finally, create a method to initialize the Bank (you can copy this code from the `buildbank.txt` file included with the sample code):

```
public void buildBank() {
    /* Get the bank from the controller */
    itso.atm.model.Bank bank = getController().getBank();
    /* Create the customers */
    itso.atm.model.Customer customer1 = new itso.atm.model.Customer();
    itso.atm.model.Customer customer2 = new itso.atm.model.Customer();
    /* Add the customers to the bank */
```

```
bank.getCustomers().addElement(customer1);
bank.getCustomers().addElement(customer2);
/* Create the ATM cards */
itso.atm.model.Card customer1Card = new itso.atm.model.Card();
itso.atm.model.Card customer2Card = new itso.atm.model.Card();
customer1Card.setCardNumber("100001");
customer1Card.setPinNumber("3405");
customer2Card.setCardNumber("100002");
customer2Card.setPinNumber("0033");
/* Add the cards to the customers */
customer1.getCards().addElement(customer1Card);
customer2.getCards().addElement(customer2Card);
/* Set the customer information */
customer1.setCustomerId("3056978");
customer1.setLastName("Doe");
customer1.setFirstName("John");
customer1.setTitle("Mr.");
customer2.setCustomerId("6979304");
customer2.setLastName("Smith");
customer2.setFirstName("Anne");
customer2.setTitle("Ms.");
/* Create the accounts */
itso.atm.model.CheckingAccount checkingAccountCustomer1 = new
itso.atm.model.CheckingAccount();
checkingAccountCustomer1.setAccountId("34759023");
checkingAccountCustomer1.setBalance(new java.math.BigDecimal(1000.));
itso.atm.model.SavingsAccount savingsAccountCustomer1 = new
itso.atm.model.SavingsAccount();
savingsAccountCustomer1.setBalance(new java.math.BigDecimal(100.));
savingsAccountCustomer1.setAccountId("34759023");
itso.atm.model.CheckingAccount checkingAccountCustomer2 = new
itso.atm.model.CheckingAccount();
checkingAccountCustomer2.setAccountId("34744442");
checkingAccountCustomer2.setBalance(new java.math.BigDecimal(10000.));
/* Add the accounts to the customers and the cards */
customer1.getAccounts().addElement(checkingAccountCustomer1);
customer1.getAccounts().addElement(savingsAccountCustomer1);
customer2.getAccounts().addElement(checkingAccountCustomer2);
((itso.atm.model.Card)
customer1.getCards().firstElement()).getAccounts().addElement(checkingAccountCustomer1)
;
((itso.atm.model.Card)
customer1.getCards().firstElement()).getAccounts().addElement(savingsAccountCustomer1);
((itso.atm.model.Card)
customer2.getCards().firstElement()).getAccounts().addElement(checkingAccountCustomer2)
;
}
```

Create an event-to-code connection from the initialize event on the AtmView free-form surface to the buildbank() method. Figure 143 shows the AtmView with the completed connections.

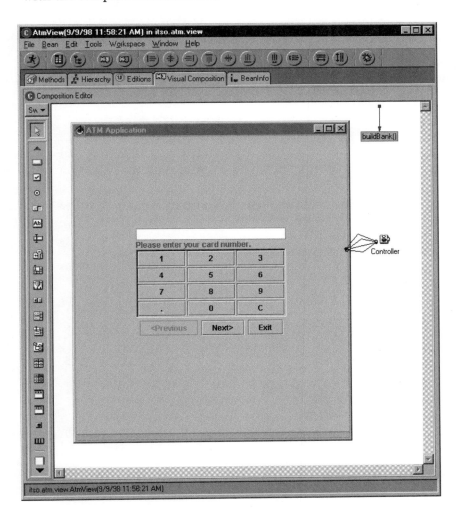

Figure 143. AtmView Bean with Connections

You can test the ATM. Use the following card numbers and PINs to test the ATM:

Customer 1— Card ID number: 100001, PIN: 3405

Customer 2 — Card ID number: 100002, PIN: 0033

Is Your ATM Working Correctly?

If it is, congratulations. The ATM is not a trivial application, and constructing it should help you with other programming projects. If your ATM is not working, here are some pointers:

❑ Check that the beans you dropped on the free-form surface are the correct Bean Type (Class or Variable).

❑ Check that the direction and source and target events of the connections are correct.

❑ Uncomment the handleException method in the AtmView to see whether any exceptions are being thrown.

❑ Load the ATM application from the sample code and compare it with your implementation.

❑ Now that you know how to use the debugger and inspectors, place breakpoints in the code and inspect suspect objects:

   • ControllerVariable - make sure each ControllerVariable instance is set with the Controller value.

   • Keypad - make sure the valueAsString property is being set and firing events.

   • Make sure the balance property is being set and firing correctly.

Now that the ATM is working, why not improve it? It would be nice if you could use keys to enter the numbers. The next section shows you how to add that function.

Figure 144 shows the flow of the application.

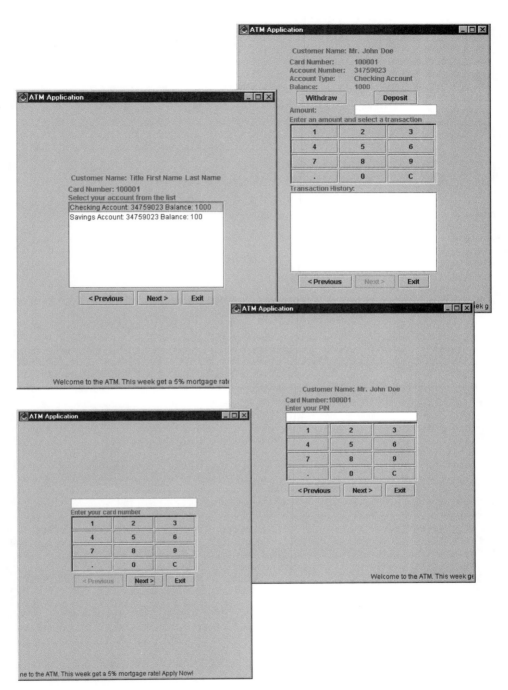

Figure 144. ATM Application Flow

Adding Keyboard Input to the ATM Application

It is easy to enable the keyboard to enter the card number, PIN, and amounts in the ATM. The Keypad is ready to deal with keyboard input; all you have to do is add it as a listener for the keyboard input.

The ATM application has three Keypads, which have to start listening for input as they are shown on the screen and stop listening when they are hidden.

Add two new methods to the AtmController and then add them as method features, using **Add Available Features**. The method bodies are:

```
public void addKeyListener( Keypad keypad) {
    getFrame().addKeyListener( keypad.getController());
}
public void removeKeyListener( Keypad keypad) {
    getFrame().removeKeyListener( keypad.getController());
}
```

To use the Keypad in the AtmWelcomePanel as a key listener, add six new connections to the AtmWelcomePanel (Table 15).

Table 15. AtmWelcomePanel Connections

Connection Number	Connection Type	Connection from	Connection to
1	EtoM	ControllerVariable,this	ControllerVariable, addKeyListener
2	PfromP	Connection 1 keypad parameter	Keypad,this
3	EtoM	AtmWelcomePanel, componentShown	ControllerVariable, addKeyListener
4	PfromP	Connection 3 keypad parameter	Keypad,this
5	EtoM	AtmWelcomePanel, componentHidden	ControllerVariable, removeKeyListener
6	PfromP	Connection 5 keypad parameter	Keypad,this

Notes:
1. You can deduce the type of feature from the connection type where P stands for property, E for Event, M for Method, and C for Code.

To add the keyboard handling in the AtmPinPanel and AtmTransactionPanel, create connections 3 – 6 from Table 15 in each panel.

Now run the ATM application. You can use the keys as well as the buttons to enter numbers.

7 Making Your Data Persistent

So far you have created the data you need for your Java programs by using special code (the customers and accounts in the ATM application) or applet parameters (the titles and URLs in the Bookmark List). In the real world you have to store the data somewhere when the program is not running. In other words you have to make the data persistent.

Most programs need some sort of persistence, ranging from a simple initialization file for user preferences to a large database that stores records for a utility company. Java supports these requirements, for example, through the Properties class and the JDBC interface, and provides thorough support for reading and writing files and objects.

There are many kinds of persistence. In this chapter you will focus on two kinds of persistence: serialization and relational databases. The serialization mechanism provided by Java enables programs to read and write Java objects from streams. The objects can be read from a local disk or from a machine across the network. Relational databases are probably the most widely used persistence mechanism in the world. They have been proven over many years to be secure, scalable, and efficient ways of storing data.

In this chapter you will save, or make *persistent*, your Bookmark List in two ways: using the serialization mechanism of Java and using the DB2 Universal Database, VisualAge for Java data access beans, and the Java JDBC interface.

Serialization

Each time you run the BookmarkListView applet that you created in "Visual Programming in Action" on page 124, the URLs in the list are passed as parameters to the applet. It would be much more useful if you could store the URLs in a file.

JDK 1.1 introduces *object serialization,* which enables you to convert an object to a stream of bytes that can later be restored to the original object.

In this chapter you add persistence to your Bookmark List objects. You learn how to store and read your objects to and from files, using the java.io. Serializable interface.

Serialization is designed to work not only on a single machine but also across a network. Thus, you can *flatten* an object on one machine and send the byte stream representation of the object over the network to another machine, that can then *resurrect* the object to use it. The object serialization mechanism and the JVM take care of any differences between operating systems or data representation on different machines.

The Serializable Interface

The Serializable interface is part of the java.io package. It provides persistence for your objects so that they can live beyond the existence of a running program. When your object is serializable, it can be written to disk and restored later when the program is run again.

The general steps to making your object serializable are (see Figure 145):

1. Implement the Serializable interface in all classes that you want to be persistent and in any classes that your objects hold as attributes that you also want to make persistent.

2. Mark any computed or redundant fields as transient. These fields will not be saved when you save the object.

3. To serialize an object, create an ObjectOutputStream object. Then use the writeObject method to serialize the object and send it to the OutputStream.

4. To deserialize an object, create an ObjectInputStream and call readObject to read the object from the InputStream.

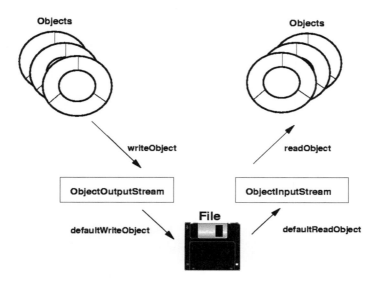

Figure 145. The Serialization Process

Serialization is achieved through the use of ObjectOutputStream and its writeObject method. The objects are written to the ObjectOutputStream (by the defaultWriteObject method) and flattened. The object's information includes the fields, type information, and references to other objects.

The restoration of the object is achieved through the use of ObjectInputStream and its readObject method. The ObjectInputStream reads the data from the file and restores the objects (type, data, and dependencies). This process is handled automatically by the defaultReadObject method.

Object Dependencies

The serialization mechanism serializes, or deserializes, not only the object but all its dependencies during writeObject or readObject execution. Therefore if your object contains references to other objects, those objects also will be serialized as long as their classes implement the Serializable interface and have not been flagged with the transient keyword. If a class is found that is not marked transient but does not implement Serializable, the NotSerializableException will be thrown.

The serialization of the dependencies of an object can result in a lot of information being serialized along with your object. Plan your serialization early and design objects with serialization in mind. If you are serializing objects over a network, these planning and design activities are particularly important.

Behind the Scenes of Serialization

As instances of a class implementing the Serializable interface, objects have a default behavior, supplied by Java, for writing their data to an output stream. The default behavior is to write the following information:

❑ Class of the object

❑ Class signature

❑ Values of the fields of the object's superclasses

❑ Values of nontransient and nonstatic fields

When primitive types are serialized, a simple call to the corresponding OutputStream write method is made. For objects, the serialization process is done through a call to the writeObject(anObject) method of ObjectOutputStream. This method checks whether the instance implements Serializable and has an overridden writeObject method. If so, it uses the overridden method; otherwise it uses the defaultWriteObject method defined in ObjectOutputStream.

When an object is read and deserialized, the class type, class signature, and the values of the nontransient and nonstatic fields of the object's superclasses are read. Objects referenced by this object are read transitively so that a complete equivalent graph of objects is reconstructed by readObject. Then readObject returns an object of type Object. You need to cast the returned object back to the original class to use it.

The default deserialization for a class is handled by the defaultReadObject method of ObjectInputStream and can be modified by overriding the readObject of the class. The readObject method must be used in conjunction with the override of writeObject.

If you have marked some fields as transient, it is your responsibility to re-create the fields when your object is instantiated. You can do this using several methods:

1. By using lazy initialization through accessor methods. This is the process used by VisualAge for Java for access to beans. The get method generated

by VisualAge for Java for the object checks whether the object is null. If the object is null, it is instantiated by the get method.

2. By overriding the readObject method to re-create these fields after calling the defaultReadObject method to restore the nontransient fields.

Examples of transient fields are found in the property change event handling code generated by VisualAge for Java, for example, in the itso.atm.model.BankAccount class (see "Building the BankAccount Bean" on page 71). The propertyChange field is marked transient. The value of the propertyChange field would be meaningless if the object were deserialized in another location because the object refers to other objects listening for the event. The declaration of the propertyChange field is:

protected transient java.beans.PropertyChangeSupport propertyChange;

Controlling the Serialization

To gain more control during the serialization or deserialization of an object, you can provide customized read and write methods that are responsible for reading and writing the object's state. In this case the stream is only responsible for storing the name of the object's class.

The Externalizable interface identifies objects that can be saved to a stream but are responsible for saving their own state. For this purpose, externalizable objects must provide a writeExternal method for storing their state during serialization and a readExternal method for restoring their state during deserialization.

Bookmark List Serialization

In this section you make the Bookmark List persistent. You make the Bookmark class itself serializable and make changes to the BookmarkListController to support the serialization. Finally you make the connections to the init and save methods in the Visual Composition Editor to invoke the serialization.

During the init method the applet reads and restores the Bookmark List from a file containing the serialized version of the list. When the destroy method is called on the applet, the object is serialized and written to the same file.

In this example, and the next, you reuse the classes from the itso.bookmark.applet package. You copy the classes from the itso.bookmark.applet package and then modify them to provide the persistence. In a real project you could reuse more of the code, but for the purposes of these examples, it is simpler to copy and modify the code.

Create a New Package and Copy the Classes

1. Create a new package in the Programming VAJ V2 project named itso.bookmark.serialized.

2. Select the BookmarkListController and BookmarkListView classes in the itso.bookmark.applet package in the Workbench. Select **Selected→Reorganize→Copy**. Click **Browse** and then enter itso.bookmark.serialized and click **OK**. Deselect the **Rename (copy as)** checkbox and click **OK**.

   Because the applet contains a reference to the original BookmarkListController, you will see an error created by the copy. You will fix that error in "Modifying the BookmarkList Applet to Support Serialization" on page 257.

Marking the Bookmark Class as Serializable

1. Select the itso.bookmark.Bookmark class in the Workbench. Modify the class declaration to implement the Serializable interface (Figure 146):

   public class Bookmark implements java.io.Serializable

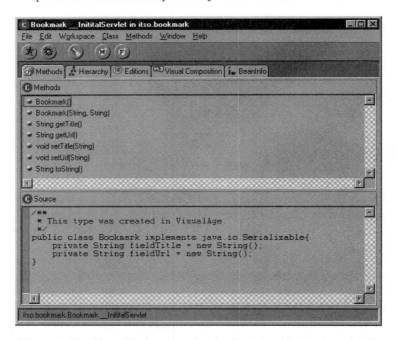

Figure 146. Class Declaration for the Serializable Bookmark Class

Modifying the BookmarkListController

1. Add the import statement; import java.io.*;, to the class declaration of itso.bookmark.serialized.BookmarkListController.

2. Add the file name of the serialized object to the itso.bookmark.serialized.BookmarkListController class declaration:

   ```
   String fileName = "bookmarks.ser";
   ```

   Files containing the serialized form of objects usually have the .ser extension. The bookmarks.ser file will be created in the project resources directory for your project. Once you have run the applet and then closed the Applet Viewer, look in project_resources\Programming VAJ V2 under the VisualAge for Java ide directory and you should see bookmarks.ser.

   The BookmarkListController controls the reading and writing of the serialized bookmarks that will be performed in the init method and a new method, save. Add both methods as method features on the BeanInfo page.

3. Create a new addEntry method that takes a Bookmark instead of strings:

   ```
   public void addEntry( Bookmark bookmark) {
       getBookmarkList().addElement( bookmark);
   }
   ```

   You need the new addEntry method to add the restored objects directly to the list.

4. Modify the init(JApplet) method so that it looks like this:

   ```
   public void init( JApplet applet)
   {
       try {
           FileInputStream fIn = new FileInputStream( fileName);
           ObjectInputStream in = new ObjectInputStream( fIn);
           while( fIn.available() > 0){
               addEntry( (Bookmark)in.readObject());
           }
           in.close();
       }
       catch( Exception e){
           System.out.println("Error in init: " + e);
       }
   }
   ```

5. Create a new save method:

   ```
   public void save()
   {
       FileOutputStream fOut = null;
       ObjectOutputStream out = null;
       try {
           fOut = new FileOutputStream( fileName);
   ```

```
              out = new ObjectOutputStream( fOut);
              for( int i = 0; i < getBookmarkList().size(); i++){
                out.writeObject( getBookmarkList().elementAt(i));
              }
              out.close();
         }
      catch( IOException e) {
            System.out.println("Error in save: " + e);
         }
      }
}
```

6. Open the BookmarkListController Class Browser to the Bean Info page.
   Check that both the init and save methods are listed as method features as
   shown in Figure 147. If they do not appear in the list, add them using **Add
   Available Features** on the **Features** menu.

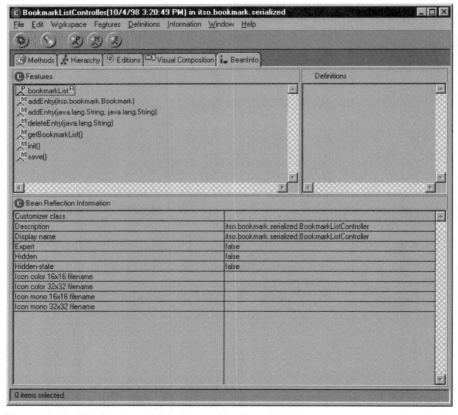

Figure 147. The BookmarkListController BeanInfo Page

Modifying the BookmarkList Applet to Support Serialization

Now you are ready to implement serialization in the BookmarkListView applet. Most of the work is already done; all you have to do is load the data when the applet starts and serialize the model before closing the applet. First, because you copied this class from the itso.bookmark.applet package, you must change the Controller to the correct class:

1. Open the BookmarkListView class in the Visual Composition Editor, select the Controller bean and then select **Morph Into** from the pop-up menu. Change the *Class name* field to: itso.bookmark.serialized.BookmarkListController and click **OK**.

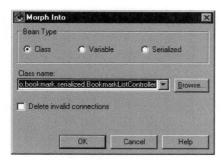

Figure 148. Morphing the Controller bean

2. Save the bean and add a new method, destroy, to the applet:

```
public void destroy() {
    getController().save();
}
```

3. Select the **Delete** button and select **Reorder Connections From** in the pop-up menu. Check that the deleteEntry connection is called first. The order may have been changed when you performed the Morph Into function. If the connection to deleteEntry is not at the top of the list, drag it to the top of the list.

Now you can test the BookmarkList applet. Run the applet and add some URLs, then close and restart it (Figure 149). The first time you run the applet you will get a message because the serialized list was not found. That is OK because the applet will create the file when the applet is destroyed.

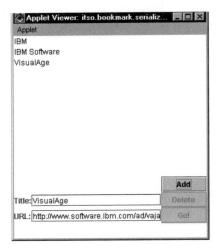

Figure 149. The Bookmark List Applet

Relational Databases

Storing program data in relational databases is probably the most common form of persistence in existence. Many of today's client-server applications are simply user interfaces to relational databases.

Relational databases provide secure, scalable, and efficient ways of storing and accessing large amounts of data. The common language for manipulating data in relational databases is the Structured Query Language (SQL). If you are new to relational databases or SQL, you may want to explore an SQL resource such as *A Guide to the Sql Standard: A User's Guide to the Standard Database Language Sql* listed in "Related Publications" on page 389.

To access relational databases, Java developers typically use JDBC. The JDBC API is a standard SQL database access interface for Java. Using JDBC, you can:

❑ Access most SQL databases

❑ Concentrate on business logic instead of database and communication programming

JDBC - Not an Acronym

Although it is widely believed that JDBC stands for Java Database Connectivity, it does not. Sun has trademarked JDBC as a separate name. It is much easier to think of it as Java Database Connectivity, however.

JDBC is similar to Microsoft's Open Database Connectivity (ODBC) API, a widely used API for accessing relational databases in Windows operating systems.

To access a particular database, an application must have access to a JDBC driver for the database. These drivers encapsulate the database-specific and platform-specific code.

JDBC Drivers

There are four kinds of JDBC drivers:

❏ JDBC-ODBC bridge: This driver provides JDBC access through most ODBC drivers. In many cases some ODBC binary code and database client code must be loaded on each client machine that uses this driver.

❏ Native-API part-Java driver: This driver converts JDBC calls into calls on the client API for the database in question. It requires that some binary code be loaded on each client machine. This type of driver supports what is commonly known as a *thick*, or *fat*, *client*: a client that requires database code to be installed.

❏ Net-protocol all-Java driver: This driver translates JDBC calls into a database independent net protocol, which is then translated to a DBMS protocol by a server. This type of driver supports what is commonly known as a *thin client*: a client that does not require database code to be installed.

❏ Native-protocol all-Java driver: This driver converts JDBC calls into the network protocol used by the DBMS.

JDBC URL Format

To access a database through JDBC, you initially use a URL to establish a database connection. The URL has different formats depending on the driver that it uses to access the database. The standard JDBC URL is jdbc:<subprotocol>:<subname>, where:

jdbc is the name of the protocol.

<subprotocol> is the name of the driver or the name of a database connectivity mechanism.

<subname> is a way of identifying the database, usually the database name.

DB2 JDBC Drivers

DB2 Universal Database supports two drivers:

Application driver: The application driver is a type 2 driver that provides support for the thick client version of DB2 JDBC access. That is, the Client Application Enabler (CAE) or the DB2 database must be installed on the machine where the Java program is running. The CAE provides a runtime environment that enables client applications to access one or more remote databases. The application driver is typically used by Java applications or servlets. The application URL is jdbc:db2:<database-name>, and the JDBC driver class is COM.ibm.db2.jdbc.app.DB2Driver.

Net driver: The net driver is a type 3 driver that provides support for a thin client. This driver is more applicable than an application driver in Web browser situations or wherever the client is unknown or constrained. The net driver does not require any database-specific code on the client platform where the Java program is running except for access to the driver itself. However, the server where the DB2 database is running must also be running the DB2 Applet Server, which provides the connection between the driver and DB2. The applet server waits for connections from applets and translates the applet's request into native DB2 requests. The URL for the net driver is jdbc:db2://host:port/<database-name>, and the driver class is COM.ibm.db2.jdbc.net.DB2Driver. The convention is to use 8888 for the port on which the Applet Server listens, but any port can be used.

JDBC Functionality

To access databases with VisualAge for Java you do not have to know too much about the JDBC interface, but an introduction to a few key areas will help. The code in the steps following this paragraphs illustrates some key points. The example connects to a database, using the thick client driver and then lists the names of the employees in the EMPLOYEE table of the SAMPLE database shipped with DB2. You can try the example yourself in the VisualAge for Java Scrapbook, but first you must add the DB2 Java JAR file to the workspace class path (see "Setting the Class Path" on page 268) and you must have DB2 running on your machine with the SAMPLE database installed.

1. Find and load the JDBC driver. Each JDBC program dynamically loads the correct driver on the basis of the URL. When a JDBC driver class is loaded, it creates an instance of the driver and registers itself with the driver manager:

   ```
   Class.forName("COM.ibm.db2.jdbc.app.DB2Driver");
   ```

2. Create a connection to the database:

   ```
   java.sql.Connection jc =
           java.sql.DriverManager.getConnection("jdbc:db2:SAMPLE");
   ```

   All ensuing SQL statements are executed in the context of this connection.

3. Create a statement object:

   ```
   java.sql.Statement stmt = jc.createStatement();
   ```

   To execute an SQL query you need a statement object.

4. Execute a query and return a result set:

   ```
   java.sql.ResultSet rs = stmt.executeQuery("Select * FROM EMPLOYEE");
   ```

   In this case, all records from the EMPLOYEE database are returned as a result set. The ResultSet class provides methods to access each column in the row and return an object.

5. Print a header for the list:

   ```
   System.out.println( "Names: ");
   ```

6. Iterate through the result set, printing two columns (FIRSTNME and LASTNAME) from each row:

   ```
   for ( int i=1; rs.next(); i++) {
       System.out.println( "\t" +  rs.getString( "FIRSTNME".trim()
               + " " + rs.getString( "LASTNAME").trim());
   }
   ```

   The ResultSet class also provides a cursor with which you can iterate through the result set by using the next method.

7. Close the connections:

   ```
   rs.close();
   stmt.close();
   jc.close();
   ```

For more information about JDBC, consult a JDBC resource such as the JavaSoft JDBC documentation or *Database Programming with JDBC and Java* or *JDBC Database Access With Java: A Tutorial and Annotated Reference* (see "Related Publications" on page 389).

Database Access Using VisualAge for Java

Using VisualAge for Java Professional you can access databases through JDBC in two ways:

❑ Code JDBC manually: You can code straight to the JDBC interface if you need that level of control over your database code.

New in V2! ➡ ❑ Use the *Data Access beans* feature: The Data Access beans feature enables you to create Data Access beans that provide access to relational databases through JDBC. The Data Access beans SmartGuides create all of the JDBC code for you.

One drawback to relational databases is that they do not store objects. They store data in rows and tables. As indicated in the example in "JDBC Functionality" on page 260, the JDBC interface does not map database rows or records to objects. Mapping the data from tables and rows to objects (object-relational mapping) is one of the tasks you face when using relational databases with Java programs.

The Data Access beans map columns to Java objects. If you have more complex data access requirements, VisualAge for Java Enterprise provides two other data access features:

VisualAge for Java Data Access Builder
> Generates Data Access Builder beans to access relational databases through JDBC. These beans map rows and result sets to Java objects.

VisualAge for Java Persistence Builder
> Generates complete object models supporting persistence

In this section you learn how to make the Bookmark List persistent, using the Data Access beans and DB2 Universal Database.

VisualAge for Java Data Access Beans

The Data Access beans feature provides two JavaBeans on the Visual Composition Editor palette:

Select
> The com.ibm.ivj.db.uibeans.Select bean is a nonvisual bean with which you can query a relational database. You can also insert, update, or delete a row in the result set and commit the changes in the database. The Select bean exposes a query property that contains a connection alias and an SQL specification for the Select bean.

DBNavigator

The com.ibm.ivj.db.uibeans.DBNavigator bean is a visual bean that is used with a Select bean. The DBNavigator bean provides a set of buttons that execute the SQL statement for the associated Select bean; perform other relational database operations, such as commit updates to the database; and navigate rows in the result set. You can use the DBNavigator bean to test your database access or in the deployed Java program.

Select Bean Features

The Select bean provides a set of events, methods, and properties for relational database access.

Events The Select bean can inform listeners before and after any of the following events:

❑ Adding a new row to the result set

❑ Committing changes to the database

❑ Closing the database connection

❑ Connecting to the database

❑ Deleting a row from the result set

❑ Disconnecting from the database

❑ Executing the SQL query

❑ Rolling back changes to the database

❑ Updating the current row in the result set

Using the Table Changed event, the Select bean can also inform listeners that the underlying database table has changed.

Methods The Select bean provides more than forty methods, many of which deal with getting and setting column values in the result set. Each column in the result set can be accessed through its index or name and returned as an object of type Object or String. As well the parameters for an SQL query can be read and set through methods on the Select bean.

Some of the other methods that the Select bean exposes are:

commit: Commit the current updates to the database.

rollback: Roll back the current updates to the database (if Auto-commit is not enabled).

execute: Execute the query defined when you created the Select bean.

firstRow, nextRow, lastRow: Navigate through the result set created by the execute method.

updateRow: Update a row in the database on the basis of the data in the current row of the result set.

deleteRow: Delete the row in the database corresponding to the current row of the result set.

Properties The Select bean exposes several properties that affect database access (the last three are expert properties):

query: The query property is where you set the connection alias and the SQL specification for your Select bean.

fillCacheOnExecute: Whether to fetch all rows of the result set of an execute method into the cache. If this is false, the maximumRows property along with the packet properties determine the number of rows to fetch.

lockRows: Specifies whether a lock is immediately acquired for the row. A value of True indicates that a lock is immediately acquired for the current row. A value of False indicates that a lock is not acquired for the row until an update request is issued. The default value is False.

readOnly: Specifies whether updates to the database are allowed. A value of True indicates that updates are disallowed even if the database manager would permit them. A value of False indicates that updates are allowed, provided that the database manager permits them. The default value is False.

For a complete description of the Data Access beans see their JavaDoc descriptions in the VisualAge for Java online documentation.

Database Access Class

During the specification of your Select bean you are asked to specify a name for the Database Access class. This class is used to hold the connection alias and SQL specification. You can reuse the same Database Access class and connection alias for several SQL specifications.

Connection Alias

A connection alias specifies the database connection characteristics for the Select bean, for example, the URL for the connection, and the user ID and password to be passed with the connection request.

As previously stated, you can reuse the same connection alias for several SQL specifications. If different Select beans specify the same connection alias, they share the database connection associated with that connection alias. If one Select bean commits updates to a database, it commits all uncommitted updates made by any Select bean sharing the database connection.

During the creation of the connection alias, you can check the **Auto-commit** checkbox if you want database updates to be automatically committed for each SQL query. If you do not check the checkbox, database updates are not automatically committed. This checkbox is checked by default.

SQL Specification

An SQL specification specifies an SQL statement for the Select bean. You can enter the SQL statement manually (through an editor) or you can use the SQL Assist SmartGuide to help you visually compose the SQL statement.

A Select bean can be associated with only one SQL specification.

Making the BookmarkList Persistent Using Data Access Beans

You have already used serialization to make the Bookmark List persistent. Now you will create a database table to hold the bookmarks from the list. When you add or delete entries from the list, they will be added or removed from the database.

The BookmarkListController encapsulates the database access, and the BookmarkListView simply accesses the controller as before. The controller uses two database queries: the first to build and return the complete Bookmark List, and the second to access an individual bookmark in the list. The two database queries require two different Select beans.

Prerequisites

To complete this example you need access to a relational database, and you have to create the database table used by the example. The example uses DB2 Universal Database running on Windows NT. If you use any other environment, modify the example as appropriate. The example assumes you have already installed DB2 successfully.

You will also need to have TCP/IP configured and running on your machine.

Creating the Bookmark List Table and Starting DB2

1. Make sure that DB2 and the DB2 Windows NT Security Server are started. Use the Services dialog box from the Windows NT Control Panel (Figure 150).

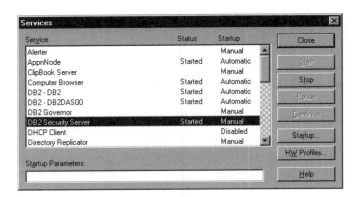

Figure 150. Starting DB2 and the DB2 Windows NT Security Server

2. Start the DB2 Applet Server from the Windows NT command line (Figure 151 on page 266) using the following statement: db2jstrt 8888. (8888 is the port where the server will listen for requests and must match the port specified in the URL.)

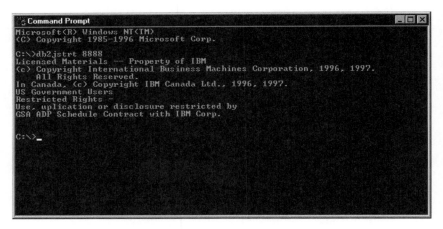

Figure 151. Starting the DB2 Applet Server

3. Open a DB2 Command Window, using **Start→Programs→DB2 for Windows NT→Command Window**.

If you are using DB2 5.2 (the evaluation version on the CD-ROM) you have to run the DB2TSART command in the Command window before proceeding to the next step.

4. From the examples directory, copy the files in the DATABEANS directory to a local drive and run the BUILDBOOKMARKS.BAT file in the DB2 Command Window.

Running the BUILDBOOKMARKS file creates a new database called BKMARKS, and a new table in the database called BOOKMARKS. The schema definition for the table is:

```
CREATE TABLE BOOKMARKS ( \
    title CHAR( 50) NOT NULL PRIMARY KEY, \
    url CHAR( 50) NOT NULL \
)
```

The BUILDBOOKMARKS file then gives public access to the table and fills the table with the bookmark list data:

```
LOAD FROM COMP.DEL OF DEL INSERT INTO bookmarks
COMMIT
GRANT BINDADD ON DATABASE TO PUBLIC
GRANT CONNECT ON DATABASE TO PUBLIC
GRANT ALL ON BOOKMARKS TO PUBLIC
CONNECT RESET
```

The list is filled with the following values:

```
IBM,http://www.ibm.com
IBM Software,http://www.software.ibm.com
Javasoft,http://www.javasoft.com
```

Adding the Data Access Beans Feature

1. In the Workbench select **File→Quick Start**, select **Features→Add Feature** and click **OK**.

2. Select **IBM Data Access Beans 1.0** from the list in the Selection Required dialog box and click **OK**.

Creating a New Package and Copying the Classes

1. To reuse the classes from the itso.bookmark.applet package, create a new package in the Programming VAJ V2 project named itso.bookmark.databeans.

2. Select the BookmarkListController and BookmarkListView classes in the itso.bookmark.applet package in the Workbench. Select **Selected→Reorganize→Copy**. Click **Browse**, then enter itso.bookmark.databeans, and click **OK**. Deselect the **Rename (copy as)** checkbox and click **OK**.

Fixing the Incorrect Controller Reference

1. Open the `itso.bookmark.databeans.BookmarkListView` applet in the Visual Composition Editor.

2. Select the `Controller` bean and then select **Morph Into** from the pop-up menu. Change the *Class name* field to `itso.bookmark.databeans.BookmarkListController` and click **OK**.

Setting the Class Path

1. In the Workbench select **Window→Options** and then select **Resources** from the list. In the *Workspace class path* field enter: `X:\sqllib\java\db2java.zip;` (where X is the drive where DB2 is installed). You can also use the **Edit** and **Add Jar/Zip** buttons to locate the file. The DB2 Zip or JAR file is required for both the applet running in the Applet Viewer and the Visual Composition Editor itself when you are specifying the connection properties.

2. In the Workbench select **itso.bookmark.databeans.BookmarkListView** and then select **Selected→Properties**. Click the **Class Path** tab. Click the **Edit** button and select the **IBM Data Access Beans** checkbox (Figure 152 on page 268). Click **OK** to exit.

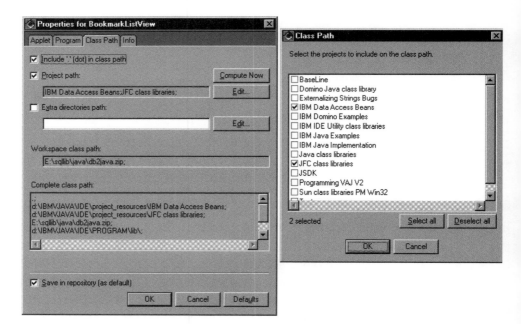

Figure 152. Setting the Class Path

Creating the Select Beans

1. Open the itso.bookmark.databeans.BookmarkListController in the Visual Composition Editor and select **Database** from the Palette Category selection pull-down menu. The Beans Palette changes to the Data Access beans: Select and DBNavigator (Figure 153 on page 269).

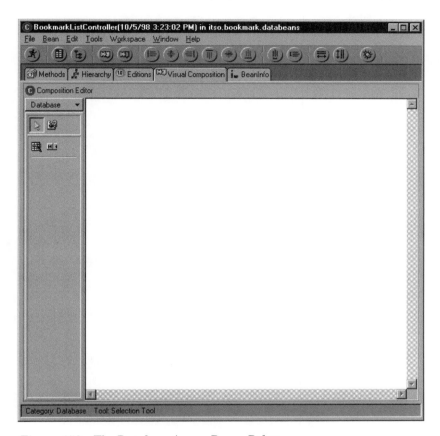

Figure 153. The Database Access Beans Palette

2. Drop a Select bean on the free-form surface. Change the *beanName* property to List.

3. Drop another Select bean on the free-form surface. Change the *beanName* property to Bookmark.

Setting the Connection Properties for the Select Beans

1. Open the Property Sheet for the List bean (Figure 154 on page 270).

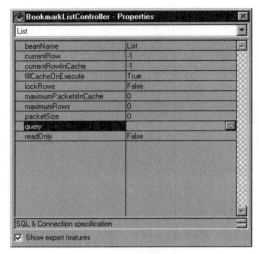

Figure 154. The Property Sheet for the List Bean

2. Click in the field to the right of *query* and then click the small button that appears.

3. Click the **New** button in the Query dialog box and fill the New Database Access Class dialog box in as follows (Figure 155 on page 270):

   Package: itso.bookmark.databeans

   Class name: DataAccess

4. Click **OK** to create the Data Access class.

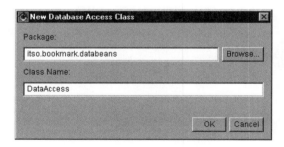

Figure 155. Setting the Class and Package of the Data Access Class

5. In the Query dialog box, click the **Add** button to the right of the *Connections* text area.

6. Fill in the Connection Alias Definition dialog box as follows (Figure 156 on page 271):

Connection Name: Bookmark (This must be a valid Java method name.)

URL: jdbc:db2://hostname:8888/BKMARKS

Substitute the host name of your machine for hostname. You can find the host name of your machine from the Network Properties dialog box or by typing hostname on the command line on most platforms.

JDBC Driver Choices: COM.ibm.db2.jdbc.net.DB2Driver

User ID: Your user ID

Password: Your password

For the purposes of the example, use your own user ID and password to access the database. This is not a recommended practice for real deployment, however.

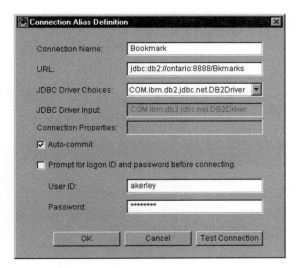

Figure 156. Setting the Connection Alias

7. Click **Test Connection**. If the connection is not successful, check the error message and then go back and check that you performed the steps correctly.

8. Click **OK** on the Connection Alias Definition dialog box.

Do not select the **OK** button on the Query Specification dialog box at this point. You want the dialog to stay open so that you can create the first SQL specification.

Setting the SQL Specification for the List Bean

In the same Query dialog:

1. Click the **SQL** tab, then click the **Add** button to the right of the SQL text field.

2. In the New SQL Specification dialog box (Figure 157 on page 272), enter SelectAll for the *SQL Name* and select the **Use SQL Assist SmartGuide (recommended)** checkbox. Click **OK**.

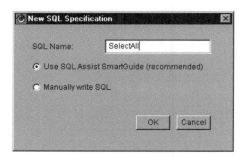

Figure 157. The New SQL Specification Dialog Box

3. In the SQL Assist SmartGuide (Figure 158 on page 272):

   a. Click the **Tables** tab and select the USERID.BOOKMARKS checkbox where USERID is your userid.

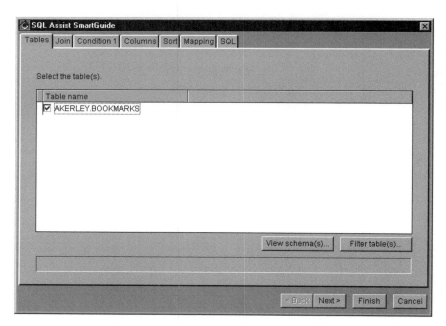

Figure 158. Specifying the Database Table

b. Under the **Columns** tab (Figure 159 on page 273) select TITLE and URL and click **Add>>**. This setting specifies the columns that will be returned in the result set.

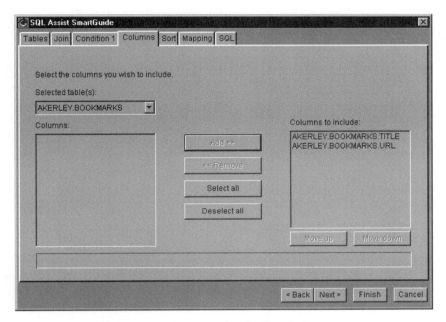

Figure 159. Specifying the Columns for the Result Set

c. Select the **SQL** tab and then select **Run SQL** to test the query (Figure 160 on page 274).

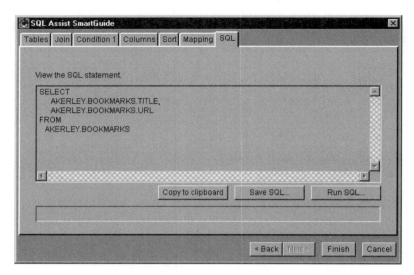

Figure 160. Testing the Query

 d. Select **Close** on the SQL Execution Result Set dialog box, then click on **Finish** in the SQL Assist Smart Guide, then **OK** in the Query dialog box.

Setting the SQL Specification for the Bookmark Bean

The steps for setting the SQL specification the Bookmark bean are very similar to those for the List bean.

1. Select the Bookmark bean on the free-form surface and open the Property sheet.

2. Click the field to the right of the *query* property and then the small button that appears in the field.

3. Select the **Bookmark** connection, click the **SQL** tab, and then click **Add**.

4. In the New SQL Specification dialog box, enter findBookmark for the *SQL Name*, select the **Manually write SQL** checkbox, and click **OK**.

See "Notice" on page 277 for better instructions.

5. In the SQL Editor, enter:

```
SELECT USERID.BOOKMARKS.TITLE, USERID.BOOKMARKS.URL FROM USERID.BOOKMARKS
WHERE ( ( USERID.BOOKMARKS.TITLE = :MYTITLE ) )
```

 where USERID is your userid, and :MYTITLE represents a variable that will be replaced through the setParameter method. You use the setParameter method to set queries or update statements with data from your program.

6. Click **OK** to exit the SQL Editor. Click **OK** to exit the Query dialog box.

7. Save the bean.

Modifying the BookmarkListController Methods

Modify the add and delete methods in the Controller to add and delete entries from the database table. You will also add a new init method, which will return the contents of the table. You can copy the code from BookmarkListController.java in the examples directory.

1. Modify the init(JApplet) method:

```java
public void init( JApplet applet)
{
    String title = new String();
    String url = new String();
    int currentRow,rows;
    try{
        getList().execute();
        getList().firstRow();
        rows=getList().getNumRows();
        for (currentRow=1;currentRow<=rows;currentRow++){
            title= getList().getColumnValueToString("BOOKMARKS.TITLE");
            url= getList().getColumnValueToString("BOOKMARKS.URL");
            Bookmark b = new Bookmark( title, url);
            getBookmarkList().addElement( b);
            getList().nextRow();
        }
    }
    catch (java.lang.Throwable ivjExc) {
        handleException(ivjExc);
    }
    return;
}
```

2. Modify the addEntry method:

```java
public void addEntry(String title, String url) {
    try{
        getBookmarkList().addElement( new Bookmark(title, url));
        getList().newRow(false);
        getList().setColumnValueFromString("BOOKMARKS.TITLE",title);
        getList().setColumnValueFromString("BOOKMARKS.URL",url);
        getList().updateRow();
    }
    catch (java.lang.Throwable ivjExc){
        handleException(ivjExc);
    }
    return;
}
```

3. Modify the deleteEntry method:

```
public void deleteEntry(String title)
{
    Enumeration e = getBookmarkList().elements();
    Bookmark b = null;
    while( e.hasMoreElements()){
        b = (Bookmark)e.nextElement();
        if( b.getTitle().equals( title)){
            getBookmarkList().removeElement(b);
        }
    }
    try{
        getBookmark().setParameterFromString("MYTITLE",title);
        getBookmark().execute();
        getBookmark().deleteRow();
    }
    catch (java.lang.Throwable ivjExc){
        handleException(ivjExc);
    }
    return;
}
```

Notice how you set the MYTITLE parameter (which you created in the SQL specification) to the current value of title.

Select the Delete button and select **Reorder Connections From** in the pop-up menu. Check that the deleteEntry connection is called first. The order may have been changed when you performed the Morph Into function. If the connection to deleteEntry is not at the top of the list, drag it to the top of the list.

Run the Example

Because you modified only the implementation of the BookmarkListController, you do not have to modify the BookmarkListView. You can simply run the example (Figure 161 on page 277).

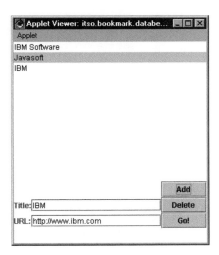

Figure 161. The itso.bookmark.databeans.BookmarkListView Applet

---

Notice

In order for the delete function to work correctly the MYTITLE parameter must be defined in the SQL specification. Instead of entering the SQL statement directly in the SQL editor, use the SQL Assist SmartGuide to generated the query. The SQL Assist SmartGuide settings are as follows:

❑ Table: userid.BOOKMARKS (where userid is the ID you are using)

❑ Condition 1: TITLE is exactly equal to :MYTITLE

❑ Columns: TITLE and URL

The final SQL statement will look the same as the original, but VisualAge for Java will generate the correct SQL specification for you.

---

8 Creating Servlets

Servlets have become a very popular way of providing Web-based functions. Not only do they benefit from the advantages of the Java language and executing in the JVM, they can be faster than other server-side Web techniques.

In VisualAge for Java Professional, you can create, run, and debug servlets within the VisualAge for Java environment. The VisualAge for Java Enterprise Edition has more powerful servlet support, including a Servlet Builder with a set of visual beans for building your HTML pages.

In this chapter you create the Bookmark List as a servlet that uses HTML pages to interact with the user.

Servlets: A Refresher

A servlet is a specialized Java program that a server invokes in response to a request from a client. Typically the server is a Web server, and the client is a Web browser.

Servlet development is supported by the Java Servlet Development Kit (JSDK) from JavaSoft, soon to be included as part of the standard JDK.

A servlet, like an applet, has a set of life-cycle methods that it must implement to provide functions (see Figure 162). Servlets extend the javax.servlet.GenericServlet and must implement the javax.servlet.Servlet interface. Most servlet developers use the javax.servlet.http.HttpServlet, which provides convenience methods and facilities specific to HTTP Web servers.

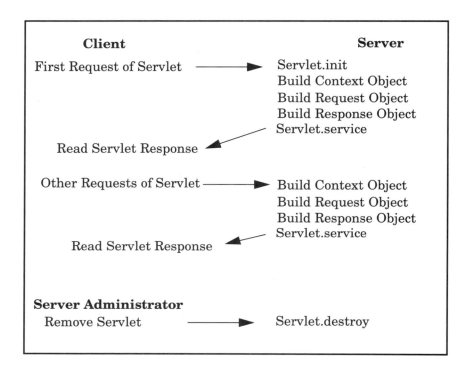

Figure 162. Servlet Architecture

The lifecycle methods are:

❏ init - Called once when the Web server loads the servlet. The Web server may load the servlet the first time a client requests the servlet, or earlier depending on the configuration of the Web server. In contrast to Common Gateway Interface (CGI) programs, servlets are long running and do not incur the cost of initialization at each request. A servlet will continue to run until it is removed from the server.

❏ service - The service method is called each time the servlet is requested. Typically most servlet developers do not use the service method, instead they use the doPost and doGet methods supplied by the HttpServlet class.

  • doPost - Invoked in response to a request from the server through the POST method, typically from an HTML form. POST methods should be used whenever the request will modify some information on the server. Examples of an HTML form using the POST method will be built in the example. The simplest form looks like this:

```
<FORM ACTION=http://localhost:8080/servlet/itso.bookmark.servlet.BookmarkListServlet
METHOD=POST>
<INPUT TYPE=HIDDEN NAME=action VALUE=save>
<INPUT TYPE=SUBMIT NAME=SaveButton VALUE=Save>
</FORM>
```

This form simply calls the servlet, passing the *action* parameter with a value of save. The servlet is invoked when the user clicks the **Save** button on the Web page.

- doGet - Invoked in response to a request from the server through the GET method, typically from a simple URL request or an HTML form. GET methods should be used whenever the request will not modify any data on the server.

  The GET method is the default when you use a URL in the Web browser. For example, clicking on the following link:

  ```
  <a href=http://localhost:8080/servlet/itso.bookmark.servlet.BookmarkListServlet>Invoke
  the servlet!</a>
  ```

  or typing:

  http://localhost:8080/servlet/itso.bookmark.servlet.BookmarkListServlet into the Location (also called Address or Netsite) field in the Web browser invokes the servlet's doGet method.

  The Web server passes two parameters to the service, doGet and doPost methods:

  HttpServletResponse: This object contains an output stream for writing information back to the Web browser as well as accessing the Hypertext Transfer Protocol (HTTP) header information.

  HttpServletRequest: This object contains an input stream for reading the browser's request as well as convenience methods for retrieving parameters from the request.

- destroy - The destroy method is called when the servlet is removed from the Web server. Release any resources in the destroy method and write any persistent data back to storage.

The ServletContext class provides information about the environment to the servlet, including the names of other servlets running in the environment and the network service under which the service is running.

For more information about the servlet classes, see the JSDK documentation.

Designing Servlet Systems

A servlet is typically used to generate dynamic HTML pages, on the basis of a simple URL link or in response to information from an HTML form. The servlet obtains any needed resources during the init method and then services requests, using one of the service methods.

The service typically consists of processing the passed data and then writing HTTP header and HTML tags to the output stream supplied in the parameters to the connection.

Separating User Interface Code from Business Logic
Mixing HTML tags with your Java code is not always a good idea. Just as you separate the user interface logic of your Java programs from the business logic, you should try and separate your HTML generation from your business logic. One approach (if your server supports it) is to use the SERVLET HTML tag. Using the this tag within server-side include files (.shtml) enables you to separate much of your HTML from your Java code. You can create your HTML pages, using your favorite tools, and then add SERVLET tags. When the servlet runs, it places the output on the page where the SERVLET tag originally was placed.

Servlets are not limited to generating dynamic HTML pages. Many servlet-based systems serve HTML pages containing APPLET tags. Once the applet is running in the Web browser, it uses the java.net.URL openStream method to communicate with the servlet. Distributed systems built in this way can transmit serialized objects between the applet and servlet without consideration for firewalls or encrypting the transmission because these issues are handled by the Web browser and server. Sophisticated servlets can also obtain the names of other servlets running on the Web server and invoke methods on them.

Servlets are inherently multithreaded. The Web server, depending on its configuration, invokes the service methods of a servlet every time a request is received. Therefore a servlet can have many requests executing the same service methods at one time. Although this brings a small amount of complexity to coding servlets, it is also a great advantage. For example, a servlet that accesses a database could create a pool of connections in the init method and then use them as requests are received. The servlet could also cache data that each service request accesses. If you do not want the servlet to be multithreaded, use the SingleThreadModel interface when creating your servlet.

When a servlet encounters errors, it should, if possible, throw a ServletException or an UnavailableException so that the Web server will send the appropriate message to the Web browser and take any other appropriate action. The HttpServlet also supplies the setStatus and sendError methods to send the status or error code back to the browser.

Making the Bookmark List a Servlet

In this section you modify the Bookmark List program to become a servlet-based program. The servlet serves dynamic HTML pages that form the user interface to the Bookmark List. Figure 163 shows the program flow.

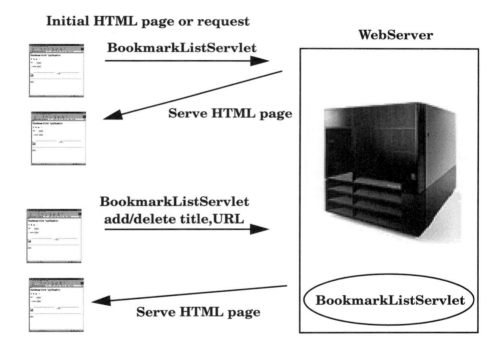

Figure 163. The BookmarkList Servlet Architecture

The servlet is a subclass of javax.servlet.http.HttpServlet and implements four methods:

❑ init: Load the current serialized Bookmark List into memory.

❑ doPost: Respond to three requests from a browser:

- Delete: Delete the element from the list and send the updated list back to the browser.
- Add: Add the element to the list and send the updated list back to the browser.
- Save: Save the current Bookmark List to disk.

❑ doGet: Respond to one request from a browser.

- Send the dynamic HTML page to the browser.

❑ destroy: Store the serialized current Bookmark List to disk.

Before building the servlet, create a new package in the Programming with VAJ V2 project: itso.bookmark.servlet. You deploy the servlet to a Web server in Chapter 10, "Deploying Your Java Programs" on page 327.

To create the servlet (as usual you can load the source from BookmarkListServlet.java):

1. Load the JSDK. To load the classes from the CD:

   a. Create a new project named JSDK. Select the new project.

   b. Select **File→Import** from the Workbench menu bar. Select the **Jar file** radio button and click **Next**. In the Select files of type .jar or .zip dialog box, select **Zip files (*.zip)** from the *Files of type* drop-down list. Browse to X:\Products\platform\JSDK, where X is your CD-ROM drive, and platform is the platform you are running on, for example, E:\Products\Windows\JSDK. Select the **jsdk.zip** file and click **Open**. Click **Finish** in the SmartGuide to start the import.

2. Create a new class in the itso.bookmark.servlet package — BookmarkListServlet — that extends javax.servlet.http.HttpServlet. Use the SmartGuide to import the javax.servlet, java.io, javax.servlet.http and java.util packages as well as the type: itso.bookmark.Bookmark.

   a. Add a string attribute to the class declaration to hold the name of the serialized Bookmark List file:

   private String SerializedBookmarkFileName = "C:\\TEMP\\BOOKMARK.SER";

   Make sure you change the above pathname to an appropriate location on your machine.

   b. Add an attribute to hold the servlet URL (you dynamically set the string during the request):

   private String ServletURL = null;

   c. You will use a Vector to hold the list. Use the BeanInfo page to add a nonbound Vector property named bookmarkList to hold the list.

   Figure 164 shows the class declaration.

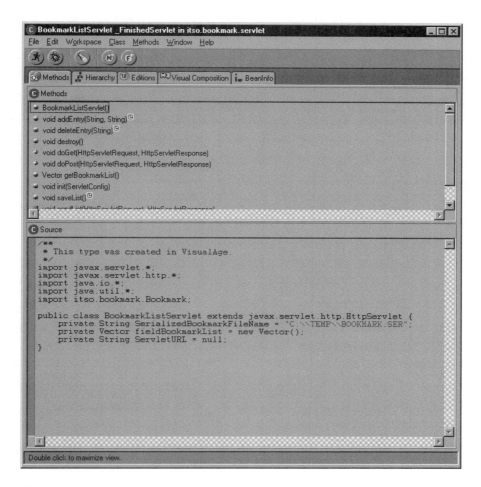

Figure 164. BookmarkListServlet Class Declaration

3. If you have not already made the itso.bookmark.Bookmark class serializable, do so now:

    public class Bookmark implements java.io.Serializable

Figure 165 shows the class declaration.

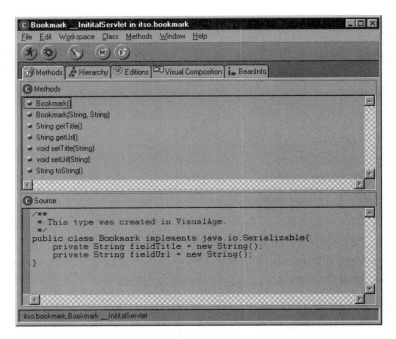

Figure 165. Modified Bookmark Class Declaration

4. Copy the addEntry and deleteEntry methods from the BookmarkListController you created in "Building the BookmarkListController" on page 126. You can almost use these methods as is to add and delete entries from the bookmarkList vector. To copy the methods (Figure 166):

   a. Select the addEntry and deleteEntry methods from the itso.bookmark.applet.BookmarkListController in the Workbench.

   b. Select **Selected→Reorganize→Copy**, click **Browse** and begin typing BookmarkListServlet. Select BookmarkListServlet, click **OK**, and deselect the **Rename (Copy as)** checkbox.

   c. Click **OK**.

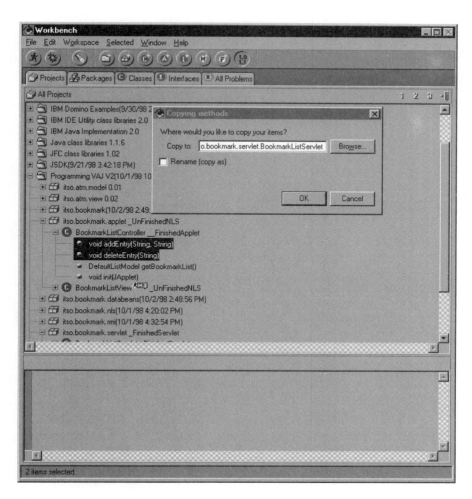

Figure 166. Copying the addEntry and deleteEntry Methods

5. Make the addEntry and deleteEntry methods thread-safe. These methods must be synchronized to keep the list from being corrupted. Change the class declarations to add the synchronized keyword:

```
public  synchronized void addEntry(String title, String url)
public  synchronized void deleteEntry(String title)
```

This is a very simple use of synchronization. In a production application you probably would also want to synchronize the reading with the writing of the Bookmark List and use separate read and write locks to improve performance.

6. Add the init method that reads the serialized Bookmark List from disk. The init method tries to load the serialized file from disk. If the file does not exist, a new Bookmark List is created. Making the Bookmark List persistent is simple when you use the Java serialization facilities.

```
public void init(ServletConfig config) throws ServletException
{
    try{
        FileInputStream fIn = new FileInputStream(      SerializedBookmarkFileName);
        ObjectInputStream in = new ObjectInputStream( fIn);
        setBookmarkList((Vector)in.readObject());
    }
    catch( FileNotFoundException e){
        setBookmarkList( new Vector());
    }
    catch( Exception e){
        log( "Error initializing servlet: " + e);
        throw new ServletException( "Error initializing servlet: " + e);
    }
}
```

7. Add the sendList method. This method is invoked during the doGet and doPost methods. The sendList method sends a dynamic HTML page back to the browser. The page contains:

- HTML title and heading tags

- A list of all bookmarks, each implemented as an HTML form with a Delete button

- The Add function implemented as another form

- A Save button to write the serialized Bookmark List to disk

The sendList method encapsulates all of the HTML generation that the servlet performs.

All the HTML forms invoke the servlet using the hidden HTML action tag to specify the action for the servlet to take. All the forms use the METHOD=POST directive which causes the doPost method on the servlet to be invoked.

The code for the sendList method is:

```
private void sendList(HttpServletRequest req, HttpServletResponse resp)
{
    PrintWriter pOut = null;
    ServletURL = req.getScheme() + "://" + req.getServerName() + ":" +
        req.getServerPort() + req.getServletPath();
    try{
        resp.setContentType( "text/html");
        pOut = new PrintWriter( resp.getOutputStream());
        pOut.println("<TITLE>BookmarkList Application</TITLE>");
```

```
      pOut.println("<H1>BookmarkList Application</H1>");
      pOut.println("<H2>Bookmarks:</H2>");
      pOut.println("<TABLE>");
      for( int i = 0; i < getBookmarkList().size(); i++){
        String Url = ((Bookmark)getBookmarkList().
            elementAt(i)).getUrl();
        String Title = ((Bookmark)getBookmarkList().
            elementAt(i)).getTitle();
        pOut.println("<TR>");
        pOut.println("<TD VALIGN=TOP>");
        pOut.println("<A HREF=" + Url + ">" + Title + "</a>");
        pOut.println("<TD>");
        pOut.println("<FORM ACTION=" + ServletURL + " METHOD=POST>");
        pOut.println("<INPUT TYPE=HIDDEN NAME=action VALUE=delete>");
        pOut.println("<INPUT TYPE=HIDDEN NAME=title VALUE=\""
            + Title + "\">");
        pOut.println("<INPUT TYPE=SUBMIT NAME=DeleteButton
    VALUE=Delete>");
        pOut.println("</FORM>");
        pOut.println("</TR>");
      }
      pOut.println("</TABLE>");
      pOut.println("<HR>");
      pOut.println("<FORM ACTION=" + ServletURL + " METHOD=POST>");
      pOut.println("<INPUT TYPE=HIDDEN NAME=action VALUE=add>");
      pOut.println("<b>Title:</b>");
      pOut.println("<INPUT TYPE=TEXT NAME=title SIZE=30>");
      pOut.println("<b>URL:</b>");
      pOut.println("<INPUT TYPE=TEXT NAME=url SIZE=30 VALUE=http://>");
      pOut.println("<INPUT TYPE=SUBMIT NAME=AddButton VALUE=Add>");
      pOut.println("</FORM>");
      pOut.println("<HR>");
      pOut.println("<FORM ACTION=" + ServletURL + " METHOD=POST>");
      pOut.println("<INPUT TYPE=HIDDEN NAME=action VALUE=save>");
      pOut.println("<INPUT TYPE=SUBMIT NAME=SaveButton VALUE=Save>");
      pOut.println("</FORM>");
      resp.setStatus( HttpServletResponse.SC_OK);
      pOut.close();
    }
    catch( IOException e)
    {
      pOut.close();
      log("Error writing to browser: " + e);
    }
}
```

Look at the fourth line in the sendList method:

```
ServletURL = req.getScheme() + "://" + req.getServerName() + ":" +
    req.getServerPort() + req.getServletPath();
```

Using the HttpServletRequest object, you build the URL to the servlet dynamically. Thus you can move the servlet to different servers or different locations on a server or change the port that the Web server is listening on, without changing the servlet code.

The seventh line of the sendList method tells the browser to expect an HTML page:

```
resp.setContentType( "text/html");
```

The eighth line of the sendList method returns a stream that the servlet uses to write to the browser:

```
pOut = new PrintWriter( resp.getOutputStream());
```

The rest of the method builds the dynamic HTML page that contains the HTML forms providing the interface to the Bookmark List. Once you have finished the example, look at the generated HTML in your Web browser, using the View Source capability.

8. Add the saveList method:

```
public synchronized void saveList()
{
    try{
      FileOutputStream fOut = new FileOutputStream(
        SerializedBookmarkFileName);
      ObjectOutputStream out = new ObjectOutputStream( fOut);
      out.writeObject( getBookmarkList());
      out.close();
    }
    catch( IOException e){
      log("Error saving list: " + e);
    }
}
```

The saveList method writes a serialized version of the Bookmark List to disk. It must be synchronized so that it does not write the wrong version of the list.

9. Add the destroy method, which simply saves the list when the servlet is destroyed:

```
public void destroy()
{
    saveList();
}
```

10. Add the doPost method:

```
protected void doPost(HttpServletRequest req,
        HttpServletResponse resp)
        throws ServletException, IOException
{
```

```
boolean sendTheList = true;
String action = req.getParameter("action");
String title = req.getParameter("title");
String url = req.getParameter("url");
if( action.equals("add")){
  addEntry( title, url);
}
else if( action.equals("delete")){
  deleteEntry( title);
}
else if( action.equals("save")){
  saveList();
}
else{
  sendTheList = false;
  log("Bad request");
}
if( sendTheList){
  sendList( req, resp);
}
}
```

The doPost method accesses the passed values, using the getParameter method and, depending on the value of the action field, adds or deletes an entry or saves the list and then always sends it back.

You specify the action field in the HTML form, using:

`<INPUT TYPE=HIDDEN NAME=action VALUE=delete>`

If the form data is incorrect, the servlet simply writes a message to the servlet log of the server.

11. Add the doGet method:

```
protected void doGet(HttpServletRequest req,
      HttpServletResponse resp)
      throws ServletException, IOException
{
    sendList( req, resp);
}
```

The doGet method simply returns the current Bookmark List when a browser invokes the URL of the servlet.

Testing the Servlet

To test the servlet you use the Servlet Runner that is included in the JSDK. You will need to have TCP/IP installed and running on your machine, and you must be able to successfully run the ping localhost command. If the command is not working, see the documentation on installing the VisualAge for Java Help system which has the same requirements. (The Hlp.txt file in the IBMVJAVA\EAB\RELNOTES directory may help.) You must run the Servlet Runner on an unused TCP/IP port (8080 by default).

Select the sun.servlet.http.HttpServer class and **Selected→Properties**. Click the **Program** tab and enter -v in the *Command line arguments* field. Click the **Class Path** tab and add the Programming VAJ V2 project to the *Project Path*.

Click the **Run** button, and the Console will show the running server.

Figure 167. Servlet Runner Output in the VisualAge for Java Console

Start a Web browser and enter the following URL:

http://localhost:8080/servlet/itso.bookmark.servlet.BookmarkListServlet

You can set breakpoints in the servlet code and debug the servlet as you interact with it through the Web browser. Figure 168 on page 293 shows the Bookmark List in the Web browser.

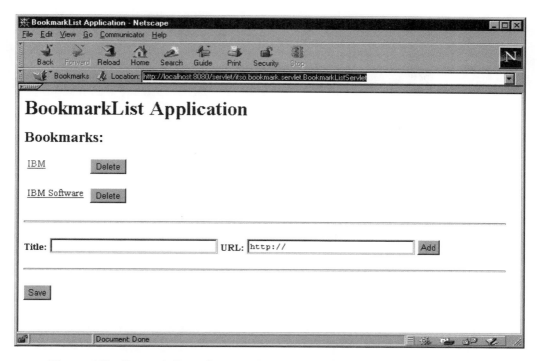

Figure 168. Dynamic Page Generated by Bookmark List Program

9 Internationalization

With the expansion of the Internet, the whole world can have access to your applet or servlet, and you may want to deploy applications anywhere in the world. Thus, it is important that you provide internationalization support for your programs. By making your Java program international, people all over the world can use it in their own language and with the correct format of specific data such as date, currency, and time.

Programs that support different languages and conventions are usually called *National Language Support* (NLS) enabled or *international* applications.

In this chapter you will learn what the JDK provides to help you write international Java programs and how international support is integrated into VisualAge for Java. Once you have learned the concepts you will make your BookmarkListView applet international and work with several other examples.

Java Internationalization Framework

To simplify the support of international applications, the JDK provides the Internationalization framework. This framework was originally developed in C++ by Taligent, a former IBM company, and has since been ported to the

Java environment. Sun adopted this framework without major modifications and made it part of the official JDK since Version 1.1.

The main components of the Internationalization framework are *locales* and *resource bundles*.

Locales

Java uses the term *locale* to identify a geographic or political region for which spoken language and format conventions are specific. The Internationalization framework defines the java.util.Locale class to support this framework. Locale objects contain information about supported geographic or political regions.

Classes that provide support for different locales are known as *locale-sensitive* classes. These classes use either a default or a specific locale to determine which locale to support. The approach is very flexible. If the particular locale is not supported, the locale hierarchy is traversed until a supported locale is found or the default locale is reached.

To create a Locale object, you specify a language, and optionally a country and variant. For example, to create a Locale object for British English, you would use the following statement:

Locale myLocale = new Locale ("en", "UK", "");

All Locale List Sample

The classes in both the java.text and the java.util.Calendar packages provide the getAvailableLocales method that returns an array of all locales that are supported by the class. This list of locales can be used to list different languages associated with the locales.

Follow these steps to create an applet that lists the different languages supported by the NumberFormat class:

1. Create a JApplet named AllLocaleList in a new package named itso.nls in the Programming VAJ V2 project and open it in the Visual Composition Editor.

2. Drop a JScrollPane on the middle of the applet and drop a JList in the JScrollPane.

3. Drop a DefaultListModel bean and a DefaultListSelectionModel bean on the free-form surface and name them DefaultListModel and DefaultListSelectionModel, respectively.

4. Connect the model of the JList to the this of DefaultListModel (Figure 169).

5. Connect the selectionModel of the JList to the this of the DefaultListSelectionModel (Figure 169).

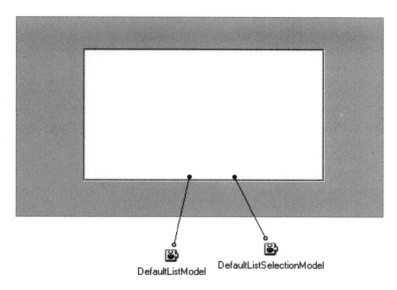

DefaultListModel   DefaultListSelectionModel

Figure 169. AllLocaleList Connections

6. Save the bean.

7. Switch to the Methods page and select the init method. Modify it to look like this:

```
public void init()
{
    try {
        setName("AllLocaleList");
        setSize(426, 240);
        setContentPane(getJAppletContentPane());
        initConnections();
        // user code begin {1}
        java.util.Locale[] allLocales =      java.text.NumberFormat.getAvailableLocales();
        java.util.Locale locale = java.util.Locale.getDefault();
        for (int i = 0; i < allLocales.length; i++) {
            /* Check if it's a valid country */
            if (allLocales[i].getDisplayCountry().length() > 0) {
            /* get name of the current Locale, add it to the list */
                getDefaultListModel().
                    addElement(allLocales[i].getDisplayName());
                /* if it's  the current setting, select it */
                if (allLocales[i].getDisplayName().
                    equals(locale.getDisplayName())) {
```

```
                getDefaultListSelectionModel().addSelectionInterval(i,i);
              }
            }
          }
          // user code end
        }
        catch (java.lang.Throwable ivjExc) {
          // user code begin {2}
          // user code end
          handleException(ivjExc);
        }
      }
    }
```

8. Change the applet width in the Properties dialog to 500 and run the applet (Figure 170).

Figure 170. AllLocaleList Applet

Resource Bundle

Java provides *resource bundle* classes that store and retrieve information, using identifiers or keys. Resource bundle classes (derived directly or indirectly from java.util.ResourceBundle) are collections of resources designed to aggregate the resources needed for a specific language. Thus you can separate the program code from the locale-specific data (for example, separate the label of a button from the code that creates it).

A naming convention is used to identify specific resource bundle classes according to their locale, so that the resource bundle methods know which resource bundle classes to select on the basis of the current locale. By using inheritance among locale resources, you can minimize resource duplication across countries and achieve graceful degradation if he exact locale does not have localized resources. For example, your program could use resources from Standard French if there is no explicit support for Canadian French.

Because a locale can be set on a per-object basis, in addition to a default, system-wide basis, it is possible to deal with more than one locale at a time in the same program.

Because java.util.ResourceBundle is an abstract class, you must create your own classes that derive from it or one of the abstract subclasses discussed below.

Accessing Resource Values

The resource bundle classes provide several methods to access resource values:

getContents

> Return the set of resource key-value pairs.

getKeys

> Return all the keys.

getObject

> Return a resource value given the key. You must cast the value to the correct type.

getString

> Return a resource value given the key. This is a convenience method for string values.

getStringArray

> Return a resource value given the key. This is a convenience method for string array values.

The two types of resource bundles are List and Property. A ListResourceBundle stores the key-value pairs in an array of objects, while the PropertyResourceBundle stores the key-value pairs in property files. You may see better performance with a ListResourceBundle than a PropertyResourceBundle because use of the PropertyResourceBundle implies a file access for each bundle. However when you use the ListResourceBundle, application code is being modified during translation work, which is not always desirable.

List Resource Bundles

The java.util.ListResourceBundle class is an abstract class that derives from ResourceBundle. It stores the localized data in an array of Object types. Therefore the localized data can be of any type, for example, Image.

When localizing your program, you subclass ListResourceBundle with your own classes, that must override the getContents method and provide an array, where each item in the array is a pair of objects. The first element of each pair is a String key, and the second is the value associated with that key.

A sample ListResourceBundle class might look like this:

```
import java.util.*;
public class MyResources extends ListResourceBundle
{
    public Object[][] getContents()
    {
        return contents;
    }
    static final Object[][] contents = {
        {"GreetingLabel", "Hello World!"},
        {"AddButton", "Add"},
    };
}
```

Property Resource Bundles

The PropertyResourceBundle class is an abstract subclass of ResourceBundle that manages resources for a locale through a set of strings loaded from a property file. Property files must have a .properties extension. They contain keys and their corresponding values. You can use those keys in your source code to call ResourceBundle.getString in order to retrieve the associated values.

Unlike ListResourceBundle, PropertyResourceBundle can be used to store strings only, not other objects.

Internationalization in VisualAge for Java

New in V2!

VisualAge for Java supports internationalization through the Externalize String function. Given a string property (in the Visual Composition Editor) or a class containing strings, VisualAge for Java can generate code that references the string indirectly through a resource bundle (property or list) and create the bundle for you. Note that strings that VisualAge for Java generates in user code blocks will not be externalized, and you should move them into separate methods.

VisualAge for Java adds an entry (composed of the key and value) in the array or property file at each point in your code where a string was directly referenced, for example:

```
JTextField1.setText("A string");
```

The string parameter will be replaced by a call to the resource bundle:

JTextField1.setText(getResourceBundle1(getString("AStringLabel")).);

International Edition of VisualAge for Java
This chapter covers how you can make your Java programs international. This is not the same as using the international edition of VisualAge for Java that supports developers working in their native languages, including French, German, Spanish, Chinese, Japanese, Korean, Italian, and Portuguese.

Externalizing All Strings in a Class

The steps to externalize all the strings in a class at one time are:

1. From the Projects page of the Workbench, select the class whose strings you want to externalize.

2. Select **Selected→Externalize Strings**. Or, click mouse button 2 and select **Externalize Strings** from the pop-up menu.

The Externalizing dialog box appears, with a list of hardcoded strings found in the class (Figure 171). As you can see in the figure, not all strings need to be externalized; for example, the "Center" string is a parameter to a call adding the component to a BorderLayout and should not be externalized.

If the same value appears more than once, VisualAge for Java will associate the same key with the value.

Figure 171. Externalizing Strings

3. Specify the type of resource bundle by selecting one of the following radio buttons:

   • List resource bundle

   • Property resource file

4. Specify the name of the resource bundle:
   Use the **Browse** button to choose an existing resource bundle, or use the **New** button to create a new bundle.

5. Under **Strings to be separated**, you can mark an item by clicking the iconic checkbox to the left of the column. By default all strings are marked for externalization so no action is required to externalize the string.

   • For strings that are never to be externalized, click once and a red *X* appears (Figure 171). The string will be removed from the *Strings to be separated* list.

   • To leave the string hardcoded for now, click twice and a *?* should appear. The string will not be removed from the **Strings to be separated** list.

   If you are not sure of a string, review it in the Context field. Then click **OK** to proceed with the externalization.

Removing the Externalization Information
VisualAge marks each item that you have chosen to externalize or never to externalize with a special comment. To make a string appear in the externalization list once again, find the accessor for the string resource or the string itself in the code and delete the comment at the end of the line: //$NON-NLS-1$. Then perform the steps 1 through 5 again.

Externalizing a String Property

If you need more control over the externalization of individual strings, you can externalize each string property separately. The steps to externalize a string property are:

1. In the Visual Composition Editor, open the Property sheet for the bean that contains the string property you want to externalize. Select the value field to the right of the property name. A small button with three dots appears to the right of the text field.

2. Select the button. The Text dialog box appears (Figure 172).

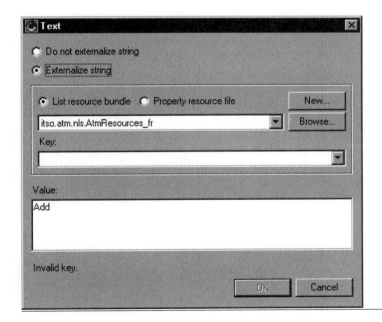

Figure 172. String Externalization Editor

3. Select the appropriate radio button:

- **Do not externalize string**
- **Externalize string**

4. If you select **Do not externalize string**, you are finished. Just click **OK** to close the window. Use this selection if the string value is long or runs over multiple lines. You must use the Text dialog to enter the string but you do not have to externalize the string.

5. If you select **Externalize string**, specify the type of resource bundle by selecting one of the following radio buttons:

   - **List resource bundle**
   - **Property resource file**

6. Specify the name of the resource bundle:

   - Use the **Browse** button or the drop-down list to choose an existing resource bundle, or use the **New** button to create a new bundle.
   - The name of the bundle appears in the bundle list.

7. To define a new resource, type its name in the *Key* field. The existing resources can be accessed through the pull-down list on the key field. The *Value:* text area contains the current value of the string property. If a key is selected, the text area contains the current value of the selected key. Click **OK** to close the window.

The next time you save the class, VisualAge for Java modifies the generated get methods for the beans so that the text property is set from the resource bundle.

Making the BookmarkListView Applet International

In this section you will add international capabilities for your BookmarkListView applet. Specifically you will add support for English, French, and Italian. When the applet starts, the strings loaded for the user interface will be in the language of the current locale for the computer.

Externalizing the Strings

1. Create a new package in the Programming with VAJ V2 project: itso.bookmark.nls.

2. Select the BookmarkListController and BookmarkListView classes in the itso.bookmark.applet package in Workbench. Select **Selected→Reorganize→Copy**. Click **Browse** and then enter

itso.bookmark.nls and click **OK**. Deselect the **Rename (copy as)** checkbox and click **OK**.

Because the applet contains a reference to the original BookmarkListController, you will see an error created by the copy. Open the BookmarkListView in the Visual Composition Editor and fix the reference, using the Morph Into function and the same process as in "Modifying the BookmarkList Applet to Support Serialization" on page 257.

3. In the Visual Composition Editor, open the Property Sheet for the JLabel that has a *text* property of Title:. Select the **Title:** text in the Property sheet and then select the button that appears in the field. The button represents the property editor.

4. In the Text dialog that appears (Figure 173 on page 306), click **Externalize String,** then select the **ListResourceBundle** radio button, then click **New**. Enter itso.bookmark.nls for the *Package* and BookmarkResources for the *Class name*.

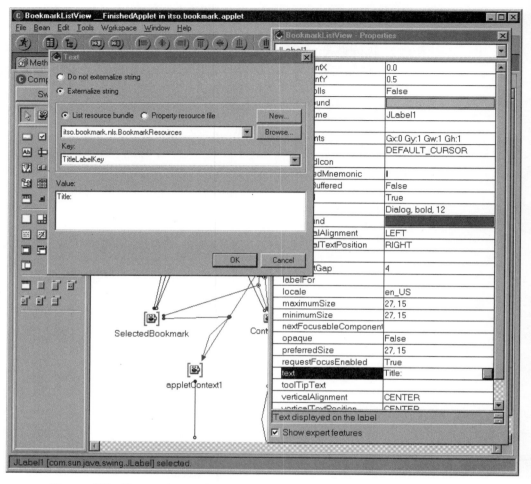

Figure 173. Externalizing the text Property

5. Enter TitleLabelKey in the *Key* field. Click **OK**.

6. For each of the three buttons, enter the key as shown in Table 16. Again select the **List resource bundle** radio button and use the same ListResourceBundle. The URL: field is not changed because the URL string is used in all the languages supported by the Bookmark List. Use the

same class, BookmarkResources, and package, itso.bookmark.nls, for all of the strings.

Table 16. Externalizing the BookmarkListView Buttons

Button	Key
Add	AddButtonKey
Delete	DeleteButtonKey
Go!	GoButtonKey

7. Now, save the bean so you can work with the generated code.

Creating the Alternate Resource Bundles

Switch to the Workbench. You see a new class, BookmarkResources, in the itso.bookmark.nls package. BookmarkResources contains an array of objects. The array contains the key-value pairs that you specified when you externalized the strings. The values of the strings in this array are the default values of the strings. Now you subclass BookmarkResources to provide the support for the other locales.

Copy BookmarkResources to another class, BookmarkResources_fr, in the same package, using **Selected→Reorganize→Copy**. Change the class declaration:

```
public class BookmarkResources_fr extends BookmarkResources{
    static final Object[][] contents = {
        {"GoButtonLabel", "Aller!"},
        {"DeleteButtonKey", "Effacer"},
        {"AddButtonkey", "Ajouter"},
        {"TitleLabelKey", "Titre:"},
    };
}
```

Notice that BookmarkResources_fr extends BookmarkResources and provides the French translations of each string. Now copy BookmarkResources_fr to BookmarkResources_it and change the values of the strings to the Italian translation:

```
public class BookmarkResources_it extends BookmarkResources{
    static final Object[][] contents = {
        {"GoButtonLabel", "Vai!"},
        {"DeleteButtonKey", "Cancella"},
        {"AddButtonkey", "Aggiungi"},
        {"TitleLabelKey", "Titolo:"},
    };
}
```

You are done. Now when the BookmarkListView applet runs, the language displayed will be that of the default locale of the machine provided that the default locale is Standard French, Standard Italian, or U.S. English.

If the locale of the machine is another version of French or Italian, the language displayed is the Standard French or Italian. If the default locale is any other locale, U.S. English will be displayed.

If you are running Windows NT, you can change your default locale through the Regional Settings. This action requires access to the NT install image and may cause VisualAge for Java to re-install some files. In the next section you build a program where the user can change the locale settings dynamically.

Figure 174 shows the running applet.

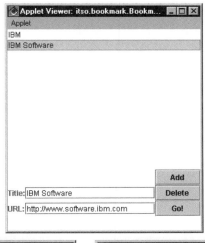

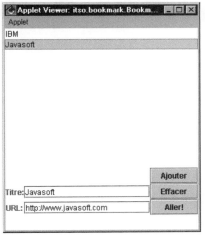

Figure 174. The Three Languages Supported in the BookmarkListView Applet

Building a Language Panel

When you created the French, Italian and U.S. English resource bundles in the last section, you probably did not change your default locale and reboot your machine just to see the different languages displayed by your applet. In this section you build a LanguagePanel that changes the display on the basis of user input.

First copy the three .gif files (frflag.gif, itflag.gif and usflag.gif) from the examples directory into the project resources directory of the Programming with VAJ V2 project (ibmvjava\ide\project_resources\Programming VAJ V2). You will use the .gif files to display the country flags of the different locales by adding an icon to a JLabel.

LanguagePanel View

1. In the itso.nls package create a LanguagePanel class that inherits from com.sun.java.swing.JFrame. Make sure you select the **Compose the class visually** checkbox to open the Visual Composition Editor.

2. Add a JLabel to the center of the panel and a JComboBox to the bottom of the panel and change the bean names to SelectLanguageLabel and LanguageChoice.

3. Change the *text* property of SelectLanguageLabel to Select Your Language of Preference. Change the *foreground* color to *Black* and ensure that *verticalAlignment* and *verticalTextPosition* are set to CENTER, *horizontalAlignment* to LEFT, and *horizontalTextPosition* to RIGHT.

4. Click the field to the right of the SelectLanguageLabel *icon* property and then click the button that appears in the right of the field. Select the **file** radio button and click **Browse**. Select **Programming with VAJ V2\usflag.gif** and click **OK**.

5. Resize the frame and the textfield to see the complete text and image (Figure 175 on page 311).

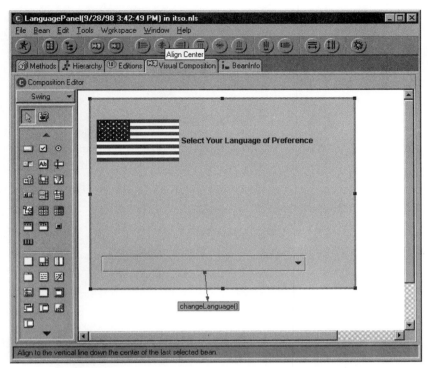

Figure 175. The LanguagePanel in the Visual Composition Editor

Creating the Resource Bundles

1. Externalize the *text* property of the SelectLanguageLabel (see Figure 176 on page 312):

   a. Select the **List resource bundle** radio button.

   b. Enter itso.nls for the *Package name* and LanguageResources for the *Class Name*.

   c. Enter SelectLanguageLabel in the *Key* field.

   d. The *Value* field should already be filled in with Select Your Language of Preference.

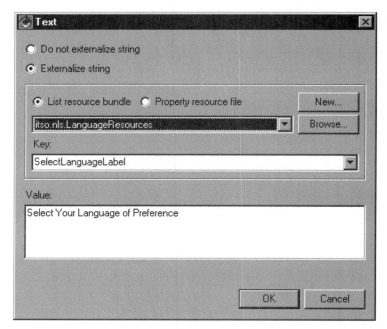

Figure 176. Externalizing the SelectLanguageLabel

In "Creating the Alternate Resource Bundles" on page 307, you created the alternate resource bundles by copying the created class. You can also use VisualAge for Java to produce the different bundles.

2. Externalize the text property of the SelectLanguageLabel again. This time choose itso.nls for the *Package* and LanguageResources_fr for the *Class name*.

   a. Enter SelectLanguageLabel in the *Key* field.

   b. Enter Choisissez une Langue de Préférence in the *Value* field.

   To create an international character, hold down the ALT key and input the ASCII code for the character, using the number pad on the right-hand side of your keyboard, then release ALT. For this example you only need the é symbol: 0233.

3. Repeat the externalization one more time, using itso.nls.LanguageResources_it for Italian:

   a. Enter SelectLanguageLabel in the *Key* field.

   b. Enter Selezionare un Linguaggio dello Preferenza in the *Value* field.

   c. Save the bean. The free-form surface shows the text field with an American flag and Italian text. Don't worry, you will fix that when the application starts.

You now have three resource bundle classes in your itso.nls package: LanguageResources, LanguageResources_fr, and LanguageResources_it. To use the generic resource bundle, LanguageResources, to support the default locale, English, and all the other locales that are not French or Italian, subclass the French and Italian resource bundles from LanguageResources instead of from java.util.ListResourceBundle. Add the icon for the American flag to the default language resources so the LanguageResources class looks like these:

```
public class LanguageResources extends java.util.ListResourceBundle {
    static final Object[][] contents = {
        {"SelectLanguageLabel", "Select your language of preference"},
        {"Icon",new com.sun.java.swing.ImageIcon("usflag.gif")}
    };
}
```

Modify the two subclasses to match the following code:

```
public class LanguageResources_fr extends LanguageResources {
    static final Object[][] contents = {
        {"SelectLanguageLabel", "Choisissez une Langue de Préférence"},
        {"Icon",new com.sun.java.swing.ImageIcon("frflag.gif")}};
}

public class LanguageResources_it extends LanguageResources {
    static final Object[][] contents = {
        {"SelectLanguageLabel", "Selezionare un Linguaggio dello Preferenza"},
        {"Icon",new com.sun.java.swing.ImageIcon("itflag.gif")}
    };
}
```

Dynamically Changing the Locale

In "Making the BookmarkListView Applet International" on page 304, the resource bundle for the default locale was loaded automatically when the program started. To dynamically change the locale, you have to add code to change the locale-specific components.

Loading Resource Bundles

To load a resource bundle you use the static method, getBundle, from the ResourceBundle with the name of the resource bundle base class (including package information if not in the same package as the calling application) and the preferred locale. For example:

```
ResourceBundle myBundle = ResourceBundle.getBundle("MyResources", aLocale);
```

where aLocale is your Locale object, and MyResources is the name of your resource bundle.

Number of Resource Bundles
In complex applications, you typically define many resource bundle hierarchies; for example, one for each window or one for labels, one for numbers, one for pictures, and one for sounds.

In the LanguagePanel applet, you will use only one resource bundle hierarchy. If the current locale is set to French Canadian, the getBundle method first looks for a class called MyResources_fr_CA. If it does not find the class, it looks for Standard French (MyResources_fr). If that search fails, the method loads the generic class MyResources. If the method cannot find MyResources, it throws a MissingResourceException.

Retrieving Resources from Resource Bundles

Once your resource bundle class is loaded, you can use the keys to access the stored objects. The getObject method returns an element of the static array of resources. As the resource is always returned as a java.lang.Object, you have to cast it to the correct type of your object. As you learned in "Accessing Resource Values" on page 299, a getString method is provided for convenience. For example, if you want to set a JLabel to the "HelloWorld" resource, you use:

```
myJLabel.setText(myBundle.getString("HelloWorld"));
```

When you use the ListResourceBundle class, you can also store objects other than strings. For example, you could use myBundle to retrieve the "BigNumber" resource into a variable:

```
Integer myBigNumber = (Integer)myBundle.getObject("BigNumber"));
```

Finishing the LanguagePanel

To make LanguagePanel a multilingual panel, create two methods:

❑ The changeLanguage() method is called whenever a user selects a new language from LanguageChoice. This method translates the language selected into a supported locale and calls the setLocale method by passing the new locale as a parameter.

❑ The updateGui(java.util.Locale) method retrieves a resource bundle instance and updates the GUI components according to the locale passed as a parameter.

To create the updateGui method:

1. Select LanguagePanel and **Selected→Add→Method**. Type in void updateGui(java.util.Locale aLocale) as the method name and choose private as the access modifier. Click **Finish** to create the method.

2. Select the method and modify its code:

```
private void updateGui(java.util.Locale aLocale)
{
    java.util.ResourceBundle aResourceBundle=null;
    try {
        aResourceBundle=
            java.util.ResourceBundle.getBundle("itso.nls.LanguageResources",
            aLocale);
    }
    catch (Exception e) {
        System.out.println(e);
    }
    getSelectLanguageLabel().
        setText(aResourceBundle.getString("SelectLanguageLabel"));
        getSelectLanguageLabel().setIcon((com.sun.java.swing.ImageIcon)
            aResourceBundle.getObject("Icon"));
}
```

At the beginning of the method, a local variable is created to hold the resource bundle object. Then the resource bundle instance is retrieved, using the current locale. Once the resource bundle instance has been retrieved, it is used to get the resources for each label.

To create the changeLanguage method:

1. In the Workbench, select the **LanguagePanel** class and **Selected→Add→Method** or click the **M** icon on the toolbar.

2. Enter void changeLanguage() as the method name and select **private** as the access modifier. Click **Finish** to create the method.

3. Select the method and modify its code:

```
private void changeLanguage()
{
    if( getLanguageChoice().getSelectedItem().equals(
            java.util.Locale.FRANCE.getDisplayLanguage())) {
        updateGui(java.util.Locale.FRANCE);
    }
    else if(getLanguageChoice().getSelectedItem().equals(
```

```
            java.util.Locale.US.getDisplayLanguage())) {
        updateGui(java.util.Locale.US);
    }
    else if (getLanguageChoice().getSelectedItem().equals(
            java.util.Locale.ITALY.getDisplayLanguage())) {
        updateGui(java.util.Locale.ITALY);
    }
}
```

To change the GUI when the user selects another language, just add an event-to-code connection from the itemStateChanged event of the LanguageChoice to the changeLanguage method (Figure 177). Now save the bean.

Finally, you need to populate the list of languages for the Select language drop-down list and set the GUI to the default locale on initialization. Change the initialize method to look like this:

```
private void initialize() {
    // user code begin {1}
    // user code end
    setName("LanguagePanel");
    setDefaultCloseOperation(com.sun.java.swing.WindowConstants.DISPOSE_ON_CLOS
    E);
    setSize(528, 299);
    setContentPane(getJFrameContentPane());
    initConnections();
    // user code begin {2}
    getLanguageChoice().addItem(java.util.Locale.US.getDisplayLanguage());
    getLanguageChoice().addItem(java.util.Locale.FRANCE.getDisplayLanguage());
    getLanguageChoice().addItem(java.util.Locale.ITALY.getDisplayLanguage());
    updateGui(java.util.Locale.getDefault());
    // user code end
}
```

Save and run the LanguagePanel (Figure 178).

Length of Translated Strings
One problem encountered when translating user interface elements is the relative length of strings. A translated string can be much longer or shorter than the original string. When you design your user interfaces keep this in mind and use layouts and constraints that will adjust to changing string lengths.

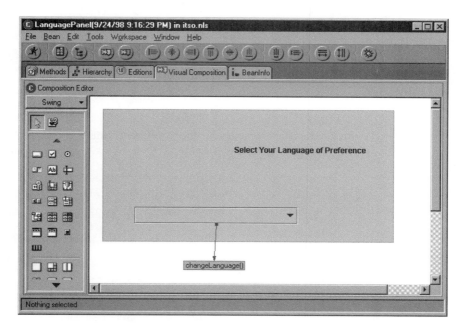

Figure 177. LanguagePanel Connection

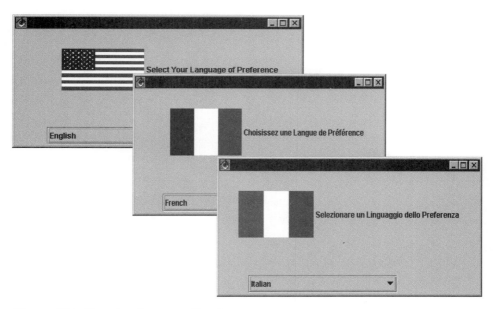

Figure 178. Running LanguagePanel

Formatting Dates and Times

The DateFormat class and its subclasses are used to handle the formatting of date and time information. You have to use the getDateTimeInstance method to get the date and time formatter or getDateInstance to get only the date formatter. The following code shows you how to use getDateInstance for a given locale attribute:

```
Date myDate = new Date("21 September 1998");
DateFormat df = DateFormat.getDateInstance(DateFormat.DEFAULT, locale);
String formattedDate = df.format(myDate);
```

The first parameter in the getDateInstance method call is used to specify the format of the date or time to be used. Refer to the JDK documentation for all possible formats.

Adding Dates to the LanguagePanel

Follow these steps to update the Language Panel with international dates and times:

1. Open your LanguagePanel class and add four JLabels and rename them: TimeLabel, Time, DateLabel, and Date. Set the text properties to Time:, TimeValue, Date:, and DateValue (place them as shown in Figure 179).

2. Save the bean.

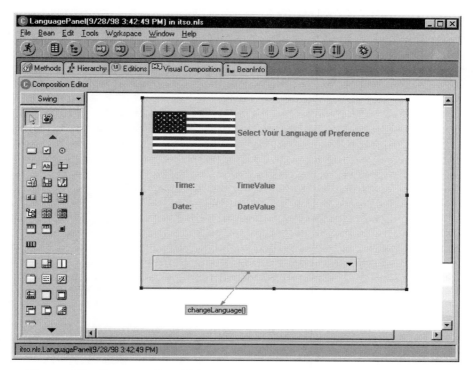

Figure 179. LanguagePanel View2

3. Externalize the TimeLabel and the DateLabel strings through their property sheets to update their appropriate values in the correct resource bundles:

LanguageResources:

Key	Value
TimeLabel	Time:
DateLabel	Date:

LanguageResources_fr:

Key	Value
TimeLabel	Heure:
DateLabel	Date:

LanguageResources_it:

Key	Value
TimeLabel	Ora:
DateLabel	Data:

4. Modify the updateGui(Locale) method in LanguagePanel:

```
private void updateGui(java.util.Locale aLocale) {
    java.util.ResourceBundle aResourceBundle=null;
    try {
        aResourceBundle=java.util.ResourceBundle.
        getBundle("itso.nls.LanguageResources",aLocale);
    }
    catch (Exception e) {
        System.out.println(e);
    }
    getSelectLanguageLabel().setText(aResourceBundle.
        getString("SelectLanguageLabel"));
    getSelectLanguageLabel().setIcon((com.sun.java.swing.ImageIcon)
        aResourceBundle.getObject("Icon"));
    getTimeLabel().setText(aResourceBundle.getString("TimeLabel"));
    getDateLabel().setText(aResourceBundle.getString("DateLabel"));
    java.text.DateFormat   dFormat, tFormat;
    dFormat = java.text.DateFormat.getDateInstance(
        java.text.DateFormat.DEFAULT, aLocale);
    tFormat = java.text.DateFormat.getTimeInstance(
        java.text.DateFormat.DEFAULT, aLocale);
    java.lang.String timeString = tFormat.format(new java.util.Date());
    java.lang.String timeZone = tFormat.getTimeZone().getID();
    getTime().setText(timeString + "   " + timeZone);
    java.lang.String dateString = dFormat.format(new java.util.Date());
    getDate().setText(dateString);
}
```

5. Save and test your work. Figure 180 shows the output.

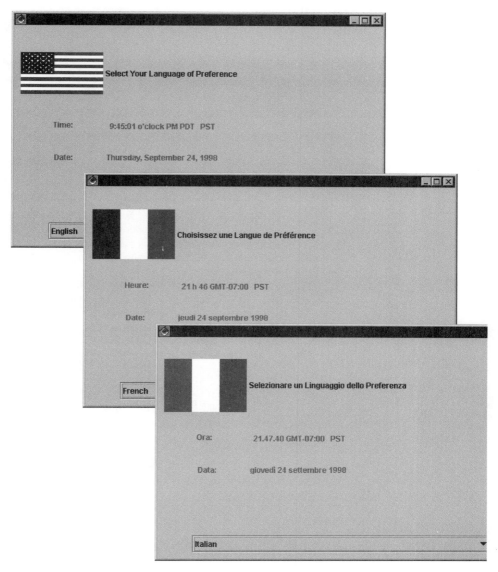

Figure 180. LanguagePanel Output with Dates and Times

Other Internationalization Considerations

This section covers resources other than strings and dates that you must consider when internationalizing your Java programs.

Using Predefined Formats

The JDK supplies the NumberFormat class and its subclasses, ChoiceFormat and DecimalFormat, for the different locale number formats. By invoking the methods provided by the NumberFormat class, you can format numbers, currencies, and percentages according to locale. However, there is a catch: NumberFormat may not support the locale you specify. To find out which locale definitions NumberFormat supports, invoke the getAvailableLocales method:

Locale[] locales = NumberFormat.getAvailableLocales();

Custom Number Formats
If NumberFormat does not support a locale that you need, you can create your own formats. You can use the DecimalFormat class to format decimal numbers into locale-specific strings. With this class you can control the display of leading and trailing zeros, prefixes and suffixes, grouping (thousands) separators, and the decimal separator. If you want to change formatting symbols such as the decimal separator, you can use the DecimalFormatSymbols class in conjunction with the DecimalFormat class. These classes offer a great deal of flexibility in the formatting of numbers, but they can make your code more complex. For more details refer to the JDK documentation.

Numbers

You can use the NumberFormat factory methods to format primitives, such as double, and their corresponding wrapper objects, such as Double.

This code example formats a Double according to locale. Invoking the getNumberInstance method returns a locale-specific instance of NumberFormat. The format method accepts the Double as an argument and returns the formatted number in a String.

```
Double amount = new Double(123456.789);
NumberFormat numberFormatter;
String amountOut;
numberFormatter = NumberFormat.getNumberInstance(currentLocale);
amountOut = numberFormatter.format(amount);
System.out.println(amountOut + "   " + currentLocale.toString());
```

The output from this example shows how the format of the same number varies with locale:

```
123 456,789 fr_FR
123.456,789 de_DE
123,456,789 en_U.S.
```

Currencies

You format currencies the same way you format numbers, except with currencies you call getCurrencyInstance to create a formatter. When you invoke the format method, it returns a String that includes the formatted number and the appropriate currency sign.

The following code example shows how to format currency in a locale-specific manner:

```
Double currency = new Double(1234567.89);
NumberFormat currencyFormatter;
String currencyOut;
currencyFormatter = NumberFormat.getCurrencyInstance(currentLocale);
currencyOut = currencyFormatter.format(currency);
System.out.println(currencyOut + "   " + currentLocale.toString());
```

Here is the output generated by the preceding lines of code:

```
1 234 567,89 F   fr_FR
1.234.567,89 DM   de_DE
$1,234,567.89 en_U.S.
```

 Converting Currencies
At first glance this output may look wrong because all of the numeric values are the same. Of course, 1 234 567,89 F is not equivalent to 1.234.567,89 DM. However, bear in mind that the NumberFormat class is unaware of exchange rates. The methods belonging to the NumberFormat class format currencies but do not convert them.

Percentages

You can also use the methods of the NumberFormat class to format percentages. To get the locale-specific formatter, invoke the getPercentInstance method. With this formatter, a fraction such as 0.75 is displayed as 75%. The following code sample shows how to format a percentage:

```
Double percent = new Double(0.75);
NumberFormat percentFormatter;
String percentOut;
percentFormatter = NumberFormat.getPercentInstance(currentLocale);
percentOut = percentFormatter.format(percent);
```

Messages

Programs often need to build messages from sequences of strings, numbers, and other data. To produce the "The disk 'MyDisk' contains 3 files." message, you would use the following code:

```
int numFiles = 3;
String diskName = "MyDisk";
String message = "The disk" + diskName + " contains"+ numFiles + "files.";
```

The above code, although easy to understand, is extremely difficult to localize because it hard codes both the strings that make up the message and the order in which they are put together. Note, for example, that the French translation of the message, "Il y a 3 fichiers sur le disque 'MyDisk'.", reverses the strings.

The MessageFormat class provides a way to build messages in a language-neutral way. It is constructed from a pattern string. The pattern string describes the structure of the message and the substitution order for the parameters. When you use a MessageFormat, the code used to create "The disk 'MyDisk' contains 3 files." would look like this:

```
Object[] arguments = new Object[2];
arguments[0] = new Integer(3);
arguments[1] = "MyDisk";
StringBuffer message = new StringBuffer();
MessageFormat fmt= new MessageFormat("Disk {0} contains {1} files.");
fmt.format(arguments, message, null);
fmt = new MessageFormat("Il y a {1} fichiers sur le disque {0} ");
fmt.format(arguments, message, null);
```

The format method formats the given arguments and substitutes the result into the pattern string to form the final message. The MessageFormat tries to format the given arguments in several ways. An array of Format objects can be passed to the MessageFormat. If the array is present, parameter n will be formatted using the nth entry of the format array. If an explicit format array has not been passed as a parameter, a default Format will be obtained. If the parameter to be formatted is a number, NumberFormat.getDefault is called. Otherwise, the parameter's toString method is called.

An additional type of Format, ChoiceFormat, is available for use in formatting the parameters of a message. A ChoiceFormat allows text to be associated with a number or range of numbers.

Collations

Applications that search or sort through text perform frequent string comparisons. A report generator performs string comparisons when sorting a list of strings in alphabetical order. However, the order of certain characters in the alphabets of different locales may be significantly different.

If your application audience is limited to people who speak English, you can probably perform string comparisons with the String.compareTo method. This method performs a binary comparison of the Unicode characters within the strings. For many languages, you cannot rely on this binary comparison to sort strings, because the Unicode values do not correspond to the relative order of the characters.

Fortunately, the Collator class allows your application to perform string comparisons for different languages. You use the Collator class to perform locale-independent comparisons. The Collator class is locale-sensitive.

To see which locales the Collator class supports, invoke the getAvailableLocales method:

Locale[] locales = Collator.getAvailableLocales();

When you instantiate the Collator class, you invoke the getInstance method and specify the locale:

Collator myCollator = Collator.getInstance(new Locale("en", "U.S."));

The getInstance method actually returns a RuleBasedCollator, which is a concrete subclass of Collator. The RuleBasedCollator class contains a set of rules that determine the sort order of strings for the locale you specify. These rules are predefined for each locale. Because the rules are encapsulated within the RuleBasedCollator, your program does not need special routines to deal with the way collation rules vary with language.

You invoke the Collator.compare method to perform a locale-independent string comparison. The method returns an integer less than, equal to, or greater than zero when the first string argument is less than, equal to, or greater than the second string argument. For example:

myCollator.compare("abc", "xyz"); // returns -1: "abc" is less than "xyz"
myCollator.compare("abc", "abc"); // returns 0: the two strings are equal
myCollator.compare("xyz", "abc"); // returns 1: "xyz" is greater than "abc"

You can use the Collator compare method when performing sort operations. The sample program (taken from the JDK Demo package) presented below uses the compare method to sort an array of English and French words. It shows what can happen when you sort the same list of words with two different collators.

Collator fr_FRCollator = Collator.getInstance(new Locale("fr","FR"));
Collator en_U.S.Collator = Collator.getInstance(new Locale("en","U.S."));

The method for sorting, called sortStrings, can be used with any Collator. Notice that the sortStrings method invokes the compare method:

```
public static void sortStrings(Collator collator, String[] words)
{
    String tmp;
    for (int i = 0; i < words.length; i++) {
        for (int j = i + 1; j < words.length; j++) {
            // Compare elements of the array two at a time.
            if (collator.compare(words[i], words[j] ) > 0 ) {
            // Swap words[i] and words[j]
            tmp = words[i];
            words[i] = words[j];
            words[j] = tmp;
            }
        }
    }
}
```

The English Collator sorts the words like this:

```
peach
pêche
péché
sin
```

According to the collation rules of the French language, the preceding list is in the wrong order. In French, "pêche" should follow "péché" in a sorted list. Therefore the French Collator sorts the array of words like this:

```
peach
péché
pêche
sin
```

10 Deploying Your Java Programs

Traditionally, you develop an application for a specific platform, test it on that platform, and create a platform-specific installation utility to deploy the application. Deploying a Java program is different; the program could be an applet, an application, or a servlet, all with different deployment techniques. In addition, the program is expected to run wherever there is a JVM.

This chapter shows you how to deploy a Java program, whether it is an applet, servlet, or application, to the runtime, or target environment.

Deploying a Java program is usually quite simple. However, because Java is "write once, run anywhere," deployment is not always trivial. The level of JDK, especially when deploying applets, can present problems as can the correct settings for CLASSPATH, and the configuration of the Web server, in the case of servlets.

It is important to test your Java programs on as many JVMs as possible. There are differences in virtual machine implementations, especially in scheduling and time-critical programs.

Deployment can become quite difficult if the Java program contains calls to nonJava code or uses nonstandard Java extensions. Writing pure Java code is necessary to ensure trouble-free deployment.

Before You Start

To complete the exercises in this chapter, you must set up the correct runtime environments for your Java programs. The requirements for the Java programs are:

Requirements for Applications

1. JDK 1.1.6

   The accompanying CD-ROM includes the JDK. Alternatively the JDK can be downloaded from:

   http://java.sun.com/products/jdk/1.1/download-jdk-windows.html

2. JFC 1.0.2

   The accompanying CD-ROM includes the JFC. Alternatively the JFC can be downloaded from:

   http://java.sun.com/products/jfc/index.html#download-swing

   For further information about using the JFC, see the README file in the Sun JFC Swing Set project resources directory.

Requirements for Servlets

1. A Web server that supports servlets

   The accompanying CD-ROM includes the Domino Go Web server. Alternatively a trial version of the Domino Go Web server can be downloaded from:

   http://www.software.ibm.com/webservers/dgw/download.htm

   Follow the links to register and download the appropriate edition for your platform and location.

2. JDK 1.1

   The Domino Go Web server includes a version of the JDK 1.1.

   The accompanying CD-ROM includes the JDK. Alternatively the JDK can be downloaded from:

   http://java.sun.com/products/jdk/1.1/download-jdk-windows.html

Requirements for Applets

1. A Web browser that supports JDK 1.1 and the JFC.

   The VisualAge for Java install image contains Netscape Navigator 4.04. For information about installing the Web browser, see the product documentation.

   To run JDK 1.1 applets in Netscape 4.04, you have to install the JDK 1.1 patch from: http://developer.netscape.com/software/jdk/download.html.

   If you are using a newer version of Netscape, ensure that full JDK 1.1 support is included in the version.

   To run applets that use JFC components, the JFC JAR file, swingall.jar, must be in the system CLASSPATH when you start the Web browser.

2. JFC 1.0.2

   The accompanying CD-ROM includes the JFC. Alternatively the JFC can be downloaded from:

   http://java.sun.com/products/jfc/index.html#download-swing

   For further information about using the JFC, see the README file in the Sun JFC Swing Set project resources directory.

3. A Web server

   You can use the Domino Go Web server. However, almost any Web server is adequate.

All of the examples in this chapter assume that you are deploying the Java programs on the machine where VisualAge for Java is installed. If you are deploying the programs on another machine, you must transfer the files to the target machine after you export them from VisualAge for Java.

Deploying an Application

A Java application is a Java program that is started from a main method. A Java object that is to be run as an application must implement a main method.

Applications have full access to the host environment. They can start programs and read and write files, and they have the same permissions as native applications. Java applications can be run on any platform that supports a JVM at the correct level.

To deploy a Java application from VisualAge for Java you have to export the Java code:

1. Choose the export type: class files or JAR file.

2. Choose that classes to include in the export:
   - Include referenced types
   - Exclude design time classes

3. Choose whether to include Debug information in the classes. Choose this option only if you are going to debug the application remotely.

 Include Referenced Types
Be careful if you select Include Referenced Types. VisualAge for Java adds all the types that your class references to the JAR file or directory export, which may include the complete JFC or JDBC hierarchies if you use those classes. You may not want to include the classes in your export.

Once you have exported the application, you should be able to run it on the target platform provided:

❑ The target platform has the same or a compatible level of the JDK installed.

❑ All classes that your application references are either packaged with your application or in the CLASSPATH on the target machine. If you have exported a JAR file, add the complete path and file name of the JAR file to the CLASSPATH. For example, if your JAR file is MyClasses.jar and you have exported it to C:\JavaClasses, the CLASSPATH entry should be C:\JavaClasses\MyClasses.jar. If you have exported class files to C:\JavaClasses, the CLASSPATH entry would simply be: C:\JavaClasses.

You may also want to package your Java application as a self-installing image. Several utilities, such as InstallShield Java Edition, are available for that purpose.

Follow these steps to deploy the finished ATM application (from Chapter 6, "Finishing the ATM Application"):

1. Install JDK 1.1.6 on your target machine and add the bin directory to your PATH statement as directed in the installation instructions.

2. Install the JFC 1.0.2 classes on the target machine.

3. Export the itso.atm.model and itso.atm.view packages as a JAR file, Atm.jar, and record the directory to which you export the file (Figure 181 on page 331). Click the **Deselect BeanInfo and Property Editor** button.

4. Set the CLASSPATH of the target machine to include the Swing classes, the JDK classes, and the JAR file you exported in Step 3. For example:

```
SET
CLASSPATH=D:\SWING-1.0.2\SWINGALL.JAR;D:\JDK1.1.6\LIB\CLASSES.ZIP;D:\JAV
ACLASSES\ATM.JAR
```

Start the application (Figure 182 on page 332) by entering java itso.atm.view.AtmView. Note that the package and class names are case-sensitive. Provided that the Java interpreter is in your PATH statement and the AtmView is in the CLASSPATH, everything should run smoothly (Figure 183 on page 332).

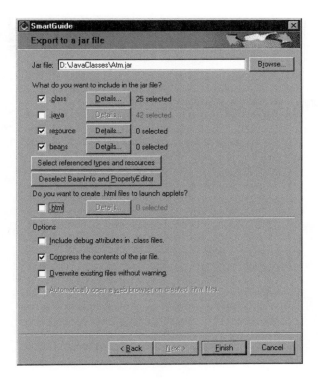

Figure 181. Exporting the ATM to a jar File

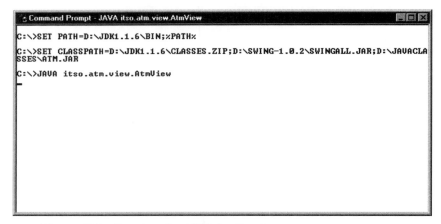

Figure 182. Starting the ATM Application

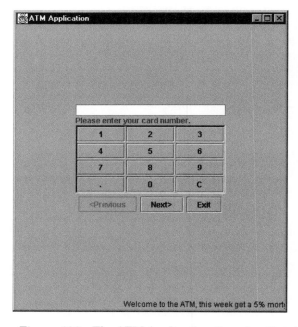

Figure 183. The ATM Application Running Outside the VisualAge for Java Environment

Deploying a Servlet

Deploying a servlet involves installing the servlet classes in the correct location on the Web server and ensuring that the Web server is correctly configured to execute servlets. You may have to install the JDK and set the CLASSPATH on the host or specifically for the Web server.

Different Web servers have different configurations, and some Web application servers, such as IBM's WebSphere, execute servlets in conjunction with a Web server.

Depending on the Web server you are using, when you deploy a servlet you can specify initialization parameters and other settings, such as where the servlet executes.

This example uses the Lotus Domino Go Web server. If you are using a different Web server or servlet environment, consult the documentation for the correct procedure.

Installing the Domino Go Web Server

To install the Domino Go Web Server, run the installation utility and follow the installation instructions. The choices you need to make are:

1. Select Components: For this example select at least the following checkboxes:
   - Lotus Domino Go Web Server
   - NT Service
   - Java Servlet

2. Target Directory: Install the Lotus Domino Go Web Server in any directory, the default, C:\WWW, is fine for the example. Note the location that you choose for the target directory.

3. Component Directories: You can leave the defaults. Note the location of the HTML directory.

4. Configuration Parameters: You have to choose an Administrator ID and Password. Using your own user ID and password is fine for the purposes of this example. Be careful with the Administrator Password though; it is echoed in the field as you type it. Record the Host Name and the Administrator ID and Password you use.

5. Reboot your computer or log out and log back in.

Starting the Lotus Domino Go Web Server

You can start the Web server from the command line, using whttpg, or from **Control Panel→Services**. If you want to see the Web server user interface, click **Startup** and then select the **Allow Service to Interact with Desktop** checkbox. Select **Lotus Domino Go Web server** and click **Start**.

Configuring the Web Server

For the purposes of the example, the default Web server configuration is fine. If you plan to use the Web server for production purposes, you should read the documentation and configure it to suit your needs.

Deploying the BookmarkListServlet

To deploy the BookmarkListServlet on the Lotus Domino Go Web server:

1. Export the itso.bookmark.servlet.BookmarkListServlet and the itso.bookmark.Bookmark classes as Java class files to the Web server default servlet directory: WWW\SERVLETS\PUBLIC (Figure 184 on page 335). In a production environment you would want to create a separate directory and define it to the Web server, but for this example the default directory is fine. You cannot export all servlet classes as a JAR file because the Web server must have the main servlet class as a .class file.

2. Make sure the Web server is running, enter the URL (http://hostname/servlet/itso.bookmark.servlet.BookmarkListServlet) in the Web browser, and you're off! Figure 185 on page 336 shows the dynamic HTML page generated by the servlet.

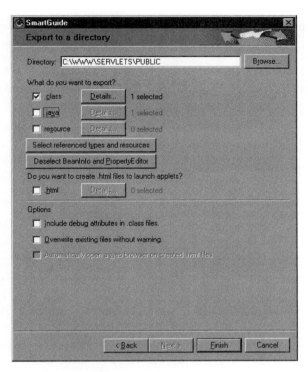

Figure 184. Exporting the Servlet Classes

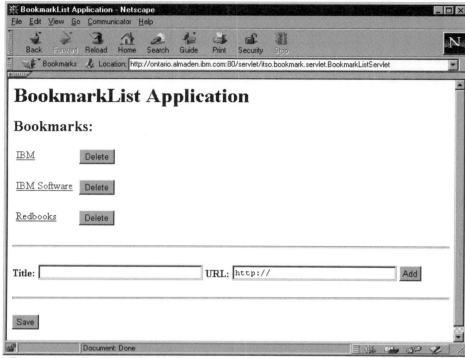

Figure 185. Running the BookmarkListServlet

Deploying an Applet

You have probably invoked many applets as you have surfed the Web, whether you were aware of it or not. Applets are Java programs that execute within a Web browser. By default they run in a "sandbox," or protected environment. Also by default, they cannot access files on your machine, and they cannot connect to other machines on the network except to the Web server from which they were accessed.

In Chapter 4, "Building User Interfaces" you created the BookmarkList applet and ran it in VisualAge for Java. VisualAge for Java provides an Applet Viewer to run and test applets within the VisualAge for Java environment. Although the Applet Viewer is good for initial testing of applets, you have to test with Web browsers to see how the applet integrates with HTML pages and whether there are any differences in the way the Web browsers display components or interact with the user.

Deploying an applet consists of two separate tasks:

1. Installing the applet on the Web server, where it can be served to a Web browser.

2. Ensuring that the correct JDK and classes are either supported by the target browsers or available from the Web server.

Web Browsers

VisualAge for Java produces JDK 1.1.6 Java code. Your Web browser must be Java enabled and must support JDK 1.1 to run the code. Another alternative is to use the Java Plug-In from JavaSoft.

Although there are many Web browsers, the vast majority of users run either Netscape Navigator or Microsoft Internet Explorer. Recent versions of both browsers support JDK 1.1 applets.

Netscape Navigator

Both Netscape Navigator 4.04 and 4.05 can support JDK 1.1 applets. However, the support is not completely straightforward:

Version 4.04:

If you are using Version 4.04, you must download and install the JDK 1.1 patch from Netscape to run JDK 1.1 applets.

Version 4.05:

A specific Netscape 4.05 version supports JDK 1.1: Preview Release 1 (AWT 1.1.5). You must install this version from http://developer.netscape.com to run JDK 1.1 applets.

To use the Navigator with applets that use JFC components, the JFC JAR file must be in the CLASSPATH when you start Netscape. For example: CLASSPATH=D:\SWING-1.0.2\SWINGALL.JAR.

For newer releases of Netscape check whether the JFC is included with the Navigator and that JDK 1.1 support is included.

Microsoft Internet Explorer

Microsoft Internet Explorer 4.01 and 5.0 support JDK 1.1 applets without modification. They do not support RMI, however. You can download RMI support for the Internet Explorer from IBM at www.alphaworks.ibm.com.

To use Internet Explorer with applets that use JFC components, the JFC JAR file must be in the CLASSPATH when you start Netscape. For example: CLASSPATH=D:\SWING-1.0.2\SWINGALL.JAR.

JavaSoft Java Plug-in

The Java Plug-in supports most versions of Netscape Navigator and Microsoft Internet Explorer and allows the use of Sun's Java Runtime Environment (JRE) or another Java Virtual Machine, instead of the browser's default Java runtime. For more information about the Java Plug-In, see the JavaSoft Web pages. The use of the Plug-in requires changes in your HTML that are dependent upon the browser being used.

CLASSPATH or CODEBASE

A Web server that serves an applet does not need to know anything about Java and therefore does not use the CLASSPATH. When you deploy your applet, you can specify the location of classes through the CODEBASE tag; otherwise the Web server, by default, searches for the classes or JAR files in the same directory as the HTML file that contains the applet. The classes are searched for in a directory relative to the codebase (or current directory) according to the package name of the class. For example, if you deploy an applet in an HTML page in the /bookmarklist directory and the applet class is itso.bookmark.applet.BookmarkListView, the Web server attempts to serve the class from the /bookmarklist/itso/bookmark/applet directory unless you specify a JAR file through the ARCHIVE tag.

Applet Tags

VisualAge for Java can create a simple .html file for your applet to run in a browser on the Internet. This file simply contains the applet tag and a title. For example:

```
<HTML>
<HEAD>
<TITLE>TestEventQCheck</TITLE>
</HEAD>
<BODY>
<H1>AppletName</H1>
<APPLET CODE=pkgname.Appletname.class WIDTH=250 HEIGHT=300>
</APPLET>
</BODY>
</HTML>
```

The complete syntax for the applet tag ([ ] means optional and the spacing is for readability) is:

```
<APPLET
        [CODEBASE = codebaseURL]
        CODE = appletFile[ALT = alternateText]
        [NAME = appletInstanceName]
```

```
        WIDTH = pixels
        HEIGHT = pixels
        [ALIGN = alignment]
        [VSPACE = pixels] [HSPACE = pixels]
        [ARCHIVE = JARFile1, JARFile2 ...]
    >
    [< PARAM NAME = appletAttribute1 VALUE = value >]
    [< PARAM NAME = appletAttribute2 VALUE = value >]
    . . .
    [alternate HTML]
</APPLET>
```

where:

- ❏ **CODEBASE = codebaseURL** is an optional attribute that specifies the base URL of the server directory that contains the applet's code. If this attribute is not specified, the document's URL is used.

- ❏ **CODE = appletFile** is a mandatory attribute that gives the name of the file that contains the applet's compiled Applet subclass. This file is relative to the base URL of the applet. It cannot be absolute.

- ❏ **ALT = alternateText** is an optional attribute that specifies any text that should be displayed if the browser understands the APPLET tag but cannot run Java applets.

- ❏ **NAME = appletInstanceName** is an optional attribute that specifies a name for the applet instance, that makes it possible for applets on the same page to find (and communicate with) each other.

- ❏ **WIDTH = pixels** and **HEIGHT = pixels** are mandatory attributes that give the initial width and height (in pixels) of the applet display area, not counting any windows or dialogs that the applet brings up.

- ❏ **ALIGN = alignment** is an optional attribute that specifies the alignment of the applet. The possible values of this attribute are the same as those of the IMG tag: left, right, top, texttop, middle, absmiddle, baseline, bottom, and absbottom.

- ❏ **VSPACE = pixels** and **HSPACE = pixels** are optional attributes that specify the number of pixels above and below the applet (VSPACE) and on each side of the applet (HSPACE). They are treated in the same way as the VSPACE and HSPACE attributes of the IMG tag.

- ❏ **ARCHIVE = JARFile1, JARFile2 ...** is an optional attribute that specifies one or several archive files to load.

  You can also use .cab or cabinet files to transfer your class files when using Microsoft Internet Explorer.

❏ **<PARAM NAME = appletAttribute1 VALUE = value>** ... is a tag that specifies an applet-specific attribute. Applets access their attributes with the getParameter method.

A Java-enabled browser that understands the <APPLET> tag ignores the [Alternate HTML] part, whereas a browser that does not support Java ignores everything until [Alternate HTML]. Thus Web pages can be created that make sense for both types of browsers.

To specify that the archive file is not in the same directory as the HTML page containing the <APPLET> tag, use the CODEBASE attribute.

Whenever a browser has to load a file needed by an applet, it looks in the directories or archives specified in the CLASSPATH of the browser first. Then it checks the applet's JAR files specified in the ARCHIVE parameter. If the browser fails to find the class file in a JAR file, it looks in the applet's codebase directory hierarchy. Any combination of JAR files and exported .class files can be used.

Deploying the BookmarkListView Applet

In this section you export the BookmarkListView applet as a JAR file and accompanying HTML file and access it from a Web browser.

Follow these steps to deploy the BookmarkListView applet:

1. Select the itso.bookmark.applet and itso.bookmark packages and select **File→Export**. In the Export to a jar file SmartGuide (Figure 186 on page 341):

   a. Click the **Jar File** radio button and then click **Next>** to continue.

   b. Select the root directory of the Web server that you have installed. For example, if you installed the Domino Go Web server into C:\WWW, select C:\WWW\HTML. If you are using or are going to use the Web server for production purposes, you may want to configure the Web server for a different directory.

   c. Name the JAR file: Bookmark.jar.

   d. Click the **Deselect BeanInfo and Property Editor** button.

   e. Select the **Do you want to create a .html files to launch applets** and the **Compress the contents of the jar file** checkboxes.

   f. Click **Finish**.

2. Set the CLASSPATH on your machine to point to the JFC classes and start the Web browser. Enter the URL

(http://hostname/BookmarkListView.html) in the location field and press **Enter**. Figure 188 on page 342 shows the running applet.

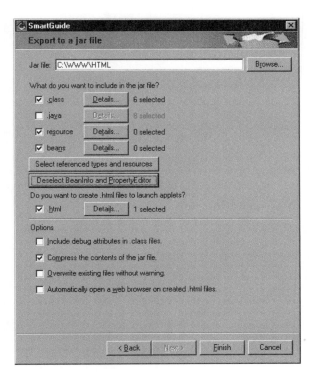

Figure 186. Exporting the BookmarkListView Applet

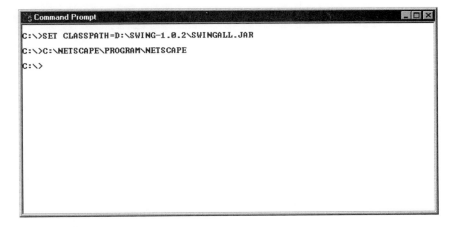

Figure 187. Starting Netscape Navigator

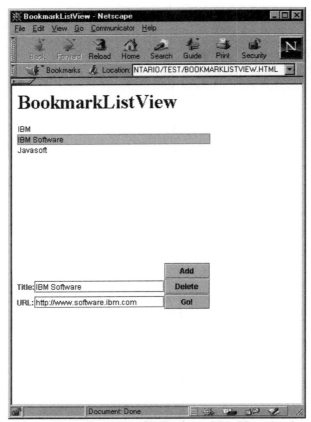

Figure 188. Running the BookmarkListView Applet

Borders

You might think that the BookmarkListView applet could use some separation from the surrounding HTML page. In the Visual Composition Editor you can set a border on Swing components using the *border* property. You can select from a list of predefined borders or code your own.

Deploying Supporting Code

Quite often you have to supply code with your Java programs that you did not create. Typically these are packaged in JAR, Zip, or CAB (for Microsoft

Internet Explorer) files. If you are deploying an applet, you can use the ARCHIVE tag to specify these other JAR files. If you are developing servlets or applications, you must place the JAR file in the CLASSPATH of the application or servlet. Deploying a program that uses the Data Access beans in VisualAge for Java is a good example.

To deploy a program that uses the Data Access beans, you must package the required JAR files with the program or make them available to the program. Programs using the Data Access beans and DB2 need access to:

❑ ivjdab.jar Data Access beans JAR file (found in IBMVJava\eab\runtime20)

❑ db2java.zip (found in SQLLIB\java)

For example, an applet using the Data Access beans might have an APPLET tag like this:

<APPLET CODE=MyDBAccessApplet.class WIDTH=250 HEIGHT=300 ARCHIVE=ivjdab.jar, db2java.zip>

In the above APPLET tag the applet class and the two JAR files would exist in the same directory as the HTML file.

To deploy an application, you would place the two JAR files in a directory (for example, C:\JAVACLASSES) and then reference the JAR files explicitly in the CLASSPATH. For example:

SET
CLASSPATH=%CLASSPATH%;C:\JAVACLASSES\ivjdab.jar;C:\JAVACLASSES\db2java.jar;

11 Advanced Topics

This chapter introduces you to these advanced features of VisualAge for Java Professional:

❑ Interface to external SCM tools

❑ AgentRunner: Lotus Domino Connection

❑ Remote Method Invocation

❑ Tool Integration Framework

For some of the exercises in this chapter you will need software that does not accompany the book. Check the Web site of the company producing the software for information about obtaining it.

Interface to External SCM Tools

Software configuration management (SCM) is the process of managing changes to the components of your software development effort. SCM helps members of a development team retrieve and build any version of an application in a consistent and repeatable manner.

VisualAge for Java provides a development environment that uses an object-based source code repository. This is VisualAge for Java's implementation of SCM; it provides software configuration support for development projects and support for multiple versions of program code.

Version control and repository management are integrated into VisualAge for Java. The repository offers excellent support for day-to-day team programming activities. However, you may want to use the interface to external SCM tools if your development process requires:

❏ Defects or features to be linked to specific code levels

❏ Documentation or other development artifacts be versioned along with the code

❏ The use of a particular SCM system or tool

❏ Automated building, packaging, and testing outside the VisualAge for Java environment

❏ That some members of the development team use an alternative Java development environment

The integration of VisualAge for Java and the SCM tool is based on importing and exporting Java source code. The editions and versions within the VisualAge for Java repository do not relate to versions within the SCM tool. For example, you can check a class into the SCM tool but still modify it within VisualAge for Java. There is no relationship between the version names in VisualAge for Java and the versions used by the SCM tool.

The development flow when working with an external SCM tool is:

1. Create the class within VisualAge for Java and then add it to the SCM tool *archive*. The term archive simply refers to the location where the SCM tool stores the files under source control.

2. Check out the class from the archive.

3. Work on the class until a desired level of functionality or a baseline is reached.

4. Check the class into the SCM tool.

Preparing to Connect to the SCM Tool from VisualAge for Java

New in V2!

VisualAge for Java Version 2 on Windows platforms offers an interface for checking source files (.java) in and out of an external SCM system. This interface is a complementary feature that you can select when you install VisualAge for Java. The interface to external SCM tools uses the MicroSoft Source Code Control (SCC) interface to communicate with SCM tools. It supports the following SCM tools:

• ClearCase 3.2 for Windows NT, from Rational Software Corporation

- PVCS Version Manager 6.0, from INTERSOLV, Inc.

- VisualAge TeamConnection Version 3.0, from IBM Corporation

Using SCM Tools

Check the Web site of the SCM tool vendor before using the interface to external SCM tools to see whether any fixes or patches to the SCM tool or SCC interface are required.

The interface to external SCM tools is fully described in the VisualAge for Java product documentation and README files.

Before you can use the interface to external SCM tools you must:

1. Install the client code for your SCM tool and any required SCC functionality on your workstation

2. Ensure that the ProviderRegKey variable in the HKEY_LOCAL_MACHINE\SOFTWARE\SourceCodeControlProvider registry entry is set to your SCM tool (Figure 189). If this variable does not appear, refer to the SCC function of your SCM tool's documentation. If you are not familiar with the Windows registry or the regedit utility, do not attempt to modify the registry.

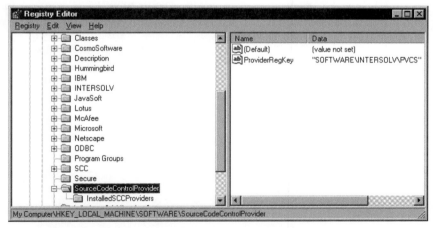

Figure 189. ProviderRegKey in the Windows NT Registry

3. Have access to at least one work directory that your SCM tool recognizes.

4. Create or have access to an organizational structure that your SCM tool will use to manage your .java files. Depending on the SCM software that

you use, one or more of the following organizational units may be required:

❑ Version object bases (VOBs) and views (ClearCase)

❑ Project files (PVCS Version Manager)

❑ Families, releases, components, and work areas (VisualAge TeamConnection)

　　You will need this organizational information when you define your SCM connection.

In addition you should:

❑ Test your native SCM client with the structure mentioned above. A good exercise is to export a few classes from VisualAge for Java to the file system and to check them in, using your native SCM client program.

❑ Be familiar with settings that your SCM tool requires, such as drive mappings, file mounts, or the creation of views.

Some SCM tools may also need to be reconfigured to handle four-character (.java) file extensions.

Setting your SCM Connection Parameters

This example uses PVCS Version Manager Version 6. If you use another SCM tool, the example may differ. If you experience problems using PVCS, run the Change Connection action before any other SCM action. You must create a PVCS project and archive directory before working with the example.

Before you can use the VisualAge for Java interface for checking classes in and out of an external SCM tool, you must set your default SCM connection parameters. Follow these steps to establish the default parameters for your external SCM connection:

1. Select any VisualAge for Java project, package, or class in the Workbench window.

2. From the pop-up menu, select **Tools→External SCM→Change Connection** (Figure 190). The SCM Connection dialog box opens (Figure 191 on page 350).

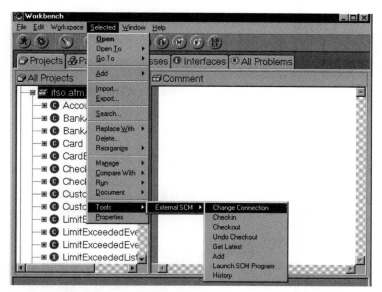

Figure 190. VisualAge for Java's Interface to External SCM Tools

3. Click **Change** to request a list of projects that your SCM tool recognizes. The term project refers to your SCM tool's basic unit of organization (see Figure 191).

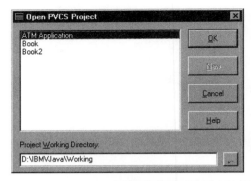

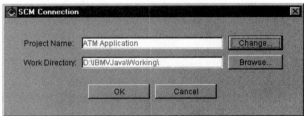

Figure 191. Changing the SCM Connection

4. Select a project from the list. (If you are using ClearCase, it does not actually matter which project you select from the list.) The SCM Connection dialog box reappears, with the Project Name field filled in (Figure 191).

5. Click **Browse** to select a default work directory that the SCM interface should use when it adds Java files to source control and checks them into the SCM repository (Figure 191).

6. Click **OK** in each dialog box.

These parameters will be passed from VisualAge for Java to your external SCM tool when you check classes in and out or perform other SCM operations.

Interface to External SCM Functions

The external SCM functions listed below are available from the **Selected→Tools** menu (Figure 192). The menu is contextual and depends on the current selection in VisualAge for Java. The Compare and Properties actions are available only for classes.

❑ Change Connection: Set up or modify the connection to the SCM tool.

❏ CheckIn: Check the source for Java classes into the SCM archive.

❏ CheckOut: Check the source for Java classes out of the SCM archive. Replace the editions that were in your workspace with the new open editions.

❏ Undo Checkout: Leave the current version in the archive and mark it as checked in.

❏ Get Latest: Retrieve the latest version from the repository but do not mark it as checked out. Replace the editions that were in your workspace with the new open editions.

❏ Add: Add new classes, that exist in VisualAge for Java, to the archive.

❏ Launch SCM Program: Start the client SCM application.

❏ Compare: Compare a Java class in VisualAge for Java with a version in the SCM tool.

❏ History: Show the SCM history for a class.

❏ Properties: Show the SCM properties for a class.

Most of the SCM functions support the selection of projects, packages, classes, or interfaces. For example, if you select a package and then **Check In**, all the types within the package are checked in to the archive.

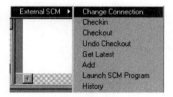

Figure 192. External SCM Functions Menu

 Visual and Bean Information
Remember that you are now working with Java source code. If you have classes that were generated in the Visual Composition Editor, make sure the **Generate meta data method** option in the Design Time section of the Options dialog box is selected. In addition, add the BeanInfo class to the archive if a BeanInfo exists for any given bean and check the bean and BeanInfo class in and out together.

Adding Classes

Before you can check classes in to and out of an SCM tool, you must add them to source control in the SCM tool's repository.

Follow these steps to add classes and interfaces from VisualAge for Java to source control in the SCM repository:

1. From the Workbench window, select one or more projects, packages, classes, or interfaces.

2. From the pop-up menu, select **Tools→External SCM→Add**. VisualAge for Java passes the list of classes and interfaces to the SCM tool, which validates the request.

3. If there are no problems, the Set Comments dialog box appears (Figure 193). Enter any comments that you want the SCM tool to log when it adds the .java files to its repository. Click **OK**.

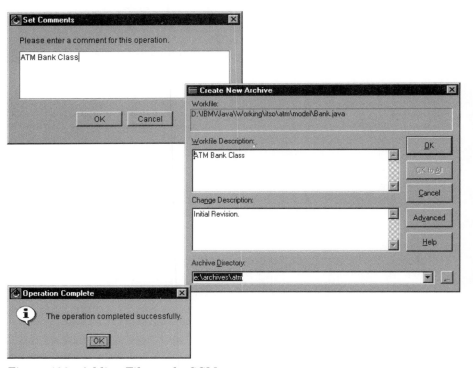

Figure 193. Adding Files to the SCM

VisualAge for Java exports the classes and interfaces to the file system on your computer, in the work directory that you specified when you set your SCM connection parameters (Figure 193). Next, VisualAge for Java invokes the SCM client function to add those source files to the SCM archive.

4. Wait for the Operation Complete dialog box (Figure 193) to appear before you do any other software configuration tasks. Click **OK** to close the Operation Complete dialog box.

Synchronizing VisualAge and the External SCM Tool
As you create new classes and interfaces in your VisualAge for Java projects and packages, remember to add them to the SCM repository as well. There is no automated relationship between the VisualAge for Java source code repository and external SCM repositories. The classes and interfaces remain in your VisualAge for Java workspace and repository. When you want to change them, remember to check them out of the SCM repository. VisualAge for Java does not enforce SCM checkout, but your SCM tool does not allow you to check in changes to program elements that you have not checked out.

Checking Out Classes

You have the choice of checking out classes, interfaces, or complete projects and packages from your SCM tool. When you can select classes and interfaces, VisualAge for Java automatically:

❑ Invokes your SCM client software to check out the most recent version of each class and interface

❑ Creates new open editions of the classes and interfaces in the VisualAge for Java repository

❑ Replaces the editions that were in your workspace with the new open editions

Follow these steps to check classes and interfaces out of your SCM tool's repository:

1. From the Workbench window, select the classes and interfaces that you want to check out, or select the projects or packages that contain the classes you want to check out.

2. From the pop-up menu, select **Tools→External SCM→Checkout**. VisualAge for Java passes the list of classes and interfaces to the SCM tool, that validates the request.

3. If there are no problems, the Set Comments dialog box appears. Enter the comments that you want the SCM tool to log when it checks the classes out of its repository. Click **OK**.

Undoing Checkout

Follow these steps to undo a previous Checkout action:

1. From the Workbench window, select the classes and interfaces for which you want to undo the checkout action.

2. From the pop-up menu, select **Tools→External SCM→Undo Checkout**.

3. VisualAge for Java passes the list of classes and interfaces to the SCM tool, that validates the request.

4. If there are no problems, the Operation Complete dialog box appears. Click **OK**.

Checking In Classes

Classes or interfaces that are checked out of your SCM tool remain checked out until you either check them back in again or undo the checkout operation. Follow these steps to check classes and interfaces from VisualAge for Java into the SCM repository:

1. From the Workbench window, select one or more projects, packages, classes, or interfaces.

2. From the pop-up menu, select **Tools→External SCM→Checkin**. VisualAge for Java passes the list of classes and interfaces to the SCM tool, that validates the request.

3. If there are no problems, the Set Comments dialog box appears. Enter any comments that you want the SCM tool to log when it checks the files into its repository. Click **OK.**

4. VisualAge for Java exports the classes and interfaces to the file system on your computer in the work directory that you specified when you set your SCM connection parameters. Next, VisualAge for Java invokes the SCM client function to check those Java files into the SCM repository.

5. If there are no problems, the Operation Complete dialog box appears. Click **OK**.

Using Undo Checkout instead of Checkin
If you have not modified a class but want to check it in to the SCM archive, use the Undo Checkout action instead of Checkin. Depending on the SCM tool that you use, when you try to check in files that have not changed, you may see an error message indicating that the SCM operation failed.

Getting the Latest Version

For testing or integration purposes you might want to have the most recent versions of classes and interfaces without checking them out. Follow these steps to get the most recently checked-in versions of classes and interfaces from your SCM repository:

1. From the Workbench window, select the classes and interfaces that you want to retrieve, or select the projects or packages whose classes you want to retrieve.

2. From the pop-up menu, select **Tools→External SCM→Get Latest**. VisualAge for Java passes the list of classes and interfaces to the SCM tool, that validates the request.

3. If there are no problems, the Operation Complete dialog box appears. Click **OK**. Open editions of the classes and interfaces are created in the VisualAge for Java repository and are added to your workspace.

As with checkout, when you get the latest classes and interfaces from your SCM library, VisualAge for Java:

❑ Retrieves the most recently checked-in versions of the classes and interfaces, from the project that you specified when you set your SCM connection parameters, and copies them to the work directory that you specified.

❑ Automatically imports the class files from the work directory to the VisualAge for Java repository and creates new open editions of the classes.

❑ Replaces the editions that were in your workspace with the new open editions.

Launching the SCM Tool from VisualAge for Java

To launch the SCM tool client:

1. From the Workbench window, select one or more projects, packages, classes, or interfaces.

2. From the pop-up menu, select **Tools→External SCM→Launch SCM Program**.

Comparing Classes

You may want to compare the edition of a checked out class that is in your workspace with a previous edition in the SCM tool's repository:

1. From the Workbench window, select the class or interface.

2. From the pop-up menu, select **Tools→External SCM→Compare**. VisualAge for Java passes the class name to the SCM tool for validation. Depending on the SCM tool, you may have several comparison options. With PVCS you have the choice of comparing (Figure 194):

   • A revision and a workfile

   • Two workfiles

   • Two revisions in one archive

   • Revisions in two archives

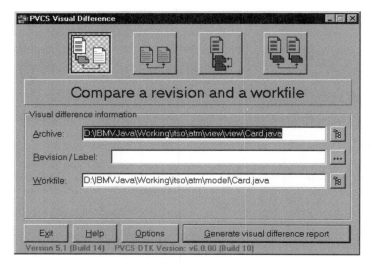

Figure 194. PVCS Compare Function

3. If there are no problems, the class is automatically exported from the VisualAge for Java repository to the file system on your workstation, in the work directory that you specified when you set your SCM connection parameters.

If the automatic export step is successful, VisualAge for Java invokes the compare function of your SCM software program.

If the export is not successful, confirm that you have checked the class out of the SCM repository. (If the file is checked in, the file status in the work directory is read-only.)

Properties

For classes, you can also view the SCM properties, that is, the classes' present status in the external SCM tool.

Follow these steps to invoke the Properties action:

1. From the Workbench window, select the class or interface.

2. From the pop-up menu, select **Tools→External SCM→Properties**. A dialog box appears with the present status and property of the selected class (Figure 195).

Figure 195. External SCM Property Function Using PVCS

SCM History

You may want a history of SCM events for selected classes and interfaces. Examples of SCM events include:

❑ Adding classes to source control

❑ Checking in and out of the SCM repository

❑ Undoing checkout

Follow these steps to request a history of the SCM events:

1. From the Workbench window, select one or more projects, packages, classes, or interfaces. You can select projects or packages as a convenient way of seeing the SCM history of all of their contained classes and interfaces at once.

2. From the pop-up menu, select **Tools→External SCM→History**. VisualAge for Java passes the list of classes and interfaces to the SCM tool, that validates the request (Figure 196). To view a detailed report click on **View Report.**

3. If there are no problems, the SCM client software on your workstation is invoked to display a history for the selected classes and interfaces.

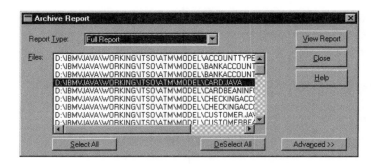

Figure 196. External SCM History Function

AgentRunner: Lotus Domino Connection

Lotus Domino is an applications and messaging server that enables you to host secure, interactive business solutions for the Internet and corporate intranets. A Domino agent is a piece of software that runs within the Domino environment and is invoked by specific actions such as receiving mail.

New in V2!

The AgentRunner included with VisualAge for Java enables you to build and debug Domino agents within VisualAge for Java while still accessing Lotus Domino. The powerful development and debugging features of VisualAge for Java can then be used to tune and perfect your agent before you export the production code to the Domino environment. Using the Domino Java Class Libraries, also included with VisualAge for Java, you develop agents and then use the AgentRunner to provide the Domino environment while debugging. For more information about the Domino Java Class Libraries see the Lotus documentation at http://www.lotus-developer.com/. For further information about the AgentRunner, see the VisualAge for Java documentation and README files.

In this section you will create a simple Domino agent that searches your mail folder for all mail that has a subject field that contains the subject field of a selected mail document. The results are mailed back to the user.

The general steps for creating a Domino agent within VisualAge for Java are:

1. Set up the VisualAge for Java and Domino environments.

2. Create the agent's classes.

3. Generate an AgentContext document in Notes.

4. Test and debug the agent in VisualAge for Java.

5. Deploy the agent.

The rest of this section demonstrates the example in a Windows NT environment, where:

❑ The Lotus Notes client is installed in: C:\LOTUS\NOTES. You need a Lotus Notes 4.6 or later client installed on your computer with access to a Lotus Domino server.

❑ VisualAge is installed in D:\IBMVJAVA. Substitute the correct pathnames for your environment as you work through the example.

Setting Up The Environment

Follow these steps to set up the VisualAge for Java and Notes environments for agent development:

1. Add the D:\IBMVJava\ide\runtime\IVJAgentRunner.jar file to the JavaUserClasses statement in your C:\WINNT\NOTES.INI file. If you do not have a JavaUserClasses statement, use this one: JavaUserClasses=D:\IBMVJava\ide\runtime\IVJAgentRunner.jar. Put the statement at the top of the notes.ini file.

   Because you have edited the notes.ini file, you must shut down and restart your Notes client so that your changes take effect.

2. Add your Notes directory (C:\LOTUS\NOTES) to your PATH environment variable. You must restart your computer or your session once you have changed your PATH statement.

3. Copy D:\IBMVJava\ide\runtime\AgentRunner.nsf to C:\lotus\notes\data. This is the database that will hold the AgentContext that the AgentRunner uses.

4. Use the **Quick Start→Add Feature** function to add the Domino Java Class Library 4.6.1 project from the repository to the environment.

Creating the Agent

The agent you create in VisualAge for Java initially must be a subclass of lotus.notes.DebugAgentBase. Once you are satisfied with the code, you will change the superclass to lotus.notes.AgentBase and deploy the agent. Follow these steps to create the agent:

1. Create a new package called itso.notes.agents in the Programming VAJ V2 project.

2. Create a new class, SearchMail, that extends lotus.notes.DebugAgentBase. Use the SmartGuide to import the lotus.notes package into SearchMail.

   Notes agents need a NotesMain method, which is invoked when the agent is started. Within the NotesMain method, the agent creates a Notes session and an agent context. Then the agent connects to the database and reads the mail.

3. Create the public void NotesMain() method in SearchMail. The code for the NotesMain method is combined in this step with the text describing the code. You can copy the complete code from the SearchMail.java file in the examples.

   All of the code must be enclosed in a try block because many of the methods in the Domino Java classes throw the NotesException.

```
public void NotesMain(){
    try{
```

Get the session from the AgentBase:

```
    Session session = getSession();
```

A Session is the root of the Notes back-end object containment hierarchy, providing access to the other Notes objects, and represents the Notes environment of the current program.

Get the agent context, that is, the agent environment of the current program:

```
    AgentContext ac = session.getAgentContext();
```

Get the current database where the agent is running:

```
    Database db = ac.getCurrentDatabase();
```

Get the currently highlighted document in the view (discontinue if there are no documents selected):

```
    Document doc = ac.getDocumentContext();
    if (doc != null) {
```

Get the Subject field of the current document (discontinue if there is no Subject field).

```
        String subject = doc.getItemValueString("Subject");
```

```
                        if (subject != null) {
```

Find all documents in the database that contain the selected document's subject (discontinue if there are no matches):

```
        DocumentCollection dc = db.FTSearch("FIELD Subject contains "
            + subject);
        if (dc.getCount() > 0) {
```

Create a new Newsletter document containing the document links:

```
        Newsletter nl = session.createNewsletter(dc);
```

Make the matched document's subject line the subject shown in the DocLink:

```
        nl.setSubjectItemName("Subject");
```

Set the format, form type, and subject and send the results to the current user:

```
        Document nlDoc = nl.formatMsgWithDoclinks(null);
        nlDoc.appendItemValue("Form", "Memo");
        nlDoc.appendItemValue("Subject",
            "Documents with subject '"
            + subject + "'");
        nlDoc.send(false, session.getUserName());
            }
        }
    }
    else{
        System.err.println("Error: No document context");
    }
}
catch( NotesException e)
{
    System.err.println("Error, Notes Exception: " + e);
}
}
```

Installing and Preparing the Agent for AgentRunner Testing

1. Export the SearchMail class to a class file (Figure 197).

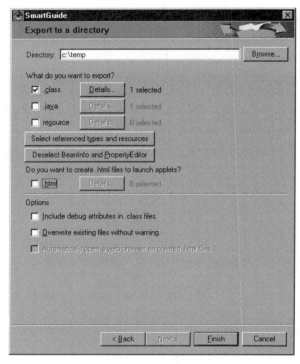

Figure 197. Exporting the SearchMail Class

2. Start your Notes client (Lotus Notes 4.6 or later and open your Mail database.

3. Select **Create→Agent** from the menu bar. The Untitled Agent dialog box appears (Figure 198):

   a. Enter a name for the agent, such as SearchMail.

   b. Select **Manually From Actions Menu** in the *When should this agent run* field.

   c. Select **Selected documents** from the *Which document(s) should it act on* field.

   d. Select the **Java** radio button for the *What should this agent run* field.

   e. Click the **Import class files** button.

   f. Select the SearchMail.class file in the directory hierarchy to which you exported it (Figure 199).

   g. Click **Add**.

   h. Click **OK**.

i. Press the **Esc** key to close the Create Agent window. When asked whether to save your changes, click **Yes**.

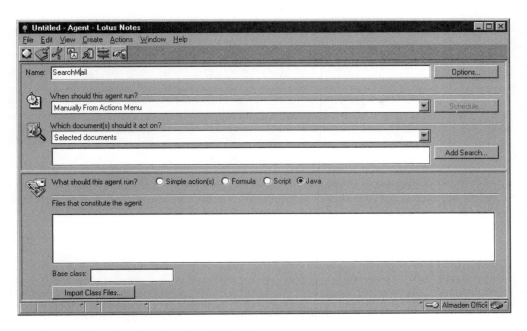

Figure 198. Creating the SearchMail Agent

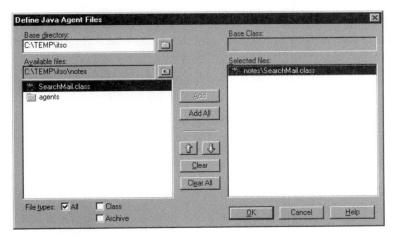

Figure 199. Importing the Class

4. Run the agent: Open the mail database, select a mail message, and select **Actions→SearchMail** from the Notes client menu bar. Running the

agent from within the Notes environment, using an agent that subclasses DebugAgentBase, will create the AgentContext document that is needed to run the agent in the VisualAge for Java IDE. It will not actually run the complete agent (getSession returns null). Figure 200 shows the AgentContext document and database.

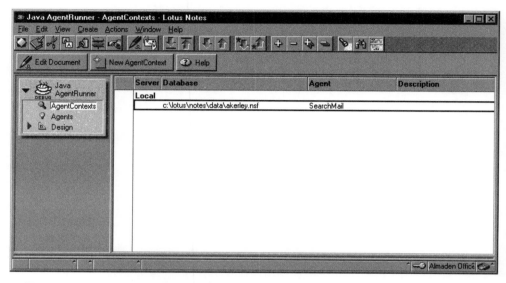

Figure 200. AgentContext Database

Testing with AgentRunner

Now that you have created your agent and the AgentContext, you can run and test the agent within VisualAge for Java:

1. Set a breakpoint somewhere within the NotesMain code.

2. Select the **SearchMail** class and then select **Selected→Tools→Agent Runner→Run.** The agent will stop at the breakpoint, and you can inspect and debug the code even though it is accessing the Notes environment (Figure 201).

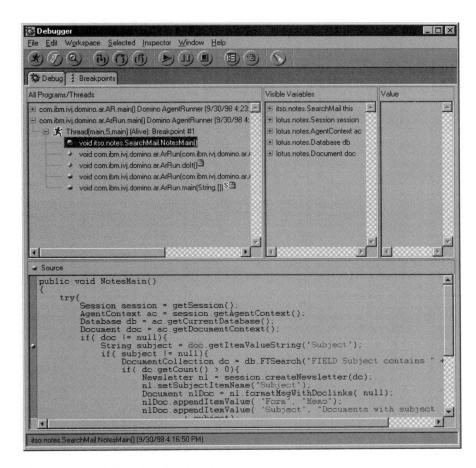

Figure 201. Debugging the Agent

3. Click the **Resume** button in the debugger. The agent will run and send you a mail message that contains links to all documents in the database that have the same subject as the document selected when you originally created the AgentContext.

If you need to change the SearchMail class, make sure you repeat these steps:

1. Export the class from VisualAge for Java.

2. Import the class into the Notes client. You can access the agent by opening the Agents view.

3. Run the agent from within Notes to regenerate the AgentContext.

You can also open the AgentContext database and delete any earlier contexts.

You can also run the agent or change the properties of the AgentContext, using **Selected→Tools→Agent Runner→Properties** (Figure 202 and Figure 203).

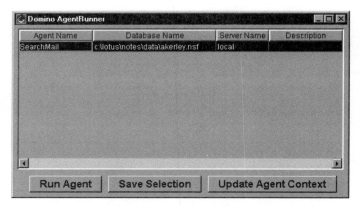

Figure 202. The AgentRunner Properties Dialog Box

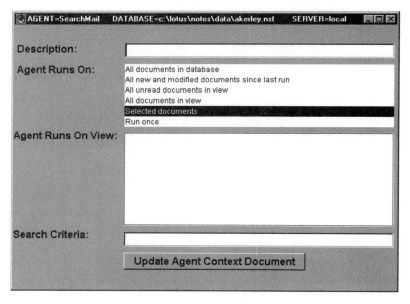

Figure 203. The AgentRunner Properties - Update AgentContext Dialog Box

Deploying the Agent

To deploy the agent, change the DebugAgentBase superclass to AgentBase and repeat the steps for changing the SearchMail class. Figure 204 shows the mail message from the agent.

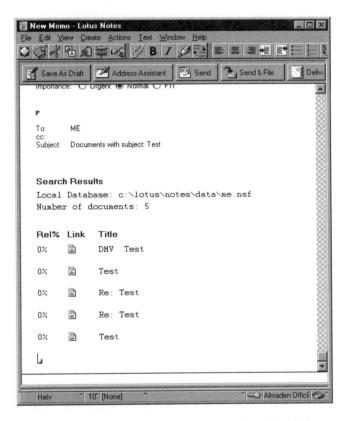

Figure 204. Mail Message Sent by the SearchMail Agent

Remote Method Invocation: A Refresher

You have seen how to use servlets to distribute the Bookmark List applet. Another option for Java distribution is RMI. Using RMI, clients can obtain references to remote objects and invoke methods on those objects.

From a conceptual point of view, RMI enables a Java application to call a remote Java object as if it were on the local machine. From an application point of view, one object invokes a method in another object, RMI provides the necessary services to locate the remote object, route the method call with all its parameters through TCP/IP to the server, invoke the method on the server object, and pass back the return object along the same path (Figure 205 on page 369).

RMI sends objects over the network. To transmit objects over the network, the RMI system serializes objects before they are transmitted and deserializes them at the other end. Therefore, any object that is to be used in RMI must implement the *java.io.Serializable* interface.

Architecture

RMI calls are handled by different layers until they eventually are communicated from the client to the server, where they cross the same number of layers until they arrive at the server object (Figure 205 on page 369).

Stub and Skeleton

The stub and skeleton classes are the interfaces between the application layer and the rest of the RMI system. The stub resides on the client and marshals the arguments, triggers the call to the remote object by calling the remote reference layer, and unmarshals return objects and exceptions.

The skeleton on the server side is responsible for unmarshaling the arguments, calling the server object, and marshaling the return objects and exceptions.

Remote Reference Layer

The remote reference layer has a client and a server component. It is responsible for maintaining a reference protocol between the components that is independent of a specific stub or skeleton. It keeps references and reconnects if a connection is lost.

Transport Layer

The transport layer creates and monitors the connections on behalf of the remote reference layer. It establishes socket connections and passes the connections to the remote reference layer. It also listens for incoming calls and sets up connections for them.

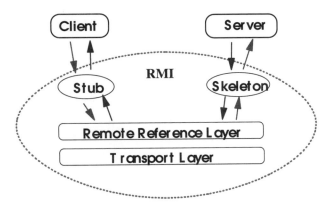

Figure 205. RMI Architecture

The high-level steps for using RMI to create a distributed system are:

1. Create a server interface that extends java.rmi.Remote.
2. Create a server implementation that extends java.rmi.UniCastRemoteObject.
3. Generate the stub and skeleton classes.
4. Create a client that obtains a remote reference to the server and performs the application functions.

To run the distributed system you must:

1. Instantiate the RMI server object on the server computer. The RMI object then:
   a. Sets a Security Manager
   b. Registers itself with the RMI Naming Registry on the server
2. Invoke the client, which:
   a. Sets a security manager, if required
   b. Obtains a remote reference to the server object

For more information, see the JDK documentation.

RMI Using VisualAge for Java

VisualAge for Java Professional supports RMI through the **RMI - Generate Stub and Skeleton** selection on the **Tools** menu. This function is much the same as using the rmic compiler in the JDK.

If you are planning on doing further RMI development, VisualAge for Java Enterprise provides more support for RMI through the RMI Proxy Builder, which builds the complete RMI infrastructure from a simple nondistributed JavaBean.

Distributing the BookmarkList

Because you created the Bookmark List by using a controller that separated the view from the data, the distribution of the BookmarkList is fairly simple. For this exercise you make the BookmarkListController a remote object that the client will access through RMI.

Follow these steps to build the distributed Bookmark List:

1. Create a new package, itso.bookmark.rmi. Copy the BookmarkListController and BookmarkListView classes from the itso.bookmark.applet package to the new itso.bookmark.rmi. Select the classes and **Selected→Reorganize→Copy**. In the Copying types dialog box (Figure 206 on page 370), enter itso.bookmark.rmi, deselect **Rename (copy as)**, and click **OK**.

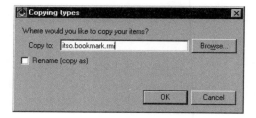

Figure 206. Copy Types Dialog

Because the BookmarkListView class uses the controller from the applet package, the copy produces an error that you will fix later.

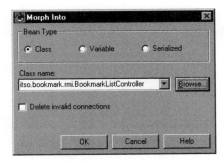

Figure 207. The Morph Into Feature

Three methods must be exposed on the BookmarkListController:

- addEntry
- deleteEntry
- getBookmarkList

2. Using the **Selected→Add→Interface** menu item, create a new interface, BookmarkListControllerI, that extends java.rmi.Remote (Figure 208). Add the three methods to the interface, specifying that each method can throw the java.rmi.RemoteException. All methods in the interface must throw this exception. The three method declarations look like this:

```
public void addEntry(String title, String url)
    throws java.rmi.RemoteException;
public void deleteEntry(String title)
    throws java.rmi.RemoteException;
public com.sun.java.swing.DefaultListModel getBookmarkList()
    throws java.rmi.RemoteException;
```

Another Shortcut for Adding Methods
You have already seen that you can create new methods by typing over an existing method. Two other ways of creating the first method in a class or interface are:
1. Use the **Selected→Method Template** menu item and then type over the method template and replace it using Shift-Control-S.
2. Create the method in the class declaration.

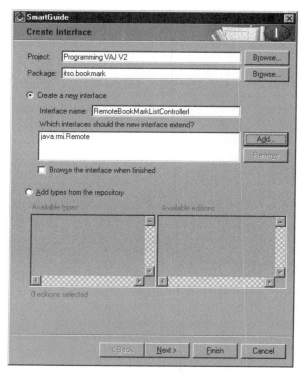

Figure 208. Creating the BookmarkListControllerI Interface

3. Change the BookmarkListController class declaration to:

```
public class BookmarkListController
        extends java.rmi.server.UnicastRemoteObject
        implements BookmarkListControllerI
```

You get an error because there is no default constructor that throws java.rmi.RemoteException.

4. Replace the default constructor:

```
public BookmarkListController() throws java.rmi.RemoteException
{
}
```

Locating the RMI Stub and Skeleton Classes
You can start the RMI registry from the VisualAge for Java Professional Options dialog box. However, unless you have exported your stub, skeleton, and interface classes and added their location to the VisualAge for Java Class Path, they will not be found.
An alternative is to start the RMI Registry in the code of the server object as you do in this example using createRegistry.

5. Add a main function to the BookmarkListController:

```
public static void main( String argv[])
{
    try{
        java.rmi.registry.LocateRegistry.createRegistry(1099);// start manually
        BookmarkListController controller = new BookmarkListController();
        System.out.println( "Registering the Security Manager ...");
        System.setSecurityManager( new java.rmi.RMISecurityManager());
        System.out.println("Publishing the server");
        java.rmi.Naming.rebind("rmi:///Controller1", controller);
        System.out.println("Controller server is ready");
    }
    catch( Exception e){
        System.out.println("Exception caught: " + e.getMessage());
    }
}
```

6. Select BookmarkListController and **Selected→Tools→RMI - Generate Stub and Skeleton** to generate:

    BookmarkListController_Skel
    BookmarkListController_Stub

7. Delete the old void init(JApplet applet) method from the BookmarkListController and the server is complete. Now you need to make a few changes in the BookmarkListView client.

8. Open the BookmarkListView class in the Visual Composition Editor and drop a variable on the free-form surface of type BookmarkListControllerI and name it RemoteController. (Always use the interface of the remote object, not the stub.) Delete the connection from AtmView.init to Controller.init. Drag the rest of the Controller's connections to the new RemoteController. Delete the original Controller.

9. Change the Source event to this on the property-to-property connection from the RemoteController.bookmarkList to URLList.model.

10. Create a new event-to-code connection from AtmView.init to a new method:

```
public BookmarkListControllerI initRMI( String serverName)
{
    BookmarkListControllerI server = null;
    try{
        String urlString = "rmi://" + serverName + "/Controller1";
        server = (BookmarkListControllerI)
            java.rmi.Naming.lookup( urlString);
    }
    catch( Exception e)
    {
        handleException(e);
    }
    return server;
}
```

11. Set the serverName parameter on the connection to your host name. Connect normalResult of the connection to RemoteController.this.

12. If you did not do so earlier, change the class declaration of the Bookmark to implement Serializable:

    public class Bookmark implements java.io.Serializable

Now the BookmarkList will work, but the updates will not be shown in the list because the client has no way of knowing the list has changed.

13. Create the connections in Table 17 to cause the list to update:

Table 17. BookmarkList Connection Details

Connection Number in Figure 209	Connection Type	Connection from	Connection to	Comments
1	EtoM	normalResult of AddButton. actionPerformed→ RemoteController. addEntry	URLList. setModel	Use connection 2 as parameter.
2	PfromP	aModel parameter on connection 1	RemoteController. bookmarkList	
3	EtoM	normalResult of AddButton. actionPerformed→ RemoteController, addEntry	URLList, repaint()	

Connection Number in Figure 209	Connection Type	Connection from	Connection to	Comments
4	EtoM	normalResult of DeleteButton, actionPerformed→ RemoteController, deleteEntry	URLList, setModel	Use connection 5 as parameter.
5	PfromP	aModel parameter on connection 4	RemoteController, bookmarkList	
6	EtoM	normalResult of DeleteButton, actionPerformed→ RemoteController, deleteEntry	URLList, repaint()	

The other option for automatically updating the URLList is to have the client implement a remote object that listens for events from the server. You can code this option manually, but VisualAge for Java Enterprise automates the construction of remote listeners for you and is a good choice if you are building RMI systems.

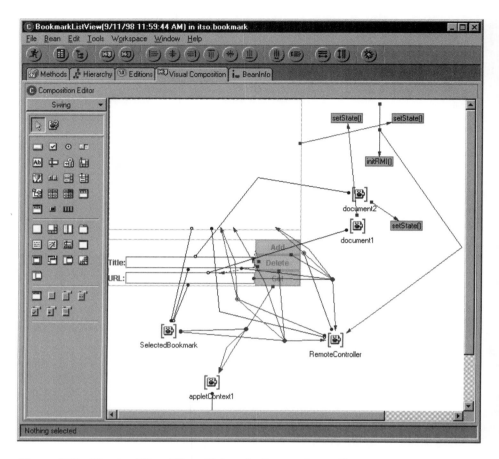

Figure 209. The AtmView Client Using the RemoteController

Testing the RMI BookmarkListView

Before starting the server, make sure the JFC Project is added to the Class Path of the BookmarkListView applet and the BookmarkListController class.

Start the server by selecting the BookmarkListController class and selecting **Selected→Run→Run main**. Then start the client by selecting the BookmarkListView class and **Selected→Run→In Applet Viewer** and test the system.

Tool Integration Framework

New in V2! With VisualAge for Java Version 2 you can add tools to the environment and programmatically access the running environment. Remember, using the Tool Integration Framework is advanced development; approach it cautiously and read the product documentation.

In this section you create the BaseLine tool, which gives the same version name to all program elements within a selected project. This is a nice feature if you are sharing code or using code for demonstration purposes. Again, this is advanced development and you should be very careful before attempting it.

You should copy the ivj.dat and ide.icx files to another location, as described in Backups on page 159, before writing code that modifies elements in your workspace.

If you do complete the exercise, you can easily improve on the BaseLine tool to take different types of program elements or to implement better error checking.

Creating the BaseLine Tool

Follow these steps to create the BaseLine tool:

1. Add the IBM IDE Utility Class Libraries project to your workspace. In the Programming with VAJ V2 project create a package called baseline. The code you are going to create for the tool is fairly simple. Create a class named BaseLine that extends com.sun.java.swing.JFrame. In the Create Class SmartGuide specify the import of the com.ibm.ivj.util.base package.

2. Open the class in the Visual Composition Editor and set the *title* of the frame to BaseLine and set the *layout* of the JFrameContentPane to GridBagLayout.

3. Add the visual beans in Table 18 to the content pane of the frame as shown in Figure 210 on page 380. Now that you have used the GridBagLayout, you should be able to use the constraints to make your GUI look like Figure 210. Using the *insets* property specifies the external padding of the component, that is, the minimum amount of space between the component and the edges of its display area. You can use the insets property if the components look "squashed" into the panel.

Table 18. Visual Beans in the BaseLine GUI

Bean Type	beanName	text
JLabel	N/A	Project Name:

Bean Type	beanName	text
JLabel	ProjectNameLabel	N/A
JLabel	N/A	Version Name:
JTextField	VersionTextField	N/A
JButton	ApplyButton	Apply
JButton	CancelButton	Cancel
JLabel	StatusLabel	Enter the version name.

4. Add a variable of type java.lang.System to the free-form surface and name it
SystemVariable, and then save the bean.

The BaseLine tool is installed into VisualAge for Java so that it can only
be invoked when you have selected one or more projects. To make the
example simple, you will not check for any errors in the project parameter
passed to the tool or for errors connecting to the workspace.

5. Add the following attribute to the class declaration:

```
Workspace ws = null;
WorkspaceModel programElement = null;
```

6. Create the following three methods (the BaseLine.java file is in the
example directory so you can also copy the code):

```
public void init( String[] args)
{
    ws = ToolEnv.connectToWorkspace();
    programElement = ws.loadedProjectNamed(args[1]);
    getProjectNameLabel().setText(programElement.getName());
    show();
}

public boolean checkVersion( String versionName)
{
    try{
        ProjectEdition[] allEditions =      ((Project)programElement).getAllEditions();
        for (int p = 0; p < allEditions.length; p++){
          if( allEditions[p].isVersion()){
            if( allEditions[p].getVersionName().equals( versionName)){
              return false;
            }
          }
        }
    }
    catch( IvjException e){
        getStatusLabel().setText( "Error checking for existing version.");
```

```
        }
        return true;
    }

    public void makeVersion( String versionName)
    {
        if( !checkVersion( versionName)){
            getStatusLabel().setText("Version already exists.");
            return;
        }
        else{
            getStatusLabel().setText("");
        }
        try{
            Project project = (Project)programElement;
            if( programElement.isVersion()){
              project.createNewEdition();
            }
            Package[] packages = project.getPackages();
            for (int p = 0; packages != null && p < packages.length; p++)
            {
              Package pkg = packages[p];
              if( pkg.isVersion()){
                pkg.createNewEdition();
              }
              Type[] types = pkg.getTypes();
              for (int t = 0; types!= null && t < types.length; t++)
              {
                Type type = types[t];
                if( type.isVersion()){
                  type.createNewEdition();
                }
                type.createVersion(versionName, true);
              }
              pkg.createVersion(versionName);
            }
            project.createVersion(versionName);
        }
        catch( IvjException e){
            getStatusLabel().setText( "Error creating new version.");
        }
    }
}
```

7. **Replace the contents of the main method with the following code:**

```
public static void main(java.lang.String[] args)
{
    BaseLine aBaseLine = new BaseLine();
    aBaseLine.init(args);
}
```

8. Make the connections indicated in Table 19.

Table 19. BaseLine Connections

Connection Number in Figure 210	Connection Type	Connection from	Connection to	Comments
1	EtoM	BaseLine, windowClosed (from free-form surface)	SystemVariable, exit()	Exit the application. You do not have to supply a parameter.
2	EtoM	CancelButton, actionPerformed	BaseLine, dispose() (to free-form surface)	Close and dispose of the frame.
3	EtoM	ApplyButton, actionPerformed	BaseLine, makeVersion()	Invoke the makeVersion method. Parameter is supplied in Connection 4.
4	PfromP	Connection 3 parameter	VersionTextField, text	

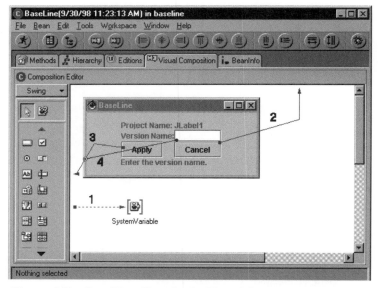

Figure 210. BaseLine Class in the Visual Composition Editor

Adding the IDE Utility Classes to the Class Path
In addition to the IBM IDE Utility class libraries project, you must add the IBMVJAVA\IDE\project_resources\IBM IDE Utility local implementation; in the *Extra directories path:* field to run tools that use the tool integration facilities.
Also, make sure the JFC classes are added to the Class Path for the BaseLine example.

Testing the BaseLine Tool in the IDE

To test the BaseLine tool you have to set the ClassPath and command line parameters to simulate VisualAge for Java invoking the tool.

On the Class Path page of the Properties dialog box in the Workbench, add the IBM IDE Utility class libraries and the JFC Class libraries project in the *Project path:* field and the X:\IBMVJAVA\IDE\project_resources\IBM IDE Utility local implementation directory in the *Extra directories path:* field, where *X* is the drive where you installed VisualAge for Java.

Adding Class Path Entries and Exporting Files
If you specified a lower-case drive letter when you installed VisualAge for Java you may encounter errors when trying to add Class Path entries by using the **Edit** and **Add Directory** buttons. VisualAge for Java informs you that it cannot access the program directory. If this happens, type the complete Class Path extension in the *Extra directories path* field.
The same error may occur when exporting files. Make sure you specify an upper-case drive letter.

On the Program page of the Properties dialog, enter -P project-name in the *Command line arguments:* field, where project-name is the name of a project in your environment. You may want to create a test project with some packages and classes to test the BaseLine tool.

The -P project-name represents the *selection_group* with which your tool will be invoked. When your tool is run in the VisualAge for Java environment, the currently selected projects are passed as the command line arguments to it.

You can choose to have your tool invoked with no arguments, or with the currently selected projects, packages, or types. Your choice will influence from which Tools menu the tool is invoked. The selection_group syntax is:

[-P project1 project2 ...] | [**-p package1 package2** ...] | [**-c type1 type2** ...]
[] optional
| exclusive or
... repeat

Now run the BaseLine class and enter the new version name for the project.

Installing the BaseLine Tool

The final step is to deploy your new tool in VisualAge for Java. In order to invoke your tool from a VisualAge for Java Tools menu, you must:

1. Create a subdirectory for the tool, called the *base directory*.
2. Copy all application classes, resource files, and HTML help into the base directory.
3. Create a control file that provides the IDE with details on the integration.
4. Optionally create additional control files for other supported languages.

Follow these steps to install the BaseLine tool:

1. Create the base directory.

   Create a directory under the IBMVJAVA\IDE\TOOLS directory. The directory name should be the complete name (package and class) of the main tool class with the periods replaced by hyphens. Create the directory: \IBMVJAVA\IDE\TOOLS\BASELINE-BASELINE.

2. Copy the tool's files to the base directory.

   Use **File→Export** and export the BaseLine.class file to the \IBMVJAVA\IDE\TOOLS\BASELINE-BASELINE directory.

3. Create the control file.

   Create the control file, default.ini, in the base directory with the following contents:

   Name = BaseLine
   Version = 1.0
   Menu-Items = BaseLine,baseline.BaseLine,-P

By placing the -P context switch in the Menu-Items line, you cause the menu item to be added to the Selected menu only when a project is selected.

The BaseLine tool is simple, it does not have any associated resource or help files, and it is not enabled for any other languages. For more information about the control file, see the product documentation.

Running the BaseLine Tool

Now restart VisualAge for Java and select the project where you want to create a baseline version. Then select **Selected→Tools→BaseLine**. Figure 211 shows the running tool.

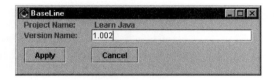

Figure 211. The Running BaseLine Tool

Notice

If you are using VisualAge for Java Enterprise, you should change the tests for products, packages, and types in the **makeVersion** method:

```
old:  if (xxxx.isVersion()) { ....
new:  if (!xxxx.isEdition() { ....
```

This is because there are also scratch editions in the Enterprise product.

You should also call the **release**() method after the **createVersion**(...) method for packages and types, for example:

```
pkg.createVersion(versionName);
pkg.release();
```

Special Notices

This publication is intended to help Java developers create Java programs with VisualAge for Java Professional. The information in this publication is not intended as the specification of any programming interfaces that are provided by VisualAge for Java. See the PUBLICATIONS section of the IBM Programming Announcement for VisualAge for Java for more information about what publications are considered to be product documentation.

References in this publication to IBM products, programs or services do not imply that IBM intends to make these available in all countries in which IBM operates.

Any reference to an IBM product, program, or service is not intended to state or imply that only IBM's product, program, or service may be used. Any functionally equivalent program that does not infringe any of IBM's intellectual property rights may be used instead of the IBM product, program or service.

This document has not been subjected to any formal review and has not been checked for technical accuracy. Results may be individually evaluated for applicability to a particular installation. You may discuss pertinent information from this document with a customer, and you may abstract pertinent information for presentation to your customers. However, any code included is for internal information purposes only and may not be given to customers. If included code is identified as incidental programming, its use must conform to the guidelines in the relevant section of the sales manual.

Any performance data contained in this document was obtained in a controlled environment based on the use of specific data and is presented only to illustrate techniques and procedures to assist IBM personnel to better understand IBM products. The results that may be obtained in other operating environments may vary significantly. Users of this document should verify the applicable data in their specific environment. No performance data may be abstracted or reproduced and given to non-IBM personnel without prior written approval by Business Practices.

The following document contains examples of data and reports used in daily business operations. To illustrate them as completely as possible, the examples contain the names of individuals, companies, brands, and products. All of these names are fictitious and any similarity to the names and addresses used by an actual business enterprise is entirely coincidental.

Reference to PTF numbers that have not been released through the normal distribution process does not imply general availability. The purpose of including these reference numbers is to alert IBM customers to specific information relative to the implementation of the PTF when it becomes available to each customer according to the normal IBM PTF distribution process.

The following terms are trademarks of the International Business Machines Corporation in the United States and/or other countries:

IBM
VisualAge
TeamConnection
WebSphere

The following terms are trademarks of other companies:

C-bus is a trademark of Corollary, Inc.

Java, JDBC and HotJava are trademarks of Sun Microsystems, Incorporated.

Microsoft, Windows, Windows NT, and the Windows 95 logo are trademarks or registered trademarks of Microsoft Corporation.

PC Direct is a trademark of Ziff Communications Company and is used by IBM Corporation under license.

Pentium, MMX, ProShare, LANDesk, and ActionMedia are trademarks or registered trademarks of Intel Corporation in the United States and other countries.

UNIX is a registered trademark in the United States and other countries licensed exclusively through X/Open Company Limited.

InstallShield and InstallShield Java Edition are trademarks or registered trademarks of InstallShield Corporation.

Netscape and Netscape Navigator are registered trademarks of Netscape Communications Corporation in the United States and other countries.

Lotus, Domino, Domino Go Webserver and Lotus Notes are registered trademarks of Lotus Development Corporation in the United States and other countries.

Related Publications

The publications listed in this section are considered particularly suitable for a more detailed discussion of the topics covered in this redbook.

International Technical Support Organization Publications

For information on ordering these ITSO publications see "How to Get ITSO Redbooks" on page 393.

❑ *Application Development with VisualAge for Java Enterprise Version 2*, SG24-5265 (to be published)

❑ *VisualAge for Java Enterprise Version 2 Team Support*, SG24-5245

❑ *Application Development with VisualAge for Java Enterprise*, SG24-5081

❑ *Unlimited Enterprise Access with Java and VisualAge Generator*, SG24-5246

❑ *Connecting the Enterprise to the Internet with MQSeries and VisualAge for Java*, SG24-2144

❑ *Factoring JavaBeans in the Enterprise*, SG24-5051

❑ *JavaBeans by Example*: *Cooking with Beans in the Enterprise*, SG24-2035, published by Prentice Hall, 1997

❑ *Using VisualAge UML Designer*, SG24-4997

Redbooks on CD-ROMs

Redbooks are also available on CD-ROMs. **Order a subscription** and receive updates 2-4 times a year at significant savings.

CD-ROM Title	Subscription Number	Collection Kit Number
Application Development Redbooks Collection	SBOF-7290	SK2T-8037

Product Documentation

The documentation from the following products may be helpful.

❑ DB2 Universal Database

  • *SQL Getting Started*, Version 5, S10J-8156-00

  • *SQL Reference*, Version 5, S10J-8165-00

❑ Lotus Domino Go WebServer

  • *Programming Guide*

  • *Webmasters Guide*

  • *Quick Beginnings*

❑ VisualAge for Java

  The VisualAge for Java documentation is available online through the product installation and at the VisualAge for Java Web site. It includes the JDK 1.1.6 documentation.

  For any other Java API documentation, see the JavaSoft Web site.

Other Publications

These publications are also relevant as further information sources:

❑ Carrel-Billiard, Marc and John Akerley. 1998. *Programming with VisualAge for Java*. Englewood Cliffs, NJ: Prentice Hall; ISBN 0-13-911371-1

❑ Nilsson Dale and Peter Jakab. 1998. *Developing JavaBeans Using VisualAge for Java*. New York, NY: John Wiley; ISBN 0-471-29788-7

❑ Sanders, Roger E. 1997. *The Developer's Handbook to DB2 for Common Servers*, New York, NY: McGraw-Hill, ISBN 0070577250

❑ Chamberlin, Don. 1998. *A Complete Guide to DB2 Universal Database*, San Francisco, CA: Morgan Kaufman; ISBN 1558604820

❑ Date, C.J. and Hugh Darwen. 1987. *A Guide to the Sql Standard : A User's Guide to the Standard Database Language Sql*, Reading, MA: Addison-Wesley Publishing Company; ISBN 0201964260

❑ Hamilton, Graham, Rick Cattell, and Maydene Fisher. 1997. *JDBC Database Access with Java: A Tutorial and Annotated Reference (Java Series)*, Reading, MA: Addison-Wesley Publishing Company; ISBN 0201309955

❑ Reese, George E. 1997. *Database Programming with JDBC and Java*, Sebastopol, CA: O'Reilly & Associates; ISBN 1565922700

❑ Horstmann. Cay S. and Gary Cornell. 1997. *Core Java 1.1: Fundamentals*, Englewood Cliffs, NJ: Prentice Hall; ISBN: 0137669577

❑ Horstmann. Cay S. and Gary Cornell. 1997. *Core Java 1.1: Advanced Features*, Englewood Cliffs, NJ: Prentice Hall; ISBN: 0137669658

❑ Flanagan, David. 1997. *Java in a Nutshell: A Desktop Quick Reference*, Sebastopol, CA: O'Reilly & Associates; ISBN: 156592262X

❑ Topley, Kim.. 1998. *Core Java Foundation Classes*, Englewood Cliffs, NJ: Prentice Hall; ISBN: 0130803014

❑ Rumbaugh, James et al. 1991. *Object-Oriented Modeling and Design*, Englewood Cliffs, NJ: Prentice Hall; ISBN: 0136298419

❑ Jacobson, Ivar. 1992. *Object-Oriented Software Engineering : A Use Case Driven Approach,* Reading, MA: Addison-Wesley Publishing Company; ISBN: 0201544350

❑ Booch, Grady. 1994. *Object-Oriented Analysis and Design with Applications* (Addison-Wesley Object Technology Series), Reading, MA: Addison-Wesley Publishing Company; ISBN: 0805353402

How to Get ITSO Redbooks

This section explains how both customers and IBM employees can find out about ITSO redbooks, CD-ROMs, workshops, and residencies. A form for ordering books and CD-ROMs is also provided.

The information in this section was current at the time of publication but is continually subject to change. For the latest information see http://www.redbooks.ibm.com.

How IBM Employees Can Get ITSO Redbooks

Employees may request ITSO deliverables (redbooks, BookManager BOOKs, and CD-ROMs) and information about redbooks, workshops, and residencies in the following ways:

- **PUBORDER** – to order hardcopies in United States

- **GOPHER link to the Internet** – type GOPHER WTSCPOK.ITSO.IBM.COM

- **Tools disks**

  To get LIST3820s of redbooks, type one of the following commands:

      TOOLS SENDTO EHONE4 TOOLS2 REDPRINT GET SG24xxxx PACKAGE
      TOOLS SENDTO CANVM2 TOOLS REDPRINT GET SG24xxxx PACKAGE (Canadian users only)

  To get lists of redbooks:

      TOOLS SENDTO USDIST MKTTOOLS MKTTOOLS GET ITSOCAT TXT

  To register for information on workshops, residencies, and redbooks:

      TOOLS SENDTO WTSCPOK TOOLS ZDISK GET ITSOREGI 1996

  For a list of product area specialists in the ITSO:

      TOOLS SENDTO WTSCPOK TOOLS ZDISK GET ORGCARD PACKAGE

- **Redbooks Web Site on the IBM Intranet**

  http://w3.itso.ibm.com/redbooks

- **IBM Direct Publications Catalog on the World Wide Web**

  http://www.elink.ibmlink.ibm.com/pbl/pbl

  IBM employees may obtain LIST3820s of redbooks from this page.

- **REDBOOKS category on INEWS**

- **On-line** – send orders to: USIB6FPL at IBMMAIL   or   DKIBMBSH at IBMMAIL

- **Internet Listserver**

  With an Internet E-mail address, anyone can subscribe to an IBM Announcement Listserver. To initiate the service, send an E-mail note to announce@webster.ibmlink.ibm.com with the keyword subscribe in the body of the note (leave the subject line blank). A category form and detailed instructions will be sent to you.

How Customers Can Get ITSO Redbooks

Customers may request ITSO deliverables (redbooks, BookManager BOOKs, and CD-ROMs) and information about redbooks, workshops, and residencies in the following ways:

- **On-line Orders** (Do not send credit card information over the Internet) – send orders to:

	IBMMAIL	**Internet**
In United States	usib6fpl at ibmmail	usib6fpl@ibmmail.com
In Canada	caibmbkz at ibmmail	lmannix@vnet.ibm.com
Outside North America	dkibmbsh at ibmmail	bookshop@dk.ibm.com

- **Telephone orders**

United States (toll free)	1-800-879-2755
Canada (toll free)	1-800-IBM-4YOU

Outside North America	(long distance charges apply)
(+45) 4810-1320 - Danish	(+45) 4810-1020 - German
(+45) 4810-1420 - Dutch	(+45) 4810-1620 - Italian
(+45) 4810-1540 - English	(+45) 4810-1270 - Norwegian
(+45) 4810-1670 - Finnish	(+45) 4810-1120 - Spanish
(+45) 4810-1220 - French	(+45) 4810-1170 - Swedish

- **Mail Orders** – send orders to:

IBM Publications	IBM Publications	IBM Direct Services
Publications Customer Support	144-4th Avenue, S.W.	Sortemosevej 21
P.O. Box 29570	Calgary, Alberta T2P 3N5	DK-3450 Allerød
Raleigh, NC 27626-0570	Canada	Denmark
USA		

- **Fax** – send orders to:

United States (toll free)	1-800-445-9269
Canada	1-800-267-4455
Outside North America	(+45) 48 14 2207 (long distance charge)

- **1-800-IBM-4FAX (United States)** or **(+1) 408 256 5422 (Outside USA)** – ask for:

    Index # 4421 Abstracts of new redbooks
    Index # 4422 IBM redbooks
    Index # 4420 Redbooks for last six months

- **Direct Services** – send note to softwareshop@vnet.ibm.com

- **On the World Wide Web**

Redbooks Web Site	http://www.redbooks.ibm.com
IBM Direct Publications Catalog	http://www.elink.ibmlink.ibm.com/pbl/pbl

- **Internet Listserver**

    With an Internet E-mail address, anyone can subscribe to an IBM Announcement Listserver. To initiate the service, send an E-mail note to announce@webster.ibmlink.ibm.com with the keyword subscribe in the body of the note (leave the subject line blank).

IBM Redbook Order Form

Please send me the following:

Title	Order Number	Quantity

First name _____ Last name _____

Company _____

Address _____

City _____ Postal code _____ Country _____

Telephone number _____ Telefax number _____ VAT number _____

☐ Invoice to customer number _____

☐ Credit card number _____

Credit card expiration date _____ Card issued to _____ Signature _____

We accept American Express, Diners, Eurocard, Master Card, and Visa. Payment by credit card not available in all countries. Signature mandatory for credit card payment.

Glossary

This glossary defines terms and abbreviations that are used in this book. If you do not find the term you are looking for, refer to the *IBM Dictionary of Computing*, New York: McGraw-Hill, 1994.

This glossary includes terms and definitions from the *American National Standard Dictionary for Information Systems*, ANSI X3.172-1990, copyright 1990 by the American National Standards Institute (ANSI). Copies may be purchased from the American National Standards Institute, 1430 Broadway, New York, New York 10018.

A

abstract class. A class that provides common behavior across a set of subclasses but is not itself designed to have instances. An abstract class represents a concept; classes derived from it represent implementations of the concept. See also *base class*.

access modifier: A keyword that controls access to a class, method, or attribute. The access modifiers in Java are public, private, protected, and package, the default.

accessor methods. Methods that an object provides to define the interface to its instance variables. The accessor method to return the value of an instance variable is called a *get* method or *getter* method, and the mutator method to assign a value to an instance variable is called a *set* method or *setter* method.

applet. A Java program designed to run within a Web browser. Contrast with application.

application. In Java programming, a self-contained, stand-alone Java program that includes a main() method. Contrast with applet.

application programming interface (API). A software interface that enables applications to communicate with each other. An API is the set of programming language constructs or statements that can be coded in an application program to obtain the specific functions and services provided by an underlying operating system or service program.

argument. A data element, or value, included as a parameter in a method call. Arguments provide additional information that the called method can use to perform the requested operation.

attribute. A specification of an element of a class. For example, a customer bean could have a name attribute and an address attribute.

B

base class. A class from which other classes or beans are derived. A base class may itself be derived from another base class. See also *abstract class*.

bean. A definition or instance of a JavaBeans component. See also *JavaBeans*.

BeanInfo. (1) A companion class for a bean that defines a set of methods that can be accessed to retrieve information on the bean's properties, events, and methods. (2) In the VisualAge for Java IDE, a page in the Class Browser that provides bean information.

beans palette. In the Visual Composition Editor, a pane that contains beans that you can select and manipulate to create programs. You can add your own categories and beans to the beans palette.

break point. A point in a computer program where the execution will be halted.

browser. (1) In VisualAge for Java, a window that provides information about program elements. There are browsers for projects, packages, classes, methods, and interfaces. (2) An Internet-based tool that lets user browse Web sites.

C

category. In the Visual Composition Editor, a selectable grouping of beans on the palette. Selecting a category displays the beans belonging to that category. See also *beans palette*.

class. A template that defines properties, operations, and behavior for all instances of that template.

class hierarchy. The relationships among classes that share a single inheritance. All Java classes inherit from the Object class.

class library. A collection of classes.

class method. See *method*.

CLASSPATH. (1) In VisualAge for Java the lists of pathnames which will be searched for dynamically loaded classes, BeanInfo information and external source for debugging. (2) In your deployment environment, the environment variable that specifies the directories in which to look for class and resource files.

client/server. The model of interaction in distributed data processing where a program at one location sends a request to a program at another location and awaits a response. The requesting program is called a *client*, and the answering program is called a *server*.

Class Browser. In the VisualAge for Java IDE, a tool used to browse the classes loaded in the workspace.

component model. An architecture and an API that allows developers to define reusable segments of code that can be combined to create a program. VisualAge for Java uses the JavaBeans component model.

composite bean. A bean that is composed of other beans. A composite bean can contain visual beans, nonvisual beans, or both. See also *bean, nonvisual bean,* and *visual bean*.

concrete class. A non-abstract subclass of an abstract class that is a specialization of the abstract class.

connection. In the Visual Composition Editor, a visual link between two components that represents the relationship between the components. Each connection has a source, a target, and other properties. See also *event-to-method connection, parameter connections,* and *property-to-property connection*.

console. In VisualAge for Java, the window that acts as the standard input (System.in) and standard output (System.out) device for programs running in the VisualAge for Java IDE.

construction from parts. A software development technology in which applications are assembled from existing and reusable software components, known as *parts*. In VisualAge for Java, parts are called *beans*.

constructor. A special class method that has the same name as the class and is used to construct and possibly initialize objects of its class type.

container. A component that can hold other components. In Java, examples of containers include Applets, Frames, and Dialogs. In the Visual Composition Editor, containers can be graphically represented and generated.

current edition. The edition of a program element that is currently in the workspace. See also *open edition*.

D

demarshal. To deconstruct an object so that it can be written as a stream of bytes. Synonym for *flatten* and *serialize*.

deserialize. To construct an object from a de-marshaled state. Synonym for *marshal and resurrect*.

double-byte character set (DBCS). A set of characters in which each character is represented by 2 bytes. Languages such as Japanese, Chinese, and Korean, which contain more symbols than can be represented by 256 code points, require double-byte character sets. Compare with *single-byte character set*.

E

edition. A specific "cut" of a program element. VisualAge for Java supports multiple editions of program elements. See also *current edition, open edition*, and *versioned edition*.

encapsulation. The hiding of a software object's internal representation. The object provides an interface that queries and manipulates the data without exposing its underlying structure.

event. An action by a user program, or a specification of a notification that may trigger specific behavior. In JDK 1.1, events notify the relevant listener classes to take appropriate actions.

event-to-method connection. A connection from an event generated by a bean to a method of a bean. When the connected event occurs, the method is executed. See also *connection*.

F

factory. A nonvisual bean capable of dynamically creating new instances of a specified bean.

feature. (1) A component of VisualAge for Java that is installed separately using the QuickStart. (2) A method, field, or event that is available from a bean's interface and to which other beans can connect.

field. See attribute

flatten. Synonymous with *demarshal*.

free-form surface. The open area of the Visual Composition Editor where you can work with visual and nonvisual beans. You add, remove, and connect beans on the free-form surface.

G

graphical user interface (GUI). A type of interface that enables users to communicate with a program by manipulating graphical features, rather than by entering commands. Typically, a GUI includes a combination of graphics, pointing devices, menu bars and other menus, overlapping windows, and icons.

H

Hypertext Markup Language (HTML). The basic language that is used to build hypertext documents on the World Wide Web. It is used in basic, plain ASCII-text documents, but when those documents are interpreted, or *rendered*, by a Web browser such as Netscape, the document can display formatted text, color, a variety of fonts, graphical images, special effects, hypertext jumps to other Internet locations, and information forms.

Hypertext Transfer Protocol (HTTP). The protocol for moving hypertext files across the Internet. Requires an HTTP client program on one end, and an HTTP server program on the other end. HTTP is the most important protocol used in the World Wide Web.

I

IDE. See Integrated Development Environment.

inheritance. (1) A mechanism by which an object class can use the attributes, relationships, and methods defined in classes related to it (its base classes). (2) An object-oriented programming technique that allows you to use existing classes as bases for creating other classes.

instance. Synonym for *object*, a particular instantiation of a data type.

integrated development environment (IDE). In VisualAge for Java, the set of windows that provide the user with access to development tools. The primary windows are Workbench, Class Browser, Log, Console, Debugger, and Repository Explorer.

interchange file. A file that you can export from VisualAge for Java that contains information about selected projects or packages. This file can then be imported into any VisualAge for Java session.

interface. A named set of method declarations that is implemented by a class. The Interface page in the Workbench lists all interfaces in the workspace.

Internet. The collection of interconnected networks that use TCP/IP and evolved from the ARPANET of the late 1960s and early 1970s.

intranet. A private *network,* inside a company or organization, that uses the same kinds of software that you would find on the public Internet. Many of the tools used on the Internet are being used in private networks; for example, many companies have Web servers that are available only to employees.

Internet Protocol (IP). The protocol that provides basic Internet functions.

IP number. An Internet address that is a unique number consisting of four parts separated by dots, sometimes called a *dotted quad* (for example: 198.204.112.1). Every Internet computer has an IP number, and most computers also have one or more domain names that are mappings for the dotted quad.

J

JDBC. In JDK 1.1, the specification that defines an API that enables programs to access databases that comply with this standard.

Java. A programming language invented by Sun Microsystems that is specifically designed for writing programs that can be safely downloaded to your computer through the Internet and immediately run without fear of viruses or other harm to your computer or files.

Java archive (JAR). A platform-independent file format that groups many files into one. JAR files are used for compression, reduced download time, and security.

JavaBeans. The specification that defines the platform-neutral component model used to represent parts. Instances of JavaBeans (often called beans) may have methods, properties, and events.

K

keyword. A predefined word reserved for Java, for example, *return*, that may not be used as an identifier.

L

listener. In JDK 1.1, a class that receives and handles events.

local area network (LAN). A computer network located on a user's establishment within a limited geographical area. A LAN typically consists of one or more server machines providing services to a number of client workstations.

log. In VisualAge for Java, the window that displays messages and warnings during development.

M

marshal. Synonymous with *deserialize*.

message. A communication from one object to another that requests the receiving object to execute a method. A method call consists of a method name that indicates the requested method and the arguments to be used in executing the method. The method call always returns some object to the requesting object as the result of performing the method. Synonym for *method call.*

method. A fragment of Java code within a class that can be invoked and passed a set of parameters to perform a specific task.

method call. Synonymous with message.

model. A nonvisual bean that represents the state and behavior of an object, such as a customer or an account. Contrast with *view*.

mutator methods. Methods that an object provides to define the interface to its instance variables. The accessor method to return the value of an instance variable is called a *get* method or *getter* method, and the mutator method to assign a value to an instance variable is called a *set* method or *setter* method.

N

named package. In the VisualAge for Java IDE, a package that has been explicitly named and created.

nonvisual bean. In the Visual Composition Editor, a bean that has no visual representation at run time. A nonvisual bean typically represents some real-world object that exists in the business environment. Compare with *model*. Contrast with *view* and *visual bean*.

O

object. (1) A computer representation of something that a user can work with to perform a task. An object can appear as text or an icon. (2) A collection of data and methods that operate on that data, which together represent a logical entity in the system. In object-oriented programming, objects are grouped into classes that share common data definitions and methods. Each object in the class is said to be an instance of the class. (3) An instance of an object class consisting of attributes, a data structure, and operational methods. It can represent a person, place, thing, event, or concept. Each instance has the same properties, attributes, and methods as other instances of the object class, although it has unique values assigned to its attributes.

object class. A template for defining the attributes and methods of an object. An object class can contain other object classes. An individual representation of an object class is called an *object*.

object-oriented programming (OOP). A programming approach based on the concepts of data abstraction and inheritance. Unlike procedural programming techniques, object-oriented programming concentrates on those data objects that constitute the problem and how they are manipulated, not on how something is accomplished.

ODBC driver. An ODBC driver is a dynamic link library that implements ODBC function calls and interacts with a data source.

Open Database Connectivity (ODBC). A Microsoft-developed C database API that allows access to database management systems calling callable SQL, which does not require the use of an SQL preprocessor. In addition, ODBC provides an architecture that allows users to add modules (database drivers) that link the application to their choice of database management systems at run time. Applications no longer need to be directly linked to the modules of all the database management systems that are supported.

open edition. An edition of a program element that can still be modified; that is, the edition has not been versioned. An open edition may reside in the workspace as well as in the repository.

operation. A method or service that can be requested of an object.

P

package. A program element that contains related classes and interfaces.

palette. See *beans palette*.

parameter connection. A connection that satisfies a parameter of an action or method by supplying either a property's value or the return value of an action, method, or script. The parameter is always the source of the connection. See also *connection*.

parent class. The class from which another bean or class inherits data, methods, or both.

part. An existing, reusable software component. In VisualAge for Java, all parts created with the Visual Composition Editor conform to the JavaBeans component model and are referred to as beans. See also non*visual bean* and *visual bean*.

primitive bean. A basic building block of other beans. A primitive bean can be relatively complex in terms of the function it provides.

private. In Java, an access modifier associated with a class member. It allows only the class itself to access the member.

process. A collection of code, data, and other system resources, including at least one thread of execution, that performs a data processing task.

program. In VisualAge for Java, a term that refers to both Java applets and applications.

program element. In VisualAge for Java, a term referring to any of the entities under source control. Program elements are projects, packages, classes, interfaces, or methods.

project. In VisualAge for Java, the topmost kind of program element. A project contains Java packages.

promotion. Within a JavaBean, to make features of a contained bean available to be used for making connections. For example, a bean consisting of three push buttons on a panel. If this bean is placed in a frame, the features of the push buttons would have to be promoted to make them available from within the frame.

property. An initial setting or characteristic of a bean; for example, a name, font, text, or positional characteristic.

property sheet. In the Visual Composition Editor, a set of name-value pairs that specify the initial appearance and other bean characteristics.

property-to-property connection. A connection from a property of one bean to a property of another bean. See also *connection*.

protected. In Java, an access modifier associated with a class member. It allows the class itself, subclasses, and all classes in the same package to access the member.

protocol. (1) The set of all messages to which an object will respond. (2) Specification of the structure and meaning (the semantics) of messages that are exchanged between a client and a server. (3) Computer rules that provide uniform specifications so that computer hardware and operating systems can communicate.

prototype. A method declaration or definition that includes the name of the method, the return type and the types of its arguments. Contrast with *signature*.

R

Remote Method Invocation (RMI). In JDK 1.1, the API that enables you to write distributed Java programs, allowing methods of remote Java objects to be accessed from other Java virtual machines.

repository. In VisualAge for Java, the storage area, separate from the workspace, that contains all editions (both open and versioned) of all program elements that have ever been in the workspace, including the current editions that are in the workspace. You can add editions of program elements to the workspace from the repository.

Repository Explorer. In VisualAge for Java, the window from which you can view and compare editions of program elements that are in the repository.

resource file. A file that is referred to from your Java program. Examples include graphics and audio files.

resurrect. Synonymous with *deserialize*.

RMI compiler. The compiler that generates stub and skeleton files that facilitate RMI communication. This compiler can be automatically invoked from the Tools menu item.

RMI registry. A server program that allows remote clients to get a reference to a server bean.

S

Scrapbook. In VisualAge for Java, the window from which you can write and test fragments of code, without having to define an encompassing class or method.

serialize. Synonymous with *demarshal*.

signature. The part of a method declaration consisting of the name of the method and the number and types of its arguments. Contrast with *prototype*.

single-byte character set. A set of characters in which each character is represented by a 1- byte code.

SmartGuide. In IBM software products, an interface that guides you through performing common tasks.

sticky. In the Visual Composition Editor, the mode that enables an application developer to add multiple beans of the same class (for example, three push buttons) without going back and forth between the beans palette and the free-form surface.

superclass. See *abstract class* and *base class*.

T

tear-off property. A property that a developer has exposed as a variable to work with as though it were a stand-alone bean.

thread. A unit of execution within a process.

type. In VisualAge for Java, a generic term for a class or interface.

U

Unicode. A character coding system designed to support the interchange, processing, and display of the written texts of the diverse languages of the modern world. Unicode characters are typically encoded using 16-bit integral unsigned numbers.

uniform resource locator (URL). A standard identifier for a resource on the World Wide Web, used by Web browsers to initiate a connection. The URL includes the communications protocol to use, the name of the server, and path information identifying the objects to be retrieved on the server. A URL looks like this:

http://www.matisse.net/seminars.html

or telnet://well.sf.ca.us.br

or news:new.newusers.question.br

user interface (UI). (1) The hardware, or software, or both that enables a user to interact with a computer. (2) The term *user interface* typically refers to the visual presentation and its underlying software with which a user interacts.

V

variable. (1) A storage place within an object for a data feature. The data feature is an object, such as number or date, stored as an attribute of the containing object. (2) A bean that receives an identity at run time. A variable by itself contains no data or program logic; it must be connected such that it receives run-time identity from a bean elsewhere in the application.

versioned edition. An edition that has been versioned and can no longer be modified.

versioning. The act of making an open edition a versioned edition; that is, making the edition read-only.

view. (1) A visual bean, such as a window, push button, or entry field. (2) A visual representation that can display and change the underlying model objects of an application. Views are both the end result of developing an application and the basic unit of composition of user interfaces. Compare with *visual bean*. Contrast with *model*.

visual bean. In the Visual Composition Editor, a bean that is visible to the end user in the graphical user interface. Compare with *view*. Contrast with *nonvisual bean*.

visual programming tool. A tool that provides a means for specifying programs graphically. Application programmers write applications by manipulating graphical representations of components.

Visual Composition Editor. In VisualAge for Java, the tool where you can create graphical user interfaces from prefabricated beans and define relationships (connections) between both visual and nonvisual beans. The Visual Composition Editor is a page in the class browser.

W

Workbench. In VisualAge for Java, the main window from which you can manage the workspace, create and modify code, and open browsers and other tools.

workspace. The work area that contains all the code you are currently working on (that is, current editions). The workspace also contains the standard Java class libraries and other class libraries.

Abbreviations

ANSI	American National Standards Institute
API	application programming interface
ATM	automated teller machine
AWT	Abstract Windowing Toolkit
CAE	Client Access Enabler
URL	uniform resource locator
CLI	call level interface
DB2	DATABASE 2
DBCS	double-byte character set
DBMS	database management system
DLL	dynamic link library
DNS	domain name server
DRDA	Distributed Relational Database Architecture
ECD	edit-compile-debug
ECI	external call interface
FTP	File Transfer Protocol
GUI	graphical user interface
HTML	Hypertext Markup Language
HTTP	Hypertext Transfer Protocol
IBM	International Business Machines Corporation
IDE	integrated development environment
IDL	interface definition language
IIOP	Internet inter-ORB protocol
IMS	Information Management System
IOR	interoperable object reference
ITSO	International Technical Support Organization
JAR	Java archive
JDK	Java Developer's Kit
JNI	Java Native Interface
JVM	Java Virtual Machine
LAN	local area network
MOFW	managed object framework
MVS	Multiple Virtual Storage
NLS	National Language Support
NT	new technology
ODBC	Open Database Connectivity
OMG	Object Management Group
OMT	object modeling technique
OO	object-oriented
OOA	object-oriented analysis
OOD	object-oriented design
ORB	Object Request Broker
OS/2	Operating System/2
OTS	object transaction service
PIN	personal identification number
RAD	rapid application development
RDBMS	relational database management system
RMI	Remote Method Invocation
SBCS	single-byte character set
SDK	Software Developer's Kit
SQL	structured query language
TCP/IP	Transmission Control Protocol/Internet Protocol
TP	transaction processing
UOW	unit of work
URL	uniform resource locator
WWW	World Wide Web

Index

Customer class
    property features 92
    testing 93
    toString method 92
Customizer class 56

D

DAT file. See interchange files
Data Access beans
    concepts 262
    Connection alias 265
    Database Access class 265
    SQL specification 265
DB2
    Applet Server 261
    JDBC drivers 260
    NT Security Server 266
Debugger
    Breakpoints page 180
    caught exceptions 184
    class trace 189
    concepts 177
    conditional breakpoints 182
    Debug page 177
    external debug 186
    opening 182
debugging
    adding breakpoints 180
    disabling breakpoints 182
    removing breakpoints 182
    removing external breakpoints 188
default package 36
deployment
    applets 336
    applications 329
    servlets 333
    supporting code 342
domain model 53
Domino agents 358

Domino Go Webserver 333
Domino Java Class Libraries 358
dynamic HTML 282
dynamic HTML pages 283

E

editions
    concepts 154
    creating 161
    loading available 162
    managing 161
    methods 161
    open 157
    replacing 162
English 313
errors
    copying classes 254, 268, 305
    in the ATM application 244
    in your code 42
event features
    BeanInfo page 66
events
    action 101
    creating 88
    creating a new interface 78
    event set 66
    firing 54
    listener interface 66
    multicast event 66
    pinChecked 87
    property change 54
    property features 55
    pseudo 140
    this 141
    unicast event 66
exceptions
    MissingResourceException 314
    NotSerializableException 252
    ServletException 283

LICENSE AGREEMENT AND LIMITED WARRANTY

READ THE FOLLOWING TERMS AND CONDITIONS CAREFULLY BEFORE OPENING THIS SOFTWARE MEDIA PACKAGE. THIS LEGAL DOCUMENT IS AN AGREEMENT BETWEEN YOU AND PRENTICE-HALL, INC. (THE "COMPANY"). BY OPENING THIS SEALED SOFTWARE MEDIA PACKAGE, YOU ARE AGREEING TO BE BOUND BY THESE TERMS AND CONDITIONS. IF YOU DO NOT AGREE WITH THESE TERMS AND CONDITIONS, DO NOT OPEN THE SOFTWARE MEDIA PACKAGE. PROMPTLY RETURN THE UNOPENED SOFTWARE MEDIA PACKAGE AND ALL ACCOMPANYING ITEMS TO THE PLACE YOU OBTAINED THEM FOR A FULL REFUND OF ANY SUMS YOU HAVE PAID.

1.   **GRANT OF LICENSE:** In consideration of your payment of the license fee, which is part of the price you paid for this product, and your agreement to abide by the terms and conditions of this Agreement, the Company grants to you a nonexclusive right to use and display the copy of the enclosed software program (hereinafter the "SOFTWARE") on a single computer (i.e., with a single CPU) at a single location so long as you comply with the terms of this Agreement. The Company reserves all rights not expressly granted to you under this Agreement.

2.   **OWNERSHIP OF SOFTWARE:** You own only the magnetic or physical media (the enclosed SOFTWARE) on which the SOFTWARE is recorded or fixed, but the Company retains all the rights, title, and ownership to the SOFTWARE recorded on the original SOFTWARE copy(ies) and all subsequent copies of the SOFTWARE, regardless of the form or media on which the original or other copies may exist. This license is not a sale of the original SOFTWARE or any copy to you.

3.   **COPY RESTRICTIONS:** This SOFTWARE and the accompanying printed materials and user manual (the "Documentation") are the subject of copyright. You may not copy the Documentation or the SOFTWARE, except that you may make a single copy of the SOFTWARE for backup or archival purposes only. You may be held legally responsible for any copying or copyright infringement which is caused or encouraged by your failure to abide by the terms of this restriction.

4.   **USE RESTRICTIONS:** You may not network the SOFTWARE or otherwise use it on more than one computer or computer terminal at the same time. You may physically transfer the SOFTWARE from one computer to another provided that the SOFTWARE is used on only one computer at a time. You may not distribute copies of the SOFTWARE or Documentation to others. You may not reverse engineer, disassemble, decompile, modify, adapt, translate, or create derivative works based on the SOFTWARE or the Documentation without the prior written consent of the Company.

5.   **TRANSFER RESTRICTIONS:** The enclosed SOFTWARE is licensed only to you and may not be transferred to any one else without the prior written consent of the Company. Any unauthorized transfer of the SOFTWARE shall result in the immediate termination of this Agreement.

6.   **TERMINATION:** This license is effective until terminated. This license will terminate automatically without notice from the Company and become null and void if you fail to comply with any provisions or limitations of this license. Upon termination, you shall destroy the Documentation and all copies of the SOFTWARE. All provisions of this Agreement as to warranties, limitation of liability, remedies or damages, and our ownership rights shall survive termination.

7.   **MISCELLANEOUS:** This Agreement shall be construed in accordance with the laws of the United States of America and the State of New York and shall benefit the Company, its affiliates, and assignees.

8.   **LIMITED WARRANTY AND DISCLAIMER OF WARRANTY:** The Company warrants that the SOFTWARE, when properly used in accordance with the Documentation, will operate in substantial conformity with the description of the SOFTWARE set forth in the Documentation. The Company does not warrant that the SOFTWARE will meet your requirements or that the operation of the SOFTWARE will be uninterrupted or error-free. The Company warrants that the

media on which the SOFTWARE is delivered shall be free from defects in materials and workmanship under normal use for a period of thirty (30) days from the date of your purchase. Your only remedy and the Company's only obligation under these limited warranties is, at the Company's option, return of the warranted item for a refund of any amounts paid by you or replacement of the item. Any replacement of SOFTWARE or media under the warranties shall not extend the original warranty period. The limited warranty set forth above shall not apply to any SOFTWARE which the Company determines in good faith has been subject to misuse, neglect, improper installation, repair, alteration, or damage by you. EXCEPT FOR THE EXPRESSED WARRANTIES SET FORTH ABOVE, THE COMPANY DISCLAIMS ALL WARRANTIES, EXPRESS OR IMPLIED, INCLUDING WITHOUT LIMITATION, THE IMPLIED WARRANTIES OF MERCHANTABILITY AND FITNESS FOR A PARTICULAR PURPOSE. EXCEPT FOR THE EXPRESS WARRANTY SET FORTH ABOVE, THE COMPANY DOES NOT WARRANT, GUARANTEE, OR MAKE ANY REPRESENTATION REGARDING THE USE OR THE RESULTS OF THE USE OF THE SOFTWARE IN TERMS OF ITS CORRECTNESS, ACCURACY, RELIABILITY, CURRENTNESS, OR OTHERWISE.

IN NO EVENT, SHALL THE COMPANY OR ITS EMPLOYEES, AGENTS, SUPPLIERS, OR CONTRACTORS BE LIABLE FOR ANY INCIDENTAL, INDIRECT, SPECIAL, OR CONSEQUENTIAL DAMAGES ARISING OUT OF OR IN CONNECTION WITH THE LICENSE GRANTED UNDER THIS AGREEMENT, OR FOR LOSS OF USE, LOSS OF DATA, LOSS OF INCOME OR PROFIT, OR OTHER LOSSES, SUSTAINED AS A RESULT OF INJURY TO ANY PERSON, OR LOSS OF OR DAMAGE TO PROPERTY, OR CLAIMS OF THIRD PARTIES, EVEN IF THE COMPANY OR AN AUTHORIZED REPRESENTATIVE OF THE COMPANY HAS BEEN ADVISED OF THE POSSIBILITY OF SUCH DAMAGES. IN NO EVENT SHALL LIABILITY OF THE COMPANY FOR DAMAGES WITH RESPECT TO THE SOFTWARE EXCEED THE AMOUNTS ACTUALLY PAID BY YOU, IF ANY, FOR THE SOFTWARE.

SOME JURISDICTIONS DO NOT ALLOW THE LIMITATION OF IMPLIED WARRANTIES OR LIABILITY FOR INCIDENTAL, INDIRECT, SPECIAL, OR CONSEQUENTIAL DAMAGES, SO THE ABOVE LIMITATIONS MAY NOT ALWAYS APPLY. THE WARRANTIES IN THIS AGREEMENT GIVE YOU SPECIFIC LEGAL RIGHTS AND YOU MAY ALSO HAVE OTHER RIGHTS WHICH VARY IN ACCORDANCE WITH LOCAL LAW.

ACKNOWLEDGMENT

YOU ACKNOWLEDGE THAT YOU HAVE READ THIS AGREEMENT, UNDERSTAND IT, AND AGREE TO BE BOUND BY ITS TERMS AND CONDITIONS. YOU ALSO AGREE THAT THIS AGREEMENT IS THE COMPLETE AND EXCLUSIVE STATEMENT OF THE AGREEMENT BETWEEN YOU AND THE COMPANY AND SUPERSEDES ALL PROPOSALS OR PRIOR AGREEMENTS, ORAL, OR WRITTEN, AND ANY OTHER COMMUNICATIONS BETWEEN YOU AND THE COMPANY OR ANY REPRESENTATIVE OF THE COMPANY RELATING TO THE SUBJECT MATTER OF THIS AGREEMENT.

Should you have any questions concerning this Agreement or if you wish to contact the Company for any reason, please contact in writing at the address below.

Robin Short
Prentice Hall PTR
One Lake Street
Upper Saddle River, New Jersey 07458

International License Agreement for Evaluation of Programs

Part 1 - General Terms

PLEASE READ THIS AGREEMENT CAREFULLY BEFORE USING THE PRO-
GRAM. IBM WILL LICENSE THE PROGRAM TO YOU ONLY IF YOU FIRST ACCEPT
THE TERMS OF THIS AGREEMENT. BY USING THE PROGRAM YOU AGREE TO
THESE TERMS. IF YOU DO NOT AGREE TO THE TERMS OF THIS AGREEMENT,
PROMPTLY RETURN THE UNUSED PROGRAM TO IBM.

The Program is owned by International Business Machines Corporation or one of its
subsidiaries (IBM) or an IBM supplier, and is copyrighted and licensed, not sold.

The term "Program" means the original program and all whole or partial copies of it. A
Program consists of machine-readable instructions, its components, data, audio-visual content
(such as images, text, recordings, or pictures), and related licensed materials.

This Agreement includes Part 1 - General Terms and Part 2 - Country-unique Terms
and is the complete agreement regarding the use of this Program, and replaces any prior oral
or written communications between you and IBM. The terms of Part 2 may replace or modify
those of Part 1.

1. License

Use of the Program

IBM grants you a nonexclusive, nontransferable license to use the Program.

You may 1) use the Program only for internal evaluation, testing or demonstration purposes, on a trial or "try-and-buy" basis and 2) make and install a reasonable number of copies
of the Program in support of such use, unless IBM identifies a specific number of copies in the
documentation accompanying the Program. The terms of this license apply to each copy you
make. You will reproduce the copyright notice and any other legends of ownership on each
copy, or partial copy, of the Program.

THE PROGRAM MAY CONTAIN A DISABLING DEVICE THAT WILL PREVENT
IT FROM BEING USED UPON EXPIRATION OF THIS LICENSE. YOU WILL NOT
TAMPER WITH THIS DISABLING DEVICE OR THE PROGRAM. YOU SHOULD TAKE
PRECAUTIONS TO AVOID ANY LOSS OF DATA THAT MIGHT RESULT WHEN THE
PROGRAM CAN NO LONGER BE USED.

You will 1) maintain a record of all copies of the Program and 2) ensure that anyone who
uses the Program does so only for your authorized use and in compliance with the terms of this
Agreement.

You may not 1) use, copy, modify or distribute the Program except as provided in this
Agreement; 2) reverse assemble, reverse compile, or otherwise translate the Program except as
specifically permitted by law without the possibility of contractual waiver; or 3) sublicense,
rent, or lease the Program.

This license begins with your first use of the Program and ends on the earlier of 1) termination of this license in accordance with the terms of this Agreement or 2) when the Program automatically disables itself. You will destroy the Program and all copies made of it within ten days of when this license ends.

2. No Warranty

SUBJECT TO ANY STATUTORY WARRANTIES WHICH CANNOT BE EXCLUDED, IBM MAKES NO WARRANTIES OR CONDITIONS EITHER EXPRESS OR IMPLIED, INCLUDING WITHOUT LIMITATION, THE WARRANTY OF NON-INFRINGEMENT AND THE IMPLIED WARRANTIES OF MERCHANTABILITY AND FITNESS FOR A PARTICULAR PURPOSE, REGARDING THE PROGRAM OR TECHNICAL SUPPORT, IF ANY. IBM MAKES NO WARRANTY REGARDING THE CAPABILITY OF THE PROGRAM TO CORRECTLY PROCESS, PROVIDE AND/OR RECEIVE DATE DATA WITHIN AND BETWEEN THE 20TH AND 21ST CENTURIES.

This exclusion also applies to any of IBM's subcontractors, suppliers or program developers (collectively called "Suppliers").

Manufacturers, suppliers, or publishers of non-IBM Programs may provide their own warranties.

3. Limitation of Liability

NEITHER IBM NOR ITS SUPPLIERS ARE LIABLE FOR ANY DIRECT OR INDIRECT DAMAGES, INCLUDING WITHOUT LIMITATION, LOST PROFITS, LOST SAVINGS, OR ANY INCIDENTAL, SPECIAL, OR OTHER ECONOMIC CONSEQUENTIAL DAMAGES, EVEN IF IBM IS INFORMED OF THEIR POSSIBILITY. SOME JURISDICTIONS DO NOT ALLOW THE EXCLUSION OR LIMITATION OF INCIDENTAL OR CONSEQUENTIAL DAMAGES, SO THE ABOVE EXCLUSION OR LIMITATION MAY NOT APPLY TO YOU.

4. General

Nothing in this Agreement affects any statutory rights of consumers that cannot be waived or limited by contract.

IBM may terminate your license if you fail to comply with the terms of this Agreement. If IBM does so, you must immediately destroy the Program and all copies you made of it.

You may not export the Program.

Neither you nor IBM will bring a legal action under this Agreement more than two years after the cause of action arose unless otherwise provided by local law without the possibility of contractual waiver or limitation.

Neither you nor IBM is responsible for failure to fulfill any obligations due to causes beyond its control.

There is no additional charge for use of the Program for the duration of this license.

IBM does not provide program services or technical support, unless IBM specifies otherwise.

The laws of the country in which you acquire the Program govern this Agreement, except 1) in Australia, the laws of the State or Territory in which the transaction is performed govern this Agreement; 2) in Albania, Armenia, Belarus, Bosnia/Herzegovina, Bulgaria, Croatia, Czech Republic, Georgia, Hungary, Kazakhstan, Kirghizia, Former Yugoslav Republic of Macedonia (FYROM), Moldova, Poland, Romania, Russia, Slovak Republic, Slovenia, Ukraine, and Federal Republic of Yugoslavia, the laws of Austria govern this Agreement; 3) in the United Kingdom, all disputes relating to this Agreement will be governed by English Law and will be submitted to the exclusive jurisdiction of the English courts; 4) in Canada, the laws in the Province of Ontario govern this Agreement; and 5) in the United States and Puerto Rico, and People's Republic of China, the laws of the State of New York govern this Agreement.

Part 2 - Country-unique Terms

AUSTRALIA: No Warranty (Section 2): The following paragraph is added to this Section:

Although IBM specifies that there are no warranties, you may have certain rights under the Trade Practices Act 1974 or other legislation and are only limited to the extent permitted by the applicable legislation.

Limitation of Liability (Section 3): The following paragraph is added to this Section:

Where IBM is in breach of a condition or warranty implied by the Trade Practices Act 1974, IBM's liability is limited to the repair or replacement of the goods, or the supply of equivalent goods. Where that condition or warranty relates to right to sell, quiet possession or clear title, or the goods are of a kind ordinarily acquired for personal, domestic or household use or consumption, then none of the limitations in this paragraph apply.

GERMANY: No Warranty (Section 2): The following paragraphs are added to this Section:

The minimum warranty period for Programs is six months.

In case a Program is delivered without Specifications, we will only warrant that the Program information correctly describes the Program and that the Program can be used according to the Program information. You have to check the usability according to the Program information within the "money-back guaranty" period.

Limitation of Liability (Section 3): The following paragraph is added to this Section:

The limitations and exclusions specified in the Agreement will not apply to damages caused by IBM with fraud or gross negligence, and for express warranty.

INDIA: General (Section 4): The following replaces the fourth paragraph of this Section:

If no suit or other legal action is brought, within two years after the cause of action arose, in respect of any claim that either party may have against the other, the rights of the concerned party in respect of such claim will be forfeited and the other party will stand released from its obligations in respect of such claim.

IRELAND: No Warranty (Section 2): The following paragraph is added to this Section:

Except as expressly provided in these terms and conditions, all statutory conditions, including all warranties implied, but without prejudice to the generality of the foregoing, all warranties implied by the Sale of Goods Act 1893 or the Sale of Goods and Supply of Services Act 1980 are hereby excluded.

ITALY: Limitation of Liability (Section 3): This Section is replaced by the following:

Unless otherwise provided by mandatory law, IBM is not liable for any damages which might arise.

NEW ZEALAND: No Warranty (Section 2): The following paragraph is added to this Section:

Although IBM specifies that there are no warranties, you may have certain rights under the Consumer Guarantees Act 1993 or other legislation which cannot be excluded or limited. The Consumer Guarantees Act 1993 will not apply in respect of any goods or services which IBM provides, if you require the goods and services for the purposes of a business as defined in that Act.

Limitation of Liability (Section 3): The following paragraph is added to this Section:

Where Programs are not acquired for the purposes of a business as defined in the Consumer Guarantees Act 1993, the limitations in this Section are subject to the limitations in that Act.

UNITED KINGDOM: Limitation of Liability (Section 3): The following paragraph is added to this Section at the end of the first paragraph:

The limitation of liability will not apply to any breach of IBM's obligations implied by Section 12 of the Sales of Goods Act 1979 or Section 2 of the Supply of Goods and Services Act 1982.

IBM INTERNATIONAL LICENSE AGREEMENT
FOR OS/2 Warp Developer's Kit for Java 1.1.6

PLEASE READ THIS AGREEMENT CAREFULLY BEFORE USING THE PROGRAM. IBM WILL ONLY LICENSE THE PROGRAM TO YOU IF YOU FIRST ACCEPT THE TERMS OF THIS AGREEMENT. REGARDLESS OF HOW YOU ACQUIRE THE PROGRAM (ELECTRONICALLY, PRELOADED, ON MEDIA OR OTHERWISE), BY USING IT YOU AGREE TO THESE TERMS.

I. LICENSE.

Subject to the terms and conditions of this Agreement, including, without limitation, the terms and conditions set forth below in Section VII "Additional Terms and Conditions" and Section VIII "Country Unique Terms", IBM grants to you a non-exclusive, non-transferable, non-assignable right, under the applicable IBM copyrights, to use one copy of the PROGRAM on only one machine at any one time. You may not copy, modify or merge copies of the PROGRAM except as provided in this Agreement. You may not rent, lease, sell, sublicense, assign, distribute or otherwise transfer the PROGRAM except as provided in this Agreement. You may not reverse compile, reverse assemble or translate any part of the PROGRAM, except as specifically permitted by law without the possibility of contractual waiver.

II. COPYRIGHT.

The PROGRAM is owned by International Business Machines or its subsidiaries (IBM) or IBM's Suppliers and is copyrighted and licensed, not sold. You may make one copy of the PROGRAM for backup purposes. You must reproduce the copyright notice(s) on such copy of the PROGRAM.

III. TERM AND TERMINATION.

You may terminate your license to the PROGRAM at any time by destroying all of your copies of the PROGRAM. In addition, IBM may terminate your license to the PROGRAM if you fail to comply with all the terms and conditions of this Agreement. Upon termination, you agree to destroy all of your copies of the PROGRAM.

IV. NO WARRANTY.

SUBJECT TO ANY STATUTORY WARRANTIES WHICH CAN NOT BE EXCLUDED, IBM MAKES NO WARRANTIES OR CONDITIONS EITHER EXPRESS OR IMPLIED, INCLUDING, WITHOUT LIMITATION, THE WARRANTY OF NON-INFRINGEMENT AND THE IMPLIED WARRANTIES OF MERCHANTABILITY AND FITNESS FOR A PARTICULAR PURPOSE, REGARDING THE PROGRAM. THE EXCLUSION ALSO APPLIES TO ANY OF IBM'S SUBCONTRACTORS, SUPPLIERS OR PROGRAM DEVELOPERS (COLLECTIVELY CALLED "SUPPLIERS").

V. LIMITATION OF LIABILITY.

NEITHER IBM NOR ITS SUPPLIERS WILL BE LIABLE FOR ANY DIRECT OR INDIRECT DAMAGES, INCLUDING WITHOUT LIMITATION, LOST PROFITS, LOST SAVINGS, OR ANY INCIDENTAL, SPECIAL, OR OTHER ECONOMIC CONSEQUENTIAL DAMAGES, EVEN IF IBM IS INFORMED OF THEIR POSSIBILITY. SOME JURISDICTIONS DO NOT ALLOW THE EXCLUSION OR LIMITATION OF INCIDENTAL OR CONSEQUENTIAL DAMAGES, SO THE ABOVE EXCLUSION OR LIMITATION MAY NOT APPLY TO YOU.

VI. GENERAL.

The laws of the country in which you acquired the PROGRAM govern this Agreement, except: (1) in Australia, the laws of the State or Territory in which the transaction is performed govern this Agreement; (2) in Central Europe and Russia, the laws of Austria govern this Agreement; (3) in Estonia, Latvia, and Lithuania, the laws of Finland govern this Agreement; (4) in Canada, the laws of the Province of Ontario govern this Agreement and (5) in the United States and Puerto Rico, and the People's Republic of China, the laws of the State of New York govern this Agreement. You agree to comply with all applicable governmental laws, regulations, orders and rules, including, without limitation, those that relate to the export of the PROGRAM. This Agreement is the complete and exclusive agreement regarding the PROGRAM and replaces any prior oral or written communications between you and IBM. For a change to be valid, both you and an authorized IBM representative must sign it.

VII. ADDITIONAL TERMS AND CONDITIONS

You may only use the PROGRAM if you are a current licensee of OS/2 Warp Version 3, OS/2 Warp Connect, OS/2 Warp Server, OS/2 Warp Server SMP, OS/2 Warp 4, or WorkSpace On-Demand and the PROGRAM may only be used in conjunction with such products.

If this PROGRAM is a "free" program under IBM Software Choice, then for each such license of OS/2 you possess, you may make a corresponding copy of the PROGRAM for use with that licensed copy. If this PROGRAM is a program reserved only for customers who have purchased an eligible upgrade offering (i.e. you need a userid and password to access the program or you received it on a CD-ROM), then for each such license of OS/2 you possess, for which you have purchased an upgrade option, you may make a corresponding copy of the PROGRAM for use with that licensed copy.

You must reproduce the copyright notice(s) on all such additional copies of the PROGRAM. The terms and conditions of this Agreement shall apply to all such additional copies of the PROGRAM. IBM may provide various program services and technical support for the PROGRAM; see the PROGRAM documentation for details.

VIII. COUNTRY UNIQUE TERMS

The following terms and conditions may replace or modify the terms and conditions set forth above if you acquired the PROGRAM in any of the countries set forth below.

AUSTRALIA:

No Warranty (Section IV): The warranties specified in this Section are in addition to any rights you may have under the Trade Practices Act or other legislation and are limited only to the extent permitted by the applicable legislation.

Limitation of Liability (Section V): The following paragraph is added to this Section: Where IBM is in breach of a condition or warranty implied by the Trade Practices Act 1974, IBM's liability is limited to: (a) where IBM supplied services, the cost of having services supplied again; or (b) where IBM supplied goods, the repair or replacement of the goods, or the supply of equivalent goods. Where that condition or warranty relates to right to sell, quiet possession or clear title, or the goods are of a kind ordinarily acquired for personal, domestic or household use or consumption, then none of the limitations in this paragraph apply.

NEW ZEALAND:

No Warranty (Section IV): The warranties specified in this Section are in addition to any rights you may have under the Consumer Guarantees Act 1993 or other legislation which cannot be excluded or limited. The Consumer Guarantees Act 1993 will not apply in respect of any goods or services which we provide, if you require the goods and services for the purposes of a business as defined in the Act.

Limitation of Liability (Section V): The following paragraph should be added to this Section:

Where products or services are not acquired for the purposes of a business as defined in the Consumer Guarantees Act 1993, the limitations in the Section are subject to the limitations in that Act.

GERMANY:

No Warranty (Section IV): The warranty for any IBM Program covers the functionality of the Program for its normal use. In case a Program is delivered without specifications, IBM will only warrant that the Program information correctly describes the Program and that the Program can be used according to the Program information. The minimum warranty period is six months.

Limitation of Liability (Section V): The limitations and exclusions specified in the Agreement will not apply to damages caused by us with intention or gross negligence. IBM is liable for assured characteristics.

IRELAND:

No Warranty (Section IV): Except as expressly provided in these terms and conditions, all statutory conditions, including warranties implied, but without prejudice to the generality of the foregoing all warranties implied by the Sale of Goods Act 1893 or the Sale of Goods and Supply of Services Act 1980 are hereby excluded.

ITALY:

(Limitation of Liability (Section V): The clause is replaced by the following: Unless otherwise provided by mandatory law, IBM is not liable for any damages which might arise.

UNITED KINGDOM:

Limitation of Liability (Section V): Add the following paragraph at the end of the first paragraph: The limitation of liability will not apply to any breach of IBM's obligations implied by Section 12 of the Sales of Goods Act 1979 or Section 2 of the Supply of Goods and Services Act 1982.

IBM LICENSE AGREEMENT FOR THE OS/2 CODE UPDATE

PLEASE READ THIS AGREEMENT CAREFULLY BEFORE USING THE PROGRAM. IBM WILL ONLY LICENSE THE PROGRAM TO YOU IF YOU FIRST ACCEPT THE TERMS OF THIS AGREEMENT. REGARDLESS OF HOW YOU ACQUIRE THE PROGRAM (ELECTRONICALLY, PRELOADED, ON MEDIA OR OTHERWISE), BY USING IT YOU AGREE TO THESE TERMS. (1) YOU AGREE THAT YOU ARE A CURRENT LICENSEE OF OS/2 WARP VERSION 3, OS/2 WARP CONNECT, OS/2 WARP SERVER, OS/2 WARP SERVER SMP, OS/2 WARP 4, OR WORKSPACE ON-DEMAND; (2) YOU MAY ONLY USE THE PROGRAM FOR MAINTENANCE PURPOSES; (3) YOU AGREE THAT FOR EACH VALID OS/2 WARP VERSION 3, OS/2 WARP CONNECT, OS/2 WARP SERVER, OS/2 WARP SERVER SMP, OS/2 WARP 4, OR WORKSPACE ON-DEMAND LICENSE YOU POSSESS, YOU MAY MAKE A CORRESPONDING COPY OF THE PROGRAM FOR USE WITH THAT LICENSED COPY OF OS/2; (4) YOU AGREE THAT THE TERMS AND CONDITIONS OF THE ORIGINAL PROGRAM LICENSE AGREEMENTS YOU RECEIVED WITH THE OS/2 PRODUCT THAT YOU ARE USING THIS PROGRAM WITH SHALL APPLY TO, AND GOVERN YOUR USE OF, EACH COPY OF THE PROGRAM; (5) YOU AGREE THAT YOUR USE OF EACH COPY OF THE PROGRAM IS CONDITIONED UPON YOU DESTROYING THOSE PORTIONS OF YOUR ORIGINAL COPIES OF OS/2 WARP SERVER, OS/2 WARP SERVER SMP, OS/2 WARP 4, OR WORKSPACE ON-DEMAND THAT THE PROGRAM IS INTENDED TO REPLACE, IF ANY; (6) YOU AGREE TO COMPLY WITH ALL APPLICABLE GOVERNMENTAL LAWS, REGULATIONS, ORDERS AND RULES INCLUDING, WITHOUT LIMITATION, THOSE THAT RELATE TO THE EXPORT OF THE PROGRAM.

About the CDs

Two CD-ROMs accompany this book. Following is a brief summary of what they contain:

CD #1: Programming with VisualAge for Java Version 2.0

This CD contains code for all the examples in the book as well as the products you need to work through the examples, including:

- VisualAge for Java, Version 2, Entry edition for Windows® and OS/2®
- DB2® Universal Database™ for Windows and OS/2 (evaluation copy)
- Lotus Domino Go Webserver for Windows and OS/2 (evaluation copy)
- Sun Microsystems JDK 1.1.6 for Windows and OS/2
- Sun Microsystems JSDK 2.0 and JFC 1.0.2

CD #2: VisualAge for Java, Professional Edition, Version 2.0

This CD contains:

- Support for JDK1.1.6, including inner classes
- Data Access Beans
- Intelligent IDE
- Integrated Debugger
- Tool Integration API
- Connect to external SCM Tools
- Context Sensitive and complete online help system

Technical Support

Prentice Hall does not offer technical support for this software. However, if there is a problem with the media, you may obtain a replacement copy by emailing us with your problem at:

discexchange@phptr.com